TESORO BOOKS

Ambassador's Journal: A Personal Account of the Kennedy Years
John Kenneth Galbraith

Here to Stay
John Hersey

The Road Back to Paris
A. J. Liebling

On Becoming American
Ted Morgan

THE ROAD BACK TO PARIS

A. J. LIEBLING

THE ROAD
BACK TO
PARIS

PARAGON HOUSE PUBLISHERS
New York

First paperback edition, 1988

Published in the United States by

Paragon House Publishers
90 Fifth Avenue
New York, NY 10011

Library of Congress Cataloging-in-Publication Data

Liebling, A. J. (Abbott Joseph), 1904-1963.
The road back to Paris.

(Tesoro books)
Reprint. Originally published: Garden City,
N.Y. : Doubleday, Doran and Co., 1944.
1. Liebling, A. J. (Abbott Joseph), 1904-1963.
2. World War, 1939-1945—Personal narratives, American.
3. War correspondents—United States—Biography.
I. Title.
D811.5.L53   1988   940.54'81'73   87-25930
ISBN 1-55778-106-0 (pbk.)

To
H. S., HORSE WATKINS
and
PINKY JOHNSON

Acknowledgment is made and thanks
are hereby expressed to the *New Yorker*
for permission to reprint such material
as has appeared in its pages

CONTENTS

Introduction xiii

BOOK I
THE WORLD KNOCKED DOWN

CHAPTER		PAGE
I	The Shape of War	3
II	Reflections in a Cul-de-sac	10
III	Toward Paris: 1939	17
IV	My Generals, My Generalissimo	25
V	Bajus Disappointed	34
VI	Vire Revisited	41
VII	Merry Christmas, Horrid New Year	45
VIII	Colonel Albatross	54
IX	Sample Supermen	57
X	The Knockdown: Paris Postscript	67
XI	Who Do Not Fight, But Run Away	84
XII	A Man Falling Downstairs	92
XIII	Once Down Is No Battle	103

BOOK II
THE WORLD ON ONE KNEE

I	No Place Like It	111
II	Rape Is Impossible	116

CONTENTS

CHAPTER   PAGE

III   Destination: United Kingdom 121

IV   Non Angeli Sed Angli 129

V   It Showed Nice Instincts 137

VI   The Long Name for the Lifeboat 147

VII   Rosie, You Be'ave Yourself 151

VIII   Dev's Double 155

XI   They Are Not Gone 161

X   Westbound Tanker 165

BOOK III
THE WORLD GETS UP

I   Toward a Happy Ending 205

II   Birds of My Country 212

III   What Do You Think That Bugle's Blowing For? . . 215

IV   The Hat of M. Murphy 224

V   Giraud Is Just a General 231

VI   The Foamy Fields 239

VII   First Act at Gafsa 279

VIII   Gafsa Revisited 284

IX   Under the Acacias 292

INTRODUCTION*

A. J. Liebling embarked on his first foreign assignment in *The New Yorker* in 1939, arriving in Paris just in time for the *drôle de guerre*, the phony war, that quiet, tense winter and spring before Hitler's forces overran Paris. The assignment was the biggest break of his career; it transformed him from a writer of New York City features into that most glamorous of journalistic creatures, a foreign correspondent, just in time to cover the choicest of all foreign stories, a major war.

Looking back on this wonderful stroke of good fortune, Liebling tried to make it sound as if he had conned the magazine into sending him. "I attracted the assignment," he wrote, "by telling McKelway** how well I could talk French. McKelway could not judge. Besides, I was a reasonable age for the job: thirty-five."

He was also an ideal choice. He could definitely speak French, with a fluency picked up during many youthful vacations in Europe when his prosperous parents had taken him along with them on grand tours of the Continent, a fluency perfected during a year spent as a student in Paris in the midtwenties.

France had become a second home for him. He had hiked across Normandy on a semiserious scholarly research project, hunting for

---

* Portions of this introduction have appeared in *Liebling Abroad* (Playboy Press, 1981) and *Wayward Reporter: The Life of A. J. Liebling* (Harper and Row, 1980). Reprinted by permission of Raymond Sokolov.
** St. Clair McKelway, an older writer at *The New Yorker*.

traces of a mythical medieval poet who had supposedly lived at Vire. There, and in the small but soigné and hearty bistros of prewar Paris, he had educated his palate and primed his appetite for substantial, serious food. And in a Left Bank café he met Angèle, the first important woman of his complex amatory career.

France had also seduced Liebling's intellect years before she got to his body. A fancy set of Maupassant on the family's shelves in the wealthy new Long Island suburb of Lawrence was this precocious boy's introduction to "adult" literature. Later, at the Columbia Journalism School, an unwilling apprentice to his future craft, Liebling cross-registered for a literature course that covered Villon and the early French classics. As a young reporter he read and reread Stendhal, who prepared him for battle.

War, indeed, had preoccupied Liebling from earliest boyhood. He memorized all the names of the marshals of France, and when, in 1916, at the age of eleven, an attack of typhoid nearly killed him, he fell into delirium and dreamt that he was a military horse decorated for valor with the Médaille Militaire by General Nivelle, the French commander at Verdun.

Probably neither St. Clair McKelway nor *The New Yorker*'s editor Harold Ross knew about any of these special credentials. Nevertheless, they did not blunder into their choice for the Paris posting. In Joe Liebling they knew they had one of the great reporters of the day. He had been seasoned by several hundred human-interest, "low-life" assignments at the New York *World-Telegram* before he switched over to America's smartest, smoothest magazine. And at *The New Yorker* Liebling had polished his technique, first as a Talk of the Town reporter, then as an increasingly skillful hand at longer features and profiles of figures in the New York entertainment world and its sleazier, Barnumesque peripheries. Liebling could report; he could write; and he knew how to function among ordinary people. Liebling did not resemble Richard Harding Davis. He was myopic and overweight and had weak feet. But Harold Ross was not looking for a swashbuckler. He wanted good, solid reporting about the everyday life of Europe in wartime, from the street and from the trenches. Liebling was his man, better than he could have hoped for.

Liebling covered the war as Ross wanted him to, from the front lines, and got the enlisted man's point of view. He found plenty of color and sharp detail of daily life, fleeing Paris in 1940, crossing the Atlantic in a submarine, dodging airborne strafers on North African battlefields, surviving the London blitz, and landing on the Normandy beaches on D day. But he did much more than bring *The New Yorker* manner to the European theater. He brought himself, a fiercely committed Francophile with a novelist's skill for crystallizing his day-to-day experiences into a profound chronicle of a "world knocked down."

In particular, it was the "world" of France that Liebling wanted fiercely to restore. Although he was a patriotic American, he viewed World War II almost exclusively as a campaign to free France. And once he had entered Paris just behind General Leclerc on liberation day, the war was essentially over for him. He stayed for a few months and then went home, well before V-E Day.

He had the French view of things, no doubt about it. And if it was a seriously limiting view, it gave unique clarity to his war reporting, much of which was later collected in this classic of the genre.

The Road Back to Paris is Liebling's collected dispatches from France, England, and North Africa. It will not instruct the young and curious who want to learn the grand outlines of the war in Europe. Liebling made no attempt to write conventional history; he did not even try to set the events he saw into their larger historical perspective, any more than he had tried to set Tallulah Bankhead in the larger perspective of Anglo-American theater and post-Reconstruction southern aristocratic eccentricity when he did a piece about her for the *World-Telegram*. He took the context for granted and then brought the reader inside it, made him feel the ominously languorous pace of battle, those still days of dreary tenting suddenly blasted into frenzy.

The Road Back to Paris helped to establish Liebling among his colleagues and with the serious reading public as the leading intelligence and stylist covering the European theater of the war. The reviews were almost uniformly favorable, but he made light of them in a letter to friend and fellow-reporter, Joe Mitchell: ". . . they took the slant 'what a relief to find a correspondent who can treat the war in the New Yorker manner' . . . Two reviewers independently hit on the idea of calling me the intellectual's Ernie Pyle, and another a sophisticated Ernie Pyle. Thank God no one suggested I was a poor man's Ernie Hemingway."

INTRODUCTION

By the 1960s the New Journalists were claiming Liebling as their godfather. He was certainly a personal journalist, taking pages to tell New Yorkers how he bought eggs in the "foamy fields" of Tunisia and then hit the dirt when the enemy dived down and shot up his makeshift desert kitchen. But the personal flavor never overwhelms the observation, the careful witnessing. Never pontificating about the progress of the battle, which he could not see himself, he focused on the things he could see. Liebling keeps himself so strictly in the background that when he does permit himself a general reaction—usually a modest one—it acquires a peculiar force.

The new phase of the Second World War began for Paris at daybreak on Friday, May 10, 1940. People had gone to bed Thursday night in their habitual state of uncertainty; the governmental crisis in London which was bringing Winston Churchill to power was still the chief subject of preoccupation. With the dawn came the air-raid sirens, startling a city that had heard no *alerte* during the daytime since the first weeks of the war. At once the little Square Louvois in front of my window took on the aspect of an Elizabethan theater, with tiers of spectators framed in the opened windows of every building. Instead of looking down at a stage, however, they all looked up. All wore nightshirts, which, since the prosperity of tenants in a walk-up is in inverse ratio to their altitude, appeared considerably dingier on the sixth and seventh floors than on the second and third.

The anti-aircraft guns were intoning such an impressive overture that startled birds flew out of the trees in at least one of the squares and circled nervously in squadrons over the roofs. As they did so, a large, formless woman in a gray nightshirt, making her *entrée* at a top-floor window, waved her right arm toward them and shouted "*Confiance!*"—putting all her neighbors in hilarious good humor.

The guns kept up their racket, and a number of tracer shells lit up the early morning sky. The noise of the airplane motors was distinctly audible, but in those pre-blitz days we could not distinguish between the sound made by bombers and that of French pursuit planes looking for Germans. At last one airplane appeared, flying so high that it looked like a charm-bracelet toy, and as it passed overhead there seemed to be a deliberate lull in the firing. People stared uneasily at the plane, as they would at a stinging insect near a ceiling, but it went away harmlessly enough, and then the guns opened up again.

INTRODUCTION

The morning air was chilly, so most of the spectators soon closed their windows and went back to bed. In the Square Louvois the neighborhood milkman, with his wagon drawn by two enormous old gray stallions, came along a few minutes after the plane, and the crash of his cans on the cobbles brought a few nervous folk back to their windows under the impression that bombing had begun.

The episode differed so from previous alarms, in which no planes were seen that nobody seemed astonished to learn from newspapers consisting mostly of headlines that the real war—the war on the western front—had begun. *"Finie la drôle de guerre,"* people said to each other with a kind of relief.

As he followed the advance of the Allies through Normandy, Liebling eventually came into Vire. Friendly fire had almost leveled the center of the town which he remembered so vividly from student days. In order for Liebling's France to be preserved, the part of it he cherished most had to be destroyed.

The irony stuck with him for the next decade, which he spent in New York as a press critic and boxing writer. These were eventful years for Liebling, who is perhaps best known today as the author of *The New Yorker*'s Wayward Press column. His incisive comments on newspaper stories and the role of the press in American life have made him a hero for all journalists. And his ringside reports of the great fights of the postwar period went beyond blow-by-blow accounts to take in the whole special world of the "sweet science," its training camps, its sociology and lingo. He became the best boxing writer in a century. But he had not forgotten his old passion; he yearned to see France again. Further prompted by the claims of the Internal Revenue Service (which offered a $20,000 deduction for expatriates) and by his second wife, who wanted a separation, Liebling went abroad again in the middle fifties.

Foreign correspondent redux, he covered British elections and racing and the Suez crisis, but his main preoccupation during this period was himself and his France.

A. J. Liebling died on December 20, 1963. At the funeral his lifelong friend Joseph Mitchell said in a eulogy:

> Shortly after I heard that Joe was dead, I went over and looked at his books in a bookcase at home. There were fifteen of them. I looked through *The Road Back to Paris* and reread "Westbound Tanker,"

INTRODUCTION

which is one of my favorite stories of his, and when I finished it I suddenly recalled, with great pleasure, a conversation I had had some years ago with the proprietor of one of the biggest and oldest stores in the Fourth Avenue secondhand bookstore district. I had been going to this store for years and occasionally had talked to the proprietor, who is a very widely read man. One day I mentioned I worked for *The New Yorker*, and he asked me if I knew A. J. Liebling. I said that I did, and he said that every few days all through the year someone, sometimes a woman, sometimes a young person, sometimes an old person, came in and asked if he had *Back Where I Came From* or *The Telephone Booth Indian* or some other book by A. J. Liebling. At that time, all of Joe's early books were out of print. "The moment one of his books turned up," the man said, "it goes out immediately to someone on my waiting list." The man went on and said that he and other veteran secondhand bookstore dealers felt that this was a sure and certain sign that a book would endure. "Literary critics don't know which books will last," he said, "and literary historians don't know, and those nine-day immortals up at the Institute of Arts and Letters don't know. *We* are the ones who know. We know which books can be read only once, if that, and we know the ones that can be read and reread and reread."

In other words, what I am getting at, Joe is dead, but he really isn't. He is dead, but he will live again. Every time anyone anywhere in all the years to come takes down one of his books and reads or rereads one of his wonderful stories, he will live again.

Liebling left several million words behind. Most of them were written about his native city, New York. But his best work, the books in which he found himself and his style most completely, was done 3,000 miles east of *The New Yorker*'s offices. Liebling abroad was Liebling at the peak of his form.

RAYMOND SOKOLOV

BOOK I

THE WORLD KNOCKED DOWN

CHAPTER I

The Shape of War

Two NEGRO SOLDIERS sat with their legs dangling into two deep parallel slit trenches in the dead-looking land between Gafsa and Sened Station one morning last winter. Each was eating a cold mixture of meat and beans out of a small shiny tin can capable of reflecting the sun's rays to a distance of several miles in that flat country, and each turned his face upward periodically, with mouth full, to stare into the hot aluminum-colored sky. When I walked up to the end of one trench its proprietor, a tan man, looked at me while the other soldier continued to regard the sky. Then the tan man looked up at the sky, and his companion looked at me. "We was dive-bummed yesterday," this second soldier, a very dark man, said to me. "Driving the infantry up to the line in two-and-a-half-ton trucks. Dive-bumming makes me sick to my stomach." I tried to sound hearty and casual as I asked, "What outfit you men out of?" "Rolling Umpty-seventh," the tan man said while the dark man took his turn looking at the sky. The Umpties are a motor-truck regiment whom I had first met under happier circumstances, in England. "How you doing?" I asked, for want of a better question. "Really, sir, I don't belong on this battlefield at all," the tan soldier answered. "I'm strictly a non-combat man." I thought to myself we were two of a kind.

It was the second day of an offensive that we had started in the direction of Maknassy, the first all-American venture of the Tunisian campaign. Sened Station was the first objective. The bulk of

3

Rommel's army was still only a little west of Tripoli, and there was a long, tempting, thinly held corridor between him and Von Arnim. The men making the attack believed that they would go on from Sened to Maknassy and from Maknassy to the coast of the Gulf of Tunis, cutting Rommel's line of supply and retreat. The major general in command had told the war correspondents he was going on to Maknassy at least and "draw the pucker string tight." We had understood from his manner that he meant to go farther than that if he got the chance.

I asked the colored soldiers how far the front of the battle was from where we then were. I put into my voice an implication that I wanted to rush right into the middle of things. The men did not know exactly where the battle was. Soldiers seldom and war correspondents almost never do. I learned afterward that the Umpties' vehicles, returning after unloading the infantry, had frightened a couple of my most dashing colleagues completely out of the battle area. They had mistaken the approaching trucks for a German tank column.

I walked back from the twin slit trenches to the jeep that had carried me out from Gafsa. Another correspondent was at the wheel. "They don't know where the battle is," I said to this other fellow. "Maybe we had better go ahead further." He said all right, so we started out across the sand again. We kept off the one road between Gafsa and Sened because there were trucks on it and they sometimes attracted strafers. The line of telephone poles along the side of the road gave us our general direction. When we had gone a short way I saw a couple of jeeps coming toward us, and we stopped. There were a couple of officers and eight men in the jeeps, all belonging to a tank-destroyer battalion that had lost its equipment earlier in the campaign. They were serving as battlefield military police, guiding traffic and waiting for prisoners to take charge of. The officers didn't know exactly where the front was either, but they invited us to have a can of coffee by a mud house a couple of miles away where the M.P.'s had set up their headquarters. There were a few scraggly olive trees around this house and a low mud wall around the trees, presumably to prevent the sand from blowing away from their roots.

One of the soldiers put a mixture of sand and gasoline in a couple of the shiny ration cans and lighted them. He filled two more ration cans with water from his canteen and placed them on the burners, and then when the water came to a boil he divided a packet of soluble coffee between the two improvised coffeepots. "The Statler people would give a million dollars to get hold of this process," he said. When the coffee had been drunk he started another batch. While I was waiting for my coffee I stood on the mud wall with one of the M.P. officers and looked over the country around. The railroad paralleled the highway, and we could see a station building with some trees around it about five miles away. It was an intermediate stop between Gafsa and Sened, needed God knows why. "Our guns were out behind there early this morning, and Jerry dropped a few shells in among those trees," the officer said, "but then our guns moved forward, 'way up toward Sened. I think you can go ahead eight or ten miles at least before you have to start to look around. You missed a good show this morning though. About twenty Stukas came over, and a dozen P-40's bounced them and shot down about eight. Boy, they were falling all over the place. They'll be back, though!" he added cheerily. When we had had our coffee we climbed back into the jeep and started forward again. The mud-house grove seemed in retrospect a pretty nice place to spend the day. Sened Station lies in a gap between two bare east-west ridges. As we moved toward it we spotted a number of dispersed scout cars and wireless-equipped jeeps, the vehicles characteristic of a reconnaissance troop. "A recon outfit!" my companion said knowingly, then, "Aren't they usually pretty well out in front of everybody?"

We drove over within fifty yards of one of the scout cars and climbed out. There were a couple of soldiers sitting with their backs against wheels of the car, reading paper books. They had their slit trenches ready dug beside them. I walked up to them and said, "What outfit is this, soldier?" One of the men, a corporal, looked up and said, "Sorry, sir, but you got any identification?" He reminded me of a stage doorman. We showed our identification cards, and the corporal explained that the recon outfit had been all the way around the enemy's position on the previous day and night and had come back to report and await another assignment. "We could have took the place, I guess," he said, "but that would not have seemed important enough." He was wrong, but reconnaissance troops, like small terriers, must have their illusions or they would lose their dash.

My companion, Boots Norgaard, who worked for the Associated Press, started taking down the names and home towns of recon soldiers. This is always a fruitful procedure for a press-association man, because he can load up his dispatches with the names and the member papers in the home towns are glad to use them. Every soldier, when he named his home town, said, "And I wish I was there now," or, "Boy, how I wish I was there this minute!" The corporal I had first spoken to asked me if it was true that Bing Crosby was dead. I said I did not know, and he asked me if Groucho Marx was dead. He said he had heard that they were and that Jack Benny was dead too. The army in Tunisia was always full of rumors about well-known people who were supposed to have died at home. Battlefields, for that matter, are always ranged by false rumors about people supposed to have died in the immediate vicinity. When my companion had written down the names of enough towns like Owensboro, Kentucky, and Central Falls, Rhode Island, we moved on again.

We had a clear view of the ridge north of Sened Station, and after we had driven a mile or so forward we saw a number of tanks coming around the end nearer us, just below the crest, and snaking down the southern slope of the ridge toward the station. There were occasional puffs of gray smoke on the slope above them, where the enemy was lobbing shells over. We could hear our own guns up ahead quite loudly now. Then we wandered in among the ammunition half-tracks of an artillery outfit. The soldiers told us that the reconnaissance troop we had just left in good health had been annihilated on the previous day. They also said that a tank-destroyer outfit had lost all its vehicles. This was a reference to the tank-destroyer battalion the military policemen belonged to. The vehicles had been lost in a quagmire in northern Tunisia a month ago, but an artillerist, garbling some conversation with an M.P., had come up with the more fascinating report that the tank busters had been ambushed during this present action. I never like the vicinity of ammo during a battle. The soldiers said two batteries out of their battalion were a mile or two ahead of us. The guns were armored 105's, six to a battery.

We came eventually to a place on the plain where a tall captain with a Red Cross brassard was standing between two jeeps both carrying Red Cross flags. We stopped to talk to him, too. The guns were in sight now, about four hundred yards farther on. The captain, whose name I remember was Bradbury, said he was battalion surgeon. Each of the jeeps had two litters slung to its sides, and when dive bombers or German counter-battery caused a casualty among the gunners Bradbury would run up in one of the jeeps and get the wounded man. He stood there looking at the guns like a spaniel watching for a ball to retrieve. "Yesterday I had seventeen," he said, "including several from the infantry that happened to be hit near us. Only three so far today. None in this position so far —we've moved half a dozen times since daybreak." All the shots we heard were going out, "boom-scream," and none coming in, "scream-boom," so we were unworried. I got out a can of Spam, and we ate it cold before continuing our advance.

"Maybe they have pulled their stuff out of Sened already," Norgaard said optimistically. I had watched the sky all day while he drove, sometimes looking straight up for Stukas and at others into the sun for strafers, but nothing had happened, and I began to hope that the P-40's had polished the local Luftwaffe off for the day.

When we had finished the Spam and said so long to Bradbury, we went on up to the guns and stopped the jeep behind them. They were in the open, because there was no cover anywhere around. They had quit shooting for the moment, probably changing a range or target, and we walked up to one gun crew who were smoking cigarettes beside their piece. As soon as we reached them an officer shouted over to them from an armored half-track to their right rear to get our identifications. "I'm sorry, sir," one soldier said, "but after all, how do we know who you are? We got no time for Ayrabs or casual strollers." We showed our identification cards, and the soldier, looking at mine, which describes me as correspondent of the *New Yorker*, said, "Huh, a *paesano*, practically. I'm from New York, too. Fourteent' Street and Avenue A. I wish I was dere now. At a movie, wit' my shoes off." Then they had to start shooting again, and we walked back toward the half-track, which we recognized from its high radio antenna as a command vehicle.

The officer who had shouted to the gunners was a square-faced fair-haired major who told us his name was Burba, executive officer of the battalion. He was in command of the two batteries, since his C.O., a lieutenant colonel, had been wounded. Major Burba said he was from McAlester, Oklahoma. He was a cool, methodical offi-

7

cer who looked as if he would have definite information about everything, so I asked him what his battery was shooting at. "Enemy guns in the grove of trees back of Sened," he said. "We think their infantry has pulled out of the town already." I asked him what range he was firing at, and he said five thousand yards. "I have one battery here," he said, "and another over about a mile to the right and slightly forward—you can see them over there," and he pointed. "Every fifth shell we fire is a smoke shell so we can see where we are hitting, and the fire of the two batteries is converging on that grove of trees. When we get all our fire together and just right, we will come down on them, and that will be the end of the battle." "Where is our infantry?" I asked in a careless tone, because I could not see any troops out in front of us. "There are two battalions in echelon in those two olive groves to the right and forward of the other battery," Burba said, pointing again. "When we have knocked out all resistance they will go forward and occupy the town. Or maybe the tanks will get there first."

The tanks, as a matter of fact, were already trying to get to the town before the infantry. They were crawling down off the southern side of the ridge where my colleague and I had observed them earlier, moving out in front of the 105's, reminding me of a file of mechanical toys that a street peddler winds up and sets down on a sidewalk. When they had deployed in front of us they turned left and rolled on toward the town. They must have been a couple of thousand yards ahead of us when something began kicking up dust and smoke, sometimes in front of and sometimes behind them. "It's those Jerry eighty-eights," Burba said. "They've got the tanks under a crossfire. We'll fix that in a few minutes." The tanks were now rolling back toward us, except for one which remained motionless out on the plain. "That's the way the infantry was yesterday," one of Burba's junior officers said. "They went up toward the firing line in trucks, and three or four of the trucks got dive-bombed before the fellows could get away from them. It was a mess. After that they couldn't get anybody back into the trucks for a while. After we knock out the opposition they will all be heroes."

"That eighty-eight's a great gun," Burba said admiringly, looking at the motionless American tank through his binoculars. "Ripped that thing just like a G.I. knife does a tin can. Flat trajectory. High muzzle velocity." "Pretty long range, hasn't it?" I asked. "Thirteen thousand five hundred yards," Burba said heartily, as if he were a salesman pushing the German gun on a reluctant prospect. Our six guns loosed off as one and the other battery followed.

Just then there was a prolonged shrieking noise and something monstrous landed a hundred yards behind us and ricocheted off toward Gafsa. It kicked up a lot of dust. It must have been an armor-piercing solid shot, because there was no explosion. Burba said, "Let's get behind the half-track," in the same tone he might have said, "Let's get out of this wind," so we moved over behind the vehicle. Something else shrieked past, through the interval between the two guns on the right flank of the battery, I thought, and I had a bitter intuition that while Burba had been explaining to us what we intended to do to the Germans, some equally competent, equally stolid German artillery officer had been outlining his plans of what he intended to do to us. "He should have snapped into it and not wasted his time talking to war correspondents," I reflected severely. But my colleague and I had an embarrassing feeling that we were not helping the battery by our presence and that if we got hit we would cause them a lot of extra trouble. We were also embarrassed by the thought that if we left too abruptly, Burba and the others might think us fair-weather friends. My colleague reminded me that he really had to get back to headquarters at Gafsa by five so he could get a fill-in on the general picture for the dispatch which he must file to catch the six-o'clock courier car to Tebessa. From there a plane would take it to the cablehead at Algiers. I didn't work for a press association and so had no bulletin to file, but we had only one jeep, and I decided that I couldn't expect the other fellow to wait. So I said, "I guess we may as well go, Major. See you some other time." Norgaard said something to the same effect, and we walked away feeling as sheepish as we ever have in our lives. We got in our jeep and drove back past the patient, expectant Captain Bradbury. We paused for a moment to say good-by to him, and I looked back and saw a column of black smoke rising from one of the gun positions, where the enemy had evidently got a hit.

Each knot of soldiers that we had passed on the way going out had seemed a friendly island that invited a prolonged stay. We were not tempted to stop to talk to any of them on the way back. "Tomorrow we will get an early start and bring out blanket rolls," I said to my companion. "That way we will be able to see more of the battle and not have to go back to Gafsa at night." He agreed. As we entered the center of Gafsa and were about to park our jeep opposite the town's one European-style hotel, which was serving as American headquarters, we saw in the street the major general who commanded the whole operation and who forty-eight hours earlier may have been thinking his name would live with Stonewall Jackson's. We stopped to ask him if the infantry had as yet entered Sened—we had been two hours on the way home—and he said they had, and Sened Station was now in our hands. "The only damned trouble," he said, "is that First Army has called off the whole offensive because there has been some kind of threat in the north. I guess we're going to play it safe and wait for Montgomery." At that time American troops were still under direct control of the British First Army. The greater part of an armored division which had been held in reserve just outside Gafsa to exploit our initial gains was sent north that night without having fought, and the great offensive went into the record as a raid.

The feeling I had had when I left the guns was the sort of thing that demands a rationalization, and I arrived at one while I was sitting on a ridge overlooking Gafsa on St. Patrick's Day, watching our people recapture the place. We had evacuated it a fortnight after the aborted offensive. The region is full of prehistoric artifacts and pieces of them, and I was trying to put together some kind of a form out of bits of flint I found on the hill. I never finished the job, but I think the result would have been ugly if I had. I thought then that I had viewed this war so long that it would be a shame to be knocked in the head before I had patched all my glimpses of it together and tried to reconstruct the shape of the beast.

CHAPTER II

Reflections in a Cul-de-sac

THERE IS AN OLD PROVERB that a girl may sleep with one man without being a trollop, but let a man cover one little war and he is a war correspondent. I belong to the one-war category. I have made no appearances for Mr. Colston Leigh, the lecture agent, either in a gas mask or out of one, and I have no fascinating reminiscences about Addis Ababa or the Cliveden set. Prior to October 1938 my only friends were prize fighters' seconds, Romance philologists, curators of tropical fish, kept women, promoters of spit-and-toilet-paper night clubs, bail bondsmen, press agents for wrestlers, horse clockers, newspaper reporters, and female psychiatrists. I was writing excellent pieces about sea-lion trainers and cigar-store proprietors for the *New Yorker,* and I was happy.

Hitler had seemed to me revolting but unimportant, like old Gómez, the dictator of Venezuela. I habitually compared him in conversation to a boor who tortured his own family because he could not cope with the outside world, a classic German type. It never occurred to me that he might destroy France, because it would have been as hard for me to prefigure a world without France as survival with one lobe of my brain gone. France represented for me the historical continuity of intelligence and reasonable living. When this continuity is broken, nothing anywhere can have meaning until it is re-established. After the Munich settlement I began to be anxious.

On Sunday, September 3, 1939, everybody with the price of a newspaper knew that Great Britain and France were about to declare war on Germany, which had already invaded Poland. I was living down on East Thirty-third Street then, but I drifted up toward the *New Yorker* office because I thought that even though it was a Sunday I might find someone there to talk to. It was a hot afternoon, I remember. Wolcott Gibbs had a radio going in his office. I went down the fire escape from the main editorial office on the nineteenth floor to the cell on the seventeenth where I did my writing and sat there for a while, at moments glad because France still had pride, at others feeling guilty because I would not share the fight or the risk. I was sorry that I had left daily newspaper work four years before then, because if I had stayed on a paper I might have a chance to go to the war. The *New Yorker* appeared a cul-de-sac.

As I sat there I thought of M. Lebourgeois, a traveling salesman I had met in the billiard room of the Hôtel du Cheval Blanc at Vire in 1926, and also of M. Perrin, the *patron* of the hotel in the

Rue de l'Ecole de Médecine at Paris, where I had lived for two years while pretending to study medieval literature, and my good friend Henri, who was the French representative of an American silk firm. All three had shared the quality of having escaped from a great danger with honor intact. None of them had come through the war unwounded, and none had achieved any great position since the armistice of 1918. But each took immense pleasure in not having been killed and in not having to be ashamed of himself.

When M. Lebourgeois had patted his stomach, while telling me of the table d'hôte at a favorite hotel in his territory, he had clearly been glad that the stomach had survived—the bullet had broken his left leg, which bothered him hardly at all except in wet weather. The merchants of the United States, M. Lebourgeois had told me, had absolutely the right idea—*le big business.* Undoubtedly, in that country of large orders, he had said, it was a pleasure to be a salesman. The retailers had vision; they were not like these retrograded types of the Department of Calvados, who bought a few articles at a time and those only with the most apparent misgivings. He had had one period of relative affluence, he had said—almost *le big business,* it had been—directly after the war, when he had gone about selling to small communities those life-size cast-iron figures of poilus which served as war memorials in most of rural Normandy. On the base of each statue was the inscription *"Morts à l'Ennemi,"* and under it the twenty or thirty names of the late heroes. The figure of the poilu was always poised on the ball of the right foot, the bayonet stuck out before him, the iron face constricted in defiance. "These opportunities don't recur often in a man's lifetime," M. Lebourgeois used to say when he told about it. "Figure to yourself—it is necessary to have a war before you can sell something in this bugger of a department." If M. Lebourgeois was sufficiently fortunate to survive this new war, he might make more sales, I figured to myself.

M. Perrin, my landlord, had taken a Chinese pleasure in disingenuous self-abasement. It was a privilege he had earned in the war. If he had deprecated himself before that, nobody would have contradicted him, because, as he used to say, he was a small, insignificant man without capacity or cultivation. Then, in order to survive, it would have been necessary for him to assert himself. He would have disliked that. But he had won the Legion of Honor for bravery under fire, and although he always shrugged away references to his decoration, he never left the ribbon off his coat. Also, he had been a captain. Intelligence is not requisite for a captain of infantry, he used to assure me. An officer of artillery or engineers, *that* required culture, but a captain of infantry, and especially one who began the war as a private, might be very stupid. It was a matter of luck, of survival, one might say. We would sit at a table in front of the Soufflet—which was later to be repiaced by a gigantic modernistic chain-store café called Dupont—watching the Danish and Rumanian students and their girls, and the little waiter with the reddish eyes and the carroty mustache would not be so brusque with M. Perrin as with the other clients. M. Perrin's suits had been shiny, but the ribbon had given him an air. Almost, one would say, an instructor at the Ecole des Chartes near by. The instructors' suits were shiny too. The possibility of such a mistake had flattered M. Perrin, and he had tried by his manner to convey to strangers the idea that his ribbon was an academic honor.

M. Perrin was a native of Lille. He had lived with his wife, a large, hot-tempered Orleanaise, his mother, who was very old, and his daughter, who was adolescent, on the street floor of the hotel. Without the red ribbon to enhance his dignity, without the head wound he had received at Douaumont to explain his flightiness, M. Perrin, it was easy to see, would have been familially submerged. "My wife is very bitter after gain," he had sometimes said over the *apero*. But he had never refused to accept payment of a bill which she had harried some student into meeting. His mother had been in Lille during the occupation of 1914–18. Her confidence had never wavered, she had once told me, since the day when she had seen some German officers eating lettuce. "They put sugar on it," she said, an indication to her of cretinism on a national scale. The reason I thought so long of M. Perrin was that he had lived in what he and I and everybody else had thought was a comfortable aftermath. Another decoration would bring him no satisfaction commensurate with the first. Neither would another head wound.

Henri had been most pleased to survive the war of any of them, because to him it had seemed especially horrible. He was a sensitive man, extremely tall, with a long, doleful countenance, watery blue eyes, and a great, drooping Gallic mustache. In 1914 he had been in the United States—it was there I had first known him—and

13

he had returned to fight. Sometimes I used to have dinner with Henri's family in their apartment on the Avenue de la Motte-Picquet, a neighborhood roughly equivalent to Central Park West, and after we had eaten, Henri would tuck a violin under his chin and his daughter Suzette would go to the piano, and then he would play and sing "J'Avais Perdu la Tête et Ma Perruque," from *Les Cloches de Corneville*. His son Jean, who had spent most of his young life in America, would sit silent, uninterested, and slightly embarrassed. Jean liked to talk about automobile engines, using a good deal of American slang. "He should be a handy man around a tank now," I thought, "he's just the right age." Henri had preferred to talk about "before the war," a period, he would say, when Paris really had been fit to live in. Eglée, his wife, had sometimes pretended to be bored by his reminiscences. I reflected that Henri, with luck, would be able to talk someday about "before the war before last." As a matter of fact he was not to survive this second war. He was to die of cold and malnutrition and chagrin, "but principally of chagrin," his daughter would later write to me, in Paris in February of 1941.

I began to think of Vire, where I had met M. Lebourgeois. It is a little city built of gray granite, and its principal street passes under a great gray clock tower that was once a gate in a wall, but all the rest of the wall is gone. The clock strikes every quarter-hour all through the night. There are two little rivers that join within the city limits, one the Vire and one the name of which I could not recall, and there is the Street of the Dyers along the bank of one of them, with old granite houses that jut over the water and low granite porches on the water level. I had once told the mayor, an anticlerical old doctor, that this street was fine, and he had said it was "an infection, a nest of microbes," and that the sooner somebody blew it up with dynamite the better it would be. The vales, *vaux,* of the two little rivers, *les vaux de Vire,* lent their names to form the word vaudeville, according to a plausible but I am now convinced inaccurate theory I had once heard told in a course in Old French at Columbia. I had arrived in Vire for the first time in 1926 because of that odd bit of information. I had always loved vaudeville at the Palace in New York. Besides, Henri had told me that during the last war he and another sergeant had brought some German prisoners from the front to a camp on the west coast, and that on the return trip they had stopped off at Vire, which was the other sergeant's home town, and that they had descended at the Cheval Blanc and eaten and drunk wonderfully well. Since I was an amateur medievalist and a vaudeville fan *and* a glutton, I had gone to Vire. On the first Sunday after my arrival I had attended some mounted trotting races that local farmers were holding at a village four miles from the city. The great heavy men on their great heavy horses—bred for sale to the field artillery—went thundering in a rough semicircle about a great cow pasture. It was easy to lose count of the number of rounds. The crowd stood inside the semicircle, most of the men amiably drunk, the women scarlet-cheeked and out of their heads with excitement, cheering their favorites. One fellow in a plaid cap led for several rounds, then his horse, a brown with a long barrel and short legs, broke into a canter. The man sawed at the horse's mouth to get it back into a trot, he kicked violently, and the horse broke into a sidling gallop and then began trying to throw him. Meanwhile another farmer, on a bay, took the lead easily without pushing his horse. The farmer had thick legs and a great heavy belly that rode in front of him like a sack of grain. He had a red face and a long mustache that drooped like a ship's ensign in a dead calm. He and his bay stallion were unexcited. They trotted in by fifty lengths. A tall old peasant standing next to me hit me on the back of the neck with the heel of his hand, a cordial gesture in Vire. "Pichart wins again!" he shouted. "It never pays to abuse a horse or a woman!"

I remembered M. Hédouin, the municipal librarian of Vire. The combined library and museum was a sort of annex of the City Hall. It was officially closed during the summertime. So I had had to pay M. Hédouin twenty francs an hour to open it for me and find books. He was a small, bent, wispy man, old, but not at all doting. There had been an early-fifteenth-century poet named Olivier Basselin in Vire, according to the *vaux-de-vire* theory which dated from about 1825. His drinking songs had become known as *vaux-de-vire,* by a transference easy to understand. Then the *r* had become an *l,* and then vaudeville had come to be a term for any gay song. The main evidence for this theory was a whole volume of Olivier Basselin's drinking songs, printed in the seventeenth century. There was no surviving manuscript. In order to have survived for two centuries outside of manuscript, the argument ran,

15

the songs must have been very popular indeed. M. Hédouin told me that a nineteenth-century critic named Armand Gasté, a native of Vire and a professor at the University of Caen—there was a street in Vire named after him—had already disposed of the question in two or three volumes. M. Hédouin fished them out of the stacks for me.

M. Gasté demonstrated by a study of the texts that the poems had been written in the seventeenth, not the fifteenth, century and by a lawyer named Jean Le Houx of Vire. Le Houx had been an outwardly serious chap who had not wanted to be known as a composer of drinking songs. He had therefore invented Basselin, as Chatterton invented Rowley and MacPherson invented Ossian, and had published his "discovery." Since the term *vaux-de-vire* had never been applied to songs before Le Houx's time, the etymology for vaudeville from *vaux-de-vire* was almost impossible, Gasté noted. The word vaudeville already occurred in the seventeenth century and was probably derived from *voix de ville,* the voice of the city. I remembered only one of his textual arguments: "Basselin" in one song compared his own nose to the red wattles of a turkey. Turkeys had not been introduced into France until well after the discovery of America, Gasté pointed out. "It was all a humbug," M. Hédouin had told me with a New England kind of malicious pleasure in destroying a pretty story. What I remembered most keenly was the play of intelligences across time, like a wireless chess game. The seventeenth-century attorney and the nineteenth-century professor had played, the old librarian in the twentieth century had marked the score.

I did not think about Germany. When I was a small child I had had a succession of German governesses all indistinguishably known to me as *Fräulein.* They had been servile to my parents and domineering to me, stupid, whining, loud, and forever trying to frighten me with stories of children who had been burned to a crisp or eaten by an ogre because they had disobeyed other Fräuleins. The fairy tales of anthropophagic stepmothers and princes turned into white mice gave me nightmares. Once when I was very small I was escorted by the current Fräulein through the torture tower in Nuremberg and made to look down a deep well into which, she told me, it was customary to throw bad little boys. It was really the place where the jolly Meistersingers had been accustomed to drop the mangled corpses of people who disagreed with them, like a slot for used razor blades. She had bought me a little miniature of the Iron Maiden as a souvenir of our promenade, complete in detail, she liked to point out. Only Germans could be so thorough, she said with pride—there were miniature spikes inside the hollow maiden's hollow eyes, just like the spikes in the big one, that pierced the victim's brain. I suppose German-lovers would have called it *gemütlich*. Banse and Goebbels and their war by fear are in the main line of German culture, not twentieth-century deviations. Only people with hollow hearts can so count on the fears of others. The Fräuleins had shared a national habit of digging their fingernails into the flesh of my arm. When I was five years old I would rather have died with my milk teeth in a governess' ankle than tie the kind of bow in my shoelaces that she had wanted to make me tie. Anybody who had had a German governess could understand Poland.

CHAPTER III

Toward Paris: 1939

THE NEW YORKER turned out to be the best possible place for a reporter who had to see the war. The magazine had always considered London and Paris, although not Newark or Chicago, within its sphere of inaction. It had run a weekly or fortnightly letter from each of these capitals for years, with an occasional Letter from Salzburg, or Megève or Berlin (during the 1936 Olympics) or Bayreuth as a seasonal variant. The editors, although annoyed by the war because it posed new problems in the selection of comic drawings, thought that the Paris-London aspect of it ought to be covered as thoroughly as a Schiaparelli opening. Harold Ross did not think we would need much on the front, because he had been on the staff of *Stars and Stripes* in Paris in 1918 and felt he knew all about the fighting end, so that it was unnecessary to send out a military expert to represent us. This was lucky for me. The trouble with the *New Yorker* from my point of view as of September 1,

1939, was that all our European coverage was already being done by Janet Flanner, who signed her dispatches "Gênet," and that I could not conceive of a reporter coming away from a story just as it broke. Unfortunately for everybody but me, Miss Flanner's mother in California got sick and Miss Flanner notified the office that she wanted to come home. I got the Paris assignment because I had spent several man-hours of barroom time impressing St. Clair McKelway, then managing editor, with my profound knowledge of France. At about the same time the *New Yorker,* through a London literary agent, acquired the services of Mollie Panter-Downes to do the London Letter. No one in the office at the time of the hiring had ever seen Mollie—the whole transaction was a great boost for the pin-through-the-program system of picking winners at horse races.

I knew very little about Lady Mendl, Elsa Maxwell, Mainbocher and Worth the dressmakers, Mr. and Mrs. Charles Bedeaux, or a number of other leading characters in Gênet's Paris dispatches, but since it seemed probable that they would lam anyway, Ross was willing to overlook this deficiency and even agreed in a halfhearted way with McKelway's idea that I write about the reactions to war of ordinary French people. "But for God's sake keep away from low-life," Ross said. Meyer Berger had once written a *New Yorker* profile of a man who fished for lost coins through subway gratings, and Ross had been trying for months to disinfect the magazine by running pieces about Supreme Court justices and the Persian Room of the Plaza. I promised to keep my end of the war reasonably clean and high-class, and the office booked me a passage on a Pan American Clipper to Lisbon. It was not hard to get an eastbound ticket that season; there were only eight passengers on my plane, including me.

After I had got what I wanted and was sure to go, I had a couple of misgivings. German planes had not yet bombarded French cities, but people here thought that they eventually would, and I shared the general Sunday-supplement idea of what bombing could accomplish. I remember a sequence in a newsreel that September that showed the panic of a London crowd when some crank started throwing rubber balls about. The people had got the idea that there was a raid on; I remember one woman throwing her children on the ground and covering them with her body. I was never to see people so frightened during a real bombing. Walking down Lexington Avenue with Joe Mitchell of the *New Yorker* one warm night shortly before I was scheduled to take off, I said, "I bet I'll wish I was back on Lex a lot of times before this thing is over." The more a man sees of war the more immediate danger has to be before he starts worrying about it. I was talking last spring to a major in Leclerc's Fighting French column who was taking a sun bath in a cup in the hills during the battle of Enfidaville. We were all temporarily trapped by mortar fire, but none of the shells had yet landed in the hollow. They were bursting on the other side of the hill, fifty yards away. I still trepidate at fifty yards, so I said to this major, "That makes me a droll of an effect." He said, "It is all a question of habit," and continued to take his sun bath. In 1939 a lot of us scared at four thousand miles.

A couple of weeks after I talked to the sun-bathing major I met a 59-year-old second lieutenant in the Corps Franc d'Afrique who was on his way to lead an infantry attack, and he said courage was a question of digestion. On the morning of October 9, 1939, when I took off for the war my digestion was excellent, but I was nervous as hell.

At that period—it sounds like talking about stagecoach days—the Clippers still left from a yacht-club setting at Port Washington, Long Island. A friend of mine named Fred Schwed, a romantic soul who had been reared on Richard Harding Davis, although in early manhood he had switched to Scott Fitzgerald, had asked to drive me out to my plane in the early morning. Passengers were supposed to be at the plane with their luggage at eight o'clock. Schwed picked me up at an hour I never had experienced while sober, at the door of the house where I was living, and headed in what I took to be the direction of Long Island because the sun was rising over it. He drove me over one bridge, which was all right, and then around a wild farming country, in which I distinctly saw a hen and on another occasion what I took to be a cow—in one jump more I figured he would have me among the coyotes and Republicans—and then over another bridge, which was all wrong because it landed us in Westchester County. By then I had only an hour or so to catch the plane, so I began to curse, which I do well. The secret of good cursing lies in cadence, emphasis, and antiphony. The basic themes are always the same. Conscious striving after variety is not to be encouraged, because it takes your mind off your cursing. By the time Schwed got me to the landing he felt what a proper swine he was for having gotten up early in the morning to take me to the plane, and if the experience had broken him of volunteering to do favors for people it would have been worth while. I rushed into the dinky frame ticket and customs office they had there, still drooling obscenity, and saw my mother, who had gotten up early in another part of Long Island and come out to see me off. Sucking back four bloody oaths that I could already feel pressing against the back of my teeth, I switched to a properly filial expression, embraced the dear woman, and got aboard the Clipper feeling like Donald Duck.

There was one woman among the passengers, a myopic young American married to a fifty-year-old Englishman who told me he raised vast quantities of broad-*a* tomatoes in the Canary Islands. The tomatist boasted of having financed Franco's airplane trip from the Canaries to Spain at the beginning of the Spanish counter-revolution. He evidently thought it had been a brilliant idea. They had a stateroom, a fact I note for its antiquarian interest: I have seldom traveled since in a plane that wasn't crowded beyond seating capacity. We all floated in luxury on that trip, with two stewards to take care of the eight of us, soundproofing that has since been eliminated even from Clippers to keep down non-essential weight, and Pullman-style berths to sleep in. The most notable passenger was a French stage and screen star going back to report for military service because, he explained to me, a French movie star who remained in Hollywood during the war would lose his popularity at home. Since he was fifty years old there was not much chance he would be taken into the army, but he had a faithful public in France which thought he was a good deal younger than that. It startled me to see him making up his face in the morning when he climbed out of his berth, but he was a nice civilized Joe. It was the first time he had ever been in an airplane, and he was pleased and excited. "Poor, sick old Europe," he kept saying to the rest of us between slugs of scotch, "poor, sick old Europe." He had just been married in America and thought it was the only country in the world that had a future. We also had on board a professional correspondent named Bob Nixon, of International News Service, a rich Peruvian kid who was going back to

Paris to finish a course at the Sorbonne, a German Jew who was a naturalized Cuban citizen and on his way to France to sell the Government a kind of blue paint to put over headlights so they would give full light but would not gleam in the blackout—there was a fortune in it, he told us all, if he could make the right connections—and a brocade manufacturer from Zurich who was going home to take up his reserve commission in the Swiss Army. The Peruvian was quiet and apparently airsick all the way across. The Swiss was a solid sort who told me that the German-speaking cantons were more anti-Nazi than the French cantons. He said he thought Switzerland could maintain her neutrality indefinitely because her army could make invasion expensive for anybody. I found this hard to believe.

When I got tired of talking to the other passengers I thought about women. I frequently do this for hours without becoming bored; they are much pleasanter than sheep to think of when you are trying to fall asleep. Thinking about women also makes you insensible to mild fright or minor discomforts. Once I was sleeping with another fellow under a pup tent in a rainstorm in Tunisia, and at about two o'clock in the morning he woke me up. I said, "What's up?" and he said, "The tent's just blown away." The rain had turned into a cloudburst, and my blankets were soaked through. I got into the front seat of a jeep and wrapped the wet blankets around me. The top and windshield afforded some help, but the water lashed in from both sides. I thought about women for four and a half hours and never even caught cold.

The Frenchman and Nixon and I took the train north from Lisbon the day after we landed. The German-Cuban had no French visa, the Peruvian had disappeared, the Swiss was to take an Italian plane to Rome and go on from there; the tomato twosome were staying on in Lisbon. There was no more feel of war—or rather, since I did not know what war felt like, of difference from peace—in Lisbon than there had been in Port Washington. As soon as the train crossed the Portuguese-Spanish frontier at Fuentes de Oñoro we recognized by the atmosphere that we were in a belligerent country. The train passed camps surrounded by barbed wire and populated either by Republican prisoners of war or Franco soldiers. The victors were so miserably dressed that it was impossible for a stranger to tell them from the vanquished. The station platforms were crowded with soldiers in cotton uniforms and canvas shoes and with officers in boots and Sam Browne belts. The officers, who paid no fare, made a practice of boarding the train and riding for a couple of stations in the wagon-restaurant, where they regaled themselves on black bread, green apples, and imitation coffee, evidently a cut above what they ordinarily got at mess. An obvious flatfoot in plain clothes stood at the end of the corridor of our first-class carriage and watched the door of our compartment, and the bare rocky country through which the railroad passed stank of poverty and ruin. At Irun all the passengers bound for France were marched through the streets to the villa of the fascist governor and kept waiting in the garden for a couple of hours until an assistant had gone through our passports. From the manner of these strutting sparrows of men you might have got the idea that they had defeated France, the United States, and Great Britain, which they had in a way, of course, but by default, and that we were captives. After the tomato fancier's protégés had finished with us, the French actor, Nixon, and I walked across the international bridge to La Hendaye. Since the Pan American people had limited us to fifty-five pounds of luggage we had no trouble carrying our stuff with us. Coming into France, where there was no strain in the faces of the lazy-looking customs guards and where there were few soldiers in evidence and plenty to eat, was like arriving in a neutral from a belligerent country.

After we had gone over to the French *gare* and gotten aboard the Sud-Express for Paris we stood looking out the carriage window at France before the train started. The actor called my attention to an erect, worthy-looking old man in a derby hat and pepper-and-salt topcoat who stood on the platform, waiting to get aboard the train. He had a clipped white mustache and a fine, honest face. The actor was much moved. "It's Pétain!" he said. "He's ambassador to Spain now. Madame lives at La Hendaye." The movie actor had been an ordinary soldier in the other war. "What a fine old boy!" he said with emotion. I had not recognized the marshal, because I had always thought of him with the long, down-sweeping mustaches of his World War I photographs. I felt constrained to agree with my companion. "A great old gent!" I said. He was the first marshal of France I had seen, and his presence seemed a link with Napoleon and a happy augury. "He is young for his age!" the actor said with admiration. I had to admit that he didn't look a day over seventy-five.

The Sud-Express, except for the blacked-out windows and the dim blue lights in the corridor after nightfall, was as fine and punctual a train as it had ever been. The only person aboard who appeared affected by the war was an attendant whom I asked for a couple of bottles of Vichy Célestin. He said, "We have only Vichy Saint-Louis on the train now. You can't get everything you want now, there's a war on!" He wore the same expression of desolation as a waiter at Lüchow's in New York last summer telling me that there was no more Gaspé salmon, only Nova Scotia salmon, on account of the war.

The train arriving at Paris stopped at the Gare d'Austerlitz, far from the center of the city, and it took me a couple of minutes to get a taxicab, but the city, a considerable portion of which we had to traverse to reach my hotel, looked much as it had in 1927 except for the strips of paper pasted across shop windows to keep the glass from flying in case of a bombardment. I don't know yet whether this dodge is of any use. I can't remember seeing any on London shops and don't know whether they gave it up before I got there or just never tried it. The taxis I had seen outside the station were all ridiculously old *tacots,* which is French for jalopies, because the newer cars had been requisitioned by the Government. They had the old-fashioned hand horns that figure in the orchestration of *The Last Time I Saw Paris.*

I had decided on the Hôtel Louvois, facing the Bibliothèque Nationale, across the little Square Louvois. The façade and the square had always attracted me when I was a student. The Louvois would have been no good for me then, being on the Right Bank, and besides the allowance that my father sent me in those days would never have permitted such an expenditure—the Louvois was marked at least *tout confort* and possibly even *deuxième catégorie* in the Hachette Guide Bleu. I figured that as a war correspondent, however, I would be able to afford it. Room and bath cost me eleven dollars a week. I took a room that fronted on the square, overlooking the fountain with heroic allegorical figures representing the rivers of France. There were four statues, all expansively female and symbolizing, I think, the Seine, Rhone, Loire, and Garonne. From my balcony on the second floor of the hotel

I had a fine view of the Garonne's navel, which was nearly big enough to hold a baseball. There were twenty-one trees, an even greater number of flowers, in season, and a *pissoir* and a *chalet de necessité* in the little park. There were also benches where lovers and nursemaids came to sit. The Rue Richelieu runs along the Bibliothèque side of the square; the Rue Chabanais with its meretricious associations begins on the hotel side. On the other two sides there were six-story buildings, one of them a hotel, with people living in them whom I saw principally when some event of general interest like a wife-beating was going on in the square, when they would all appear on the little balconies in front of their windows.

In a general way I felt that my quarter included everything between the boulevards and the river, from the Place de la Concorde around to the Place de la Bastille, but my home province in this empire was roughly bounded by Rue Saint-Augustin, Rue Sainte-Anne, Rue Richelieu (with Rue Montpensier and the Palais Royale on the other side of it), and the Place in front of the Comédie Française, with the Café de la Régence on the other side. A province of two hundred acres that included the national library, the national theater, and the national lupanar, all a bit overlaid with dust and tradition, but still sound. It was part of the Second Arrondissement, represented in the Chamber of Deputies by Paul Reynaud. He had been elected by seventeen votes. I often reflected, after he became President of the Council in March, that any nine electors from among the pharmacists' assistants, bistro proprietors, and sporting girls I got to know in the quarter might have changed the history of France and of the world by their votes.

After I had left my bag and typewriter at the hotel I went around to the Paris branch of the Guaranty Trust to get some money on a letter of credit, and met Theodore Rousseau, the director, who had once been a New York newspaperman and then secretary to Mayor John Purroy Mitchel and had since married the Princesse de Broglie. Rousseau invited me to a wartime lunch at Larue's—it turned out to be just Marennes, Pouilly Fuissé, *caille vendangeuse,* and Grands Echezeaux—and then said, "You may have got here too late, old fellow. There's a strong tip on the Bourse this morning that the war's going to be called off."

24

CHAPTER IV

My Generals, My Generalissimo

WHEN I FIRST ARRIVED IN FRANCE I was told that there were two institutions beyond suspicion, the Church and the professional army. The Church did not interest me, but the generals did. The interest did not date back only to the beginning of the war. Even at college I had occasionally risked the contempt of my fellow liberals by reading a book about a soldier. Perhaps it was because in childhood I had owned a picture book illustrated with plates representing Napoleon's battles (the Pyramids, with the Little Corporal surrounded by Mamelukes, was my favorite, and the Retreat from Moscow broke my heart) and had later read Dunn-Pattison's *Napoleon's Marshals*. I could once name all twenty-six of them—Augereau, Bernadotte, Berthier, Bessières, Brune, and then I lose the alphabetic thread. The first French general I had ever seen was Joffre, in New York during the other war; I had felt very knowing every time I referred to him as "Popper." The first I had ever spoken to was old Gouraud, who was on some sort of a cultural lecturing tour in 1928 when I met him on his way to Woonsocket, Rhode Island, which has a large French population. I was then in exile as a reporter on the Providence *Journal* and *Bulletin;* I had been fired from the sports department of the New York *Times* for frivolity, but in Providence I got all assignments bearing on European affairs because they knew I had been in Paris.

The general's train had pulled in from New York during the night, and he was sleeping in a Pullman car on a siding. I wanted to get him in time for a first-edition story for the *Bulletin,* so I went into the car and woke him up. He was in a lower berth, and his whiskers were hanging over the edge of it. I shook him by the shoulder and said firmly, *"La presse!"* He got the idea and started to get up right away. I guess he had had a lot of arguments with out-of-town reporters already. *"Nous débutons, messieurs!"* he sang out. He had a half-dozen officers concealed in uppers and lowers all around the car, and they all got up. He gave me an exclusive interview, saying he liked Americans and France wanted to be friends with the United States. I took it that it would be all right with him to say he liked Woonsocket, although he had not yet been there, so I put that in the story too, although I worried about the journalistic ethics of the procedure. In those days I was as ethical as Westbrook Pegler, although poorer.

All this will explain why I was predisposed in favor of French generals when I got to Paris in 1939, and why I have been ever since. A fellow who wanted to keep abreast with French history during the following years could not have picked a better specialty. The first project I had brought from New York with me was to write a *New Yorker* profile of General Gamelin, and that necessitated an orientation in his milieu. I looked forward to it with pleasure, like doing a piece about prize fighters or sporting women. Some fellows like to write about the stage or screen, but I never understood why. Others can contemplate without repugnance doing a profile of a politician, a newspaper publisher, or even an advertising man or somebody in the radio business, but my tastes do not run that way. Like Edward Gibbon, a military buff although he never licked anybody himself, I like to hear talk about fighting. The most sensible talk I ever heard on the subject was from Sam Langford, the old Boston Tar Baby; but a French general has something genteel and old-worldly about him that Sam lacks. A good specimen combines the charm of Raymond Weeks, my old professor of philology, and Tex Grenet, the courtly old man who used to make the morning line for the bookmakers before the pari-mutuel came to the New York tracks. Maybe it's a father fixation.

Thucydides and Plutarch saved anecdotes about generals; why should I be proud? A general once told me one about General Mittelhauser, who will be remembered only because he succeeded Weygand in Syria and then declined to continue the war by General De Gaulle's side. Mittelhauser and an aide were returning to Paris by air when the plane developed engine trouble. It began to lose altitude. Mittelhauser looked at his aide, the aide was calm. Mittelhauser thought, "There can't be anything serious. I will not show this young man I am alarmed." The aide looked at Mittelhauser. Mittelhauser appeared calm. The aide thought, "I will not show the boss I am alarmed." The pilot made a crash landing in an orchard; the plane ran between two trees and lost both wings.

"Then," said the general who told me the story, "Mittelhauser and the aide knew there had been something serious." The aide pulled Mittelhauser out of the wrecked plane. Mittelhauser said, "When does the next train leave for Paris?" The aide said, "My general, I don't even know where we are." Mittelhauser shouted in a rage, "Imbecile! You never know anything!"

Another general told me another anecdote about Weygand in the First World War. The general who was telling me the story had then been a lieutenant colonel of artillery; Weygand had been Foch's chief of staff. The artillerist had participated in an unsuccessful attack on a little hill; Weygand asked him why his guns had not been able to knock out the enemy's machine-gun positions. "Because they could not be brought to bear at that angle, my general," the artillerist had said. "You are of those who believe that infantry unsupported by artillery cannot take such positions?" "I am of those, my general." "Then bugger off," Weygand had said indignantly and stalked away.

Another old general, a fine old specimen who had been of Gamelin's *promotion* at St. Cyr, was telling me about 1894, when the Dreyfus case had split the French Army wide open. This general, by exception, had been a *Dreyfusard* as a young officer. His best friend at St. Cyr had been an anti-Dreyfusard. They had quarreled, and from that day they had stopped speaking to each other. After the war, in which both had distinguished themselves, my general was riding in a railroad train when at a station the compartment door opened and in walked his former friend, who now had 110 per cent disability for war wounds. My general had 120 per cent. The other officer sat down on the bench opposite my general without saying a word, and they glared at each other for about fifty miles. At last the former anti-Dreyfusard extended his hand and said, "Will you at least shake hands with me?" My Dreyfusard general said, "If you have arrived at better sentiments, yes."

If these stories amuse you, you may understand my obsessional interest in French generals; if not you may consider it a hobby without apparent charm, like peridromophily, which is the collection and classification of street-railway tickets.

I knew that it would be hard to get an interview with the generalissimo of all the Allied Forces while he was running such a large war, so I bespoke the good offices of William C. Bullitt, the

United States ambassador, in obtaining it. Gamelin, in all the fall of 1939, granted only one interview, and that a mass affair for all the American correspondents. Bullitt had himself been the subject of a flashy profile by Gênet. He did not know whether it had been flattering or not, and neither did I after having read it only once, but it was expedient for both of us to act as if it had been, he in order to maintain his standing as man of the world and I because I wanted him to do me a favor. He was at any rate a *New Yorker* reader; so, I afterward learned, was Paul Reynaud, and I have sometimes wondered whether Reynaud got his copies regularly in his prisons after the Armistice. I reminded Bullitt that the *New Yorker,* despite its relatively small circulation for a national magazine, went to some pretty literate people all over the country, and that our stuff was filtered down through word of mouth and reprint until it had an effect on public opinion disproportionate to the number of first readers. He said he thought the interview could be arranged, if I wasn't in too much of a hurry. He sent me to Colonel Horace A. Fuller, the military attaché, now a major general commanding a division somewhere in the Pacific, and Fuller promised to talk to Colonel Jean Petibon, Gamelin's *chef de cabinet,* for me. Before interviewing Gamelin I knew that I would have to document myself on his views, his past, and enough of his technical background and jargon to make him feel that I knew what he was talking about. The preparation is the same whether you are going to interview a diplomat, a jockey, or an ichthyologist. From the man's past you learn what questions are likely to stimulate a response; after he gets going you say just enough to let him know you appreciate what he is saying and to make him want to talk more. Everybody with any sense talks a kind of shorthand; if you make a man stop to explain everything he will soon quit on you, like a horse that you alternately spur and curb. It is all in one of Sam Langford's principles of prize fighting: "Make him lead." Only instead of countering to your subject's chin you keep him leading. Once I asked Sam what he did when the other man wouldn't lead, and he said, "I run him out of the ring." This is a recourse not open to the interviewer.

In the summer of 1940 I went up to the Hotel Carlton in Washington to talk to General John J. Pershing about the subject of a profile I was then working on. I did everything I could to get the old man to loosen up, including pretty obvious flattery. "When they started to cut down the Army after the Armistice in 1918, General," I said, "you were against it, weren't you, because you foresaw this new European crisis?" The old boy looked at me in an angry, disgusted manner and said, "Who the hell could have foreseen this?"

The worst thing an interviewer can do is talk a lot himself. Just listening to reporters in a barroom, you can tell the ones who go out and impress their powerful personalities on their subject and then come back and make up what they think he would have said if he had had a chance to say anything. One of the best preps I ever did was for a profile of Eddie Arcaro, the jockey. When I interviewed him the first question I asked was, "How many holes longer do you keep your left stirrup than your right?" Most jockeys on American tracks ride longer on their left side. That started him talking easily, and after an hour, during which I had put in about twelve words, he said, "I can see you've been around riders a lot." I had, but only during the week before I was to meet him.

A profile of course is more than a well-prepared interview. You try to get anecdotes and objective views of the subject from people who have known him at various stages of his life, and then you fit the whole business together. I figured correctly that I would have plenty of time to dig up background before I would be allowed to see the generalissimo. I began by asking M. André de Laboulaye, a former French ambassador to the United States who was now the titular head of the American section at the Hôtel Continental, to recommend a general as a guide to higher strategy and tactics. Old M. l'Ambassadeur, who had some of the charm but none of the decisiveness of a general himself, sent me to General Pujo, who had retired from the command of the Army of the Air only a year before the war began.

General Pujo was a fine average specimen of a general, with ice-blue eyes, a firm chin, a good handshake, and a vast, high-ceilinged apartment in the Rue de l'Arcade with rooms full of Sèvres vases and Empire furniture. All generals, naturally, have a tendency to furnish in Empire because that was a period when generals were appreciated. His conversation was full of nice homely phrases like "we will have them" and "we will not let go the morsel." He said that General Gamelin, an old acquaintance of his, was a man of "tranquil luminosity of mind." Finally he recommended that I buy the *Instruction for the Handling of Large Units*, a publication of the French General Staff which set forth for commanding officers the official tactical doctrine. It had been prepared while Weygand was still commander in chief of the French Army and published in 1936, but the doctrine, Pujo said, had not changed under Gamelin, Weygand's successor. He gave me a note of introduction to Berger-Levrault, the great military booksellers on the Boulevard Saint-Germain.

Berger-Levrault was a fascinating shop, surprisingly like Champion, the publisher of medieval texts on the Quai Voltaire, where I had spent good hours in my earlier Paris time. The clerks, male and female, in their gray linen dusters reminded me of Champion's. They had the same complete knowledge of stock and mental catalogue of regular customers. They regarded newcomers with the same suspicious indifference, but an introduction *"de la part du General Pujo"* had the same effect as a *de la part* of Joseph Bedier's would have had at Champion's in 1926. The French made the art of war so intellectually fascinating that the study must have stolen any reasonable general from the practice. I went in for documentation on a massive scale, putting my purchases on my expense account. General Gamelin had commanded a campaign against the Druses in the twenties; I bought and read a magnificent history of the Druses, an interesting if repulsive people, by the way, and then a detailed military history of the campaign. When I at length met the generalissimo I asked him one question based on this mass of stimulating reading, and used about one line of what he said about it.

Gamelin himself had done a bit of writing, like most French generals, and I searched Berger-Levrault's stock for Gamelin items. One phrase of his, from a textbook, particularly impressed me: "Experience should be a springboard under our feet, and not a ball and chain at our ankles." There was also a paragraph that seemed slightly stuffy in an intelligent way: "It is natural that the immediate collaborators of higher officers be allowed to express their opinions freely, it being understood that each must bow in just intellectual discipline once the decision has been made. Initiative, within the frame of intellectual discipline, is the strength of armies."

There was some difference of opinion about the generalissimo among officers of the French Army even in the early days of the war, although all admitted he was bright. The discontent came chiefly from two sources—partisans of General Weygand, who had been retired for age in 1935, and those of General George, chief of the armies in the war zone and heir apparent to Gamelin's job. The generalissimo had in turn recently attained the retirement age of sixty-seven, both parties pointed out, but they based different arguments on this fact. The Weygandists said that if the Government was going to overlook technicalities about age their man should have been kept on, especially since he was so chipper that he had been recalled at the beginning of the war and placed in command of the Army of the Levant. The Georgists said that Gamelin should have retired gracefully and handed over to George.

The only man to whom I spoke who even then predicted disaster was Charles Sweeny, an American who had been at various times a colonel in the Foreign Legion, a correspondent for the New York *World,* and a promoter of ice hockey at the Palais de Glace. He had white hair which he wore cut in a Roman bang, and he aspersed his conversation with allusions to the campaigns of Lucullus and Sulla, which perhaps led me to minimize the importance of what he said. He said that the Army was rotten because the officers were afraid to work the men hard; energetic officers were curbed by their superiors, who lived in fear of politicians. Colonel Sweeny thought also that the ten francs a day which in this war was the pay of men under fire was excessive and would lead to drunkenness and mutiny. Having all this money to spend did not seem to affect the fighting quality of French troops in Tunisia later, however, while the English have been able to fight pretty decently under the triple handicap of three bob, or sixty cents a day. The Americans have not been stopped by still higher pay, and the Australians have done all right with the highest scale of all. I think that Sweeny's political was better than his economic reasoning. At any rate he said the Army was nothing like as sound as the Army of the last war and that it would collapse at the first push. It did. Colonel Sweeny affected me like the dilapidated stranger who appears at least once in most racegoers' lives and tries to tout them onto a twenty-to-one shot, which then wins. I paid no attention to him.

My interview came to pass about two months after I had opened negotiations for it. Colonel Petibon, a hard-looking, hard-driving officer whose arrival at a colonelcy at the age of forty-five was con-

sidered precocious in the French Army, had first interviewed me in
an office like a monastic cell off a long corridor of the Hôtel des
Invalides, early in November. The colonel told me that he was a
New Yorker reader too. He evidently decided I was all right and
said I must not leave town; he would call me when the generalissimo could see me. It was just about four weeks later that he telephoned to me at my hotel.

Gamelin's headquarters was at Vincennes, which was a semi-
public secret, but he seldom received there. When he was in Paris
he used as his office a paneled Louis XV room at the Ecole Militaire
which for years had served as Joffre's study. Joffre, of course, had
been Gamelin's *grand patron*. Gamelin had risen under his aegis
in the other war, serving him in the same capacity that Petibon now
served Gamelin. The square on which the Ecole stands was re-
named the Place Maréchal-Joffre after the First World War, and
an equestrian statue of the marshal, who rode regularly and grimly
to keep his weight down, stands in the center of it, or at least did
then. The ivory-tinted walls of the generalissimo's suite, still decorated with crowns and fleurs-de-lis in gold, displayed large paintings
of the battles of Fontenoy and Lawfeldt, eighteenth-century victories of the French Army. It was a raw day, and the room was
heated by a small gas fire. In the anterooms were steel engravings of
difficult Alpine defiles captured by the French in 1800. The entire
place was reminiscent of an ancient, successful business house.

Gamelin fitted perfectly into the vaguely Dickensian setting. He
is five feet four inches tall, which is not conspicuously short for a
Frenchman. He has a good round Flemish head, his hair was blond
and parted in the middle, his cheeks were rosy pink, and he wore
a sandy mustache which had recently taken an optimistic, upward
curl. The generalissimo seemed to me to have the face of a skeptical but indulgent Dutch uncle in a Frans Hals painting, although
in newspaper photographs he often had appeared grim and strained.
I consider him one of the most intelligent and sensitive men I ever
met.

Gamelin did not favor the defensive *per se,* any more than an
experienced automobile driver favors always going in one sense of
the compass. He believed that an attack upon Germany would have
no chance of success until the Allies had accumulated a superiority
of material, including airplanes, and that only the defensive was

feasible in the interim. The strategic concept was not bad. It was that upon which Great Britain was to fight the war after the fall of France. But Gamelin's correct conclusion was based on a false premise; Great Britain and France together, with the factories they had working for them in the United States, were not outproducing Germany then. Great Britain was not training troops as fast as Germany. The discrepancy of men and materials in the Germans' favor was increasing. It is hard to believe that the generalissimo did not know this; harder to believe that, knowing it, he could have seemed so optimistic, like a somnambulist jauntily strolling off a roof. Old schoolmates of the generalissimo had told me that Gamelin from the moment of his first arrival at St. Cyr had made the same impression as an ambitious young seminarist who his colleagues at once feel is destined for a high place in the hierarchy. They had said, "He would rather be generalissimo than anything else in the world." But he could not have wanted to be remembered as the commander of a disaster.

"You can't get out of the concrete," he said to me regretfully. "There isn't enough heavy artillery in the world to get out of the concrete." This respect for fortification hardly jibed with his omission of it on the north of his line. His failure was not of concept but of execution. "Twenty-five per cent for the theoretical solution of the problem," Foch, his old professor at the War College, had told him often enough, "seventy-five per cent for the application in battle." Then, in the spring, the Allies were to abandon even the strategic defensive and move into the Low Countries.

It is not enough to say that the French paid too little attention to the use of tanks and bombers by the Germans in Poland. They believed in anti-tank defenses, in anti-tank guns, in a strong tactical air force which would control the sky over the battlefield at least, in such elementary conservative chores as keeping the men supplied with food and small-arms ammunition. Their deficiencies in all these matters had nothing to do with strategic doctrine. But in retrospect it is hard for me to associate the calm little man in the big old-fashioned room with omissions in the most elementary parts of war. It is as if I had had a long conversation with a novelist— perhaps M. Jules Romains—and a couple of years later somebody came to me and said, "You remember M. Romains? He was an illiterate."

CHAPTER V

Bajus Disappointed

THE WAR OF COURSE was not called off, but there were few indica-
tions that it was on. Paris was a city in which people were tentatively
picking up the threads of ordinary existence—tentatively and a little
sheepishly, as if ashamed of their initial agitation. Several million
Frenchmen had been mobilized, thirty-eight Communist Deputies
had been put in jail, and the newspapers carried a daily communiqué which sometimes chronicled "operations" as small as the shooting of an enemy messenger dog. People distrusted the calm, but
there was nothing they could do about it except talk. During each
fortnight the city lived through two or three periods of intense preoccupation with the war and as many of groping toward an approx-
imation of peacetime life.

Only the women clung to the hope of a continuing miracle—a
war without hard fighting. "Hitler will surely blow out his brains,"
they said, or "Just think how much money the English must be
spending for the revolution in Germany." They circulated with
grave optimism the story that a gipsy woman had got into an auto-
bus and sat down next to a Parisienne who had moved her handbag
out of the gipsy's reach. The gipsy had then said, "Why do you do
that when you have only eighteen francs in your bag?" The woman
had exactly that sum. Then the gipsy told each of the other passengers how much he or she had, down to the last *sou*. "Since you
know so much," one passenger had asked, "tell us when Hitler will
die." "On December second," the gipsy had said, and had got out
at the next stop. A story like that gained currency not because
Frenchwomen were silly but because they refused to believe that
their sons and husbands would be killed—those sons and husbands
who until then had been so miraculously preserved, it seemed.
Miracles are perhaps to be distrusted; the men were being preserved
for the bitterest destiny an army ever had, but nobody then divined
it. The book of Michel Nostradamus, the old astrologer, had become a best seller. According to the exegetes of the full-length

thirty-franc version I acquired, he had predicted the destruction of Paris by "birds from the East," and its reconquest a year later by a French king after a great victory in the Valley of the Loire, but there was some confusion about the dates for which he had predicted these events. Maybe Hitler will die on a December second —the odds are only 364 to 1 against it; perhaps there will be a battle of the Loire on the way back to Paris. Then the gipsy woman and Nostradamus will get credit for having seen clear, like experts on European affairs.

I was told that in September there had been emotion manifest in Paris; air raids had been expected hourly, reservists went to the front expecting to be hurled into counterattacks against an invader; the Poles had been the darlings of the public. But now that was all over. When people thought of the war it was with cold exasperation; there was a self-conscious distrust of phrases like "heroic poilu," "sacred soil," and "accursed Boche," but it had become clear that as long as Germany was free to mess up Europe every twenty years life would be barely supportable. Not quite everybody realized that life would not be supportable at all. It was the psychology of a defensive war; none other is possible to a decent people until it has suffered much, when a retributive counteroffensive spirit can be aroused. If all the newspaper files and foreign correspondents' books and White and Gray and Mauve Papers of a dozen governments were to be destroyed forever, the fact that the French fought would remain as proof they must have been right. They hated it so, and in the beginning they had had so clear an idea of the odds against them.

André Chamson, in his journal of the war at the front, wrote, "Hitler thought he would have us as he had had the Social Democrats—without fighting. He awaits the disintegration of the last man. But here around me the world is full of men." The Poles and the French had ended the sequence of conquests by bluff, and in doing so made Hitler's end inevitable. His capacity for bluff had been infinite; his capacity for conquest by arms, although great, was insufficient.

In Paris it was the great age of the strategists of the Café du Commerce, the French term for the armchair kind. And the hot blood that had rushed toward the national head during the month of September receded in October toward the feet already chilled by the overtures of a winter of rationed fuel. Behind the blacked-out windows of the cafés in the evenings there was some of the promiscuous sociability of speakeasy days in prohibition-time New York and, I am told, of air-raid shelters during the London blitz. Anybody at all was willing to tell you how the war could be won, but a majority favored gradual methods like the starvation of German war industry.

General Robert-Georges Nivelle, little remembered outside France then or now, had left a deep trace upon the feeling and thinking of his country. It was Nivelle who had talked his countrymen into the great offensive in the Champagne in April of 1917, remembered as the "great bloodletting." When a café strategist complained of seeming inaction in 1939, a confrere had only to wave a finger and say, "Nivelle," to shut him up. In six days in Nivelle's battle in 1917 the French had lost 35,000 killed and 80,000 wounded. As a measure of comparison, we had less than 15,000 casualties, not counting prisoners of war, in the whole African campaign. There were no hospitals reasonably near the battlefield for so many wounded, so they had to be distributed all over France; the trains of mangled men spread despair through the country. Mutinies had followed; every Frenchman of an age to be in civilian clothes in 1939 remembered that awful time. Eventually the Germans would have to attack, the café strategists said, but then we would have them.

Sometimes there was visible a bit of the surface ebullience that my friends told me there had been in Paris in the other war. One Sunday I was walking in Montmartre with my old Henri, whose American silk firm had folded its Paris office during the depression and who had lost all his money, and on the Place Blanche we saw a great crowd of soldiers and strollers around a song plugger who was selling a new ballad. The plugger, a youth about fifteen, wore four hats one on top of another and howled into a megaphone with indelicate gaiety:

> *"Hitler n'en a pas,*
> *Du tout, du tout!*
> *Hitler n'en a pas,*
> *Pas même un tout p'tit bout!"*

The lyrics were about things like ammunition and beefsteaks and gaiety. The plugger's gestures weren't included in the lyrics.

There was an evening when I heard two pimps arguing about the war in the bar of a brothel. Each was in fact the protector of one of the two *sous-maîtresses* of the house, and each was waiting until his particular protégée accumulated enough capital and good will to start in business for herself. So they were men with an assured future. It must have been in early October, when the French still held a minuscular strip of German territory in the Saar. "Them, they're not here!" one pimp shouted. "Us, we're there! So we must be winning." A moment later, to emphasize some point or other, he started showing off his World War I wounds and yelled, "I bet I am the only pimp in France with three citations." The proprietor of the house in which they were arguing was a naturalized Italian who, his wife always said, was a perfect gentleman because he never drank anything but champagne. "Not even in the morning!" Madame Lucie would say, looking adoringly at the fat procurer— "not water, not coffee, not beer, not even *mousseux* have I ever seen him drink!" I sometimes used to watch a drop of sweat gleaming on his fat ear and wonder if it tasted of Irroy '28, his favorite. Madame Lucie never told me.

Nearly four years later I was to meet a colleague of the boys under a field ambulance tent on the way to Mateur and Bizerte. He was in the Corps Franc d'Afrique, a volunteer shock-troop outfit. When the nurses had cut his uniform jacket away they had found a tricolor wrapped around his chest. It sounds like the verse of a maudlin song, but it's true. A hunk of shrapnel had gone through the white part of the flag, which was now rust-red. The lower half of a tattooed female extended down toward his scrotum from the place where the flag stopped. When I asked him where he came from he didn't bother saying "Paris"—just "Nineteenth Arrondissement." That's Belleville—the stockyards. He had been wounded in the fighting around La Maison Forestière, in the high brush east of Cap Serrat. He had a mouthful of gold teeth and a tough chin. I asked him, foolishly, what he had done in civil life. He said, "I lived on my income."

I do not want to give the impression that I covered Paris for the *New Yorker* entirely from cafés and brothels. I took the responsibilities of my new career so seriously that I joined the Anglo-

American Press Association of Paris and went at least once a week to the Hôtel Continental, where the French had set up their equivalent of the British Ministry of Information, although they did not give it the status of a full ministry until the following spring. My sponsors in the Press Association were H. R. Knickerbocker, then with International News Service, and Percy Philip of the New York *Times*. Knick was by way of being a popular hero in Paris because he had broken a big exclusive story about how Nazi leaders had opened bank accounts in a number of neutral countries, including several they were subsequently to take over. He was enthusiastic about the war, meeting me, his apartment on the Ile St-Louis, the sound of the French language, which he could not speak, and the womanhood of Texas. On subsequent occasions I was to meet him being enthusiastic about Winston Churchill, the heroism of the English people, the inspirational gifts of Major General Terry Allen, and the sweetness and fortitude of American army nurses. He and a rear admiral named Clark Howell Woodward are the only two men I ever met in my life who admitted they liked making speeches.

I went up to Knick's apartment one evening with Robert de Saint-Jean of the American section of the Hôtel Continental. Nobody can say Knick wasn't catholic in his choice of guests; it included Edgar Ansel Mowrer on one end of the political scale and on the other a pathological little Frenchman named Jean Fontenoy who wore a turtle-neck sweater with a lounge suit and moaned, whenever he could collect an audience, because the Government refused to call him up for service in the Army. He had been a notorious sucker-around-Abetz and pro-Nazi before the war, a fellow who wrote books boasting of the misery of his peasant parents and preaching that misery was good for working people. It kept them honest, according to him. He, of course, considered he had had a quasi-divine call to the masters' table. He kept on moaning in drugged tones now because he could not get a commission, but he was destined to make collaborationist speeches in theaters after the Armistice and to be found in the Seine with his throat cut. He was the first overt European-type fascist I had ever seen in the flesh, and he had a horrid fascination for me, like the first man a kid sees wearing lipstick and long black stockings. The tomato man on the Clipper had been respectable by comparison. There were not many like Fontenoy to be seen about Paris, and those who did appear in public pretended, like him, that everything had changed for them with the beginning of the war and they were now great patriots. The uncostumed collaborationist types got along swimmingly. Only the turtle-neck sweater boys got into a little trouble, and they not nearly enough. The others had had sense enough to stop talking when the war began, and newspapers friendly to them urged the Government as a national duty to accept them in positions of trust.

The Communists had been inept; they had publicly announced their position against the war, and they were being hunted down as traitors, in many cases by Rightist policemen who were more dangerous types than their quarry. The Maurrases and Lavals, the blackmailers and libelists of *L'Action Française* and *Gringoire,* used the Communists skillfully to divert suspicion from themselves. It was Henri de Kerillis, a Rightest himself, who in a speech in the Chamber of Deputies called attention to "the former apologists for the Nazis who are now trying to turn the whole war into a crusade against Stalin." The press almost unanimously reproved him for endangering national unity.

You cannot keep your mind indefinitely on a war that does not begin. Toward the end of the year many of the people who three months before had been ready to pop into their cellars like prairie dogs at the first purring of an airplane motor, expecting Paris to be expunged between dark and dawn, were complaining because restaurants did not serve beefsteak on Mondays, Tuesdays, and Fridays, and because the season had produced no new plays worth seeing. There was even a certain disappointment among the less reflective elements of the population; the appetite for disaster in some human beings is so strong that they feel let down when nothing terrible happens. Cartoonists had developed a number of wartime civilian characters in the genre of Caspar Milquetoast. One of them, a petit bourgeois called Bajus, was shown in a December comic strip listening to a radio address by Hitler. At each howl from the radio set ("I will destroy England before breakfast," "I will show the French what total war means") little Bajus' hair stood on end, and at the close of the speech he turned to his radio, saying, "Oh, please, Adolf, don't stop; frighten me again." Thousands of Bajuses felt deprived of the terror which had become the most interesting component of their daily lives.

There was, even during the fall and winter of 1939, one occasional feature of Paris life that provided a brief reminder of the war in progress. This was the firing of the anti-aircraft guns at German planes that came over on reconnaissance or to drop dirty pictures. The pictures showed British Tommies making love to naked French girls while a poilu died tangled in barbed wire. They fetched a good price from souvenir collectors. The planes never dropped any bombs, but the sound of guns fired in anger and the sight of searchlights combing the night sky is the beginning of a non-combatant's habituation to war. We were being broken in very gently.

The year slid to an end through a nearly normal Paris Christmas season, with carillons and lifesize mechanical figures in the windows of the Galeries Lafayette, postcard hucksters' stalls along the boulevards, and a special Christmas circus at the Medrano, with the three Fratellinis appearing as guest stars. The Medrano was the most delightful little circus in the world, with one ring that had a cushion around it like a billiard table. The liberty horses waved their hoofs in the faces of the spectators in front-row seats. The clowns, clown proper, *auguste* and *grotesque,* shared the hegemony of the ring with the equestrians, according to tradition. The great Fratellinis were not as limber as they had been in my student time, and they took fewer falls, but they had some good mechanical gags and their marvelous faces. The oldest brother got one of the big laughs of the evening when he made his entrance carrying a gas mask. In September every member of his audience had been carrying a similar affair.

The French like old favorites. They go to see them over and over again to observe how time is treating them, and if a performer appears to be in good health they are delighted. They have a weakness for old generals, too, old frock coats, old airplanes. They forget that even the best material wears out. Once Lieutenant Colonel Vincent Sheean and I were riding in an old French airplane in Algeria and the door blew off. There was no particular reason except that it was an old plane and an old door—the wind blew it away. The co-pilot laughed and grabbed my typewriter just as it was about to slide out of the hole the door had left. The conservative spirit is susceptible of exaggeration.

The Medrano was one of my favorite diversions that year. Another was walking along the quais, where the fishermen and book merchants of the Seine pursued the placid, even tenor of their lives. A third was passing one afternoon a week in the hushed interior of the Hamman, the old Turkish bath behind the opera. The Hamman had a dome of colored glass like a mosque and a plunge three strokes long. The icy water plashed into the plunge through the mouths of metal frogs. When you lay on your couch afterward, dozing, you could hear the soothing, nostalgic water-sound like a broken toilet in a New York rooming house. Old François, my favorite rubber, was a tall, stooped Parisian with a face like a rummy Vercingetorix. He was an urban fellow, like me. One day I told him that I was going to the country. He appeared worried, but finally said, "The country, yes. I have heard that it is simply swarming with oxygen."

CHAPTER VI

Vire Revisited

VIRE, like hundreds of other little French cities, showed little outward evidence of the war. About eight hundred of the 6,900 inhabitants Larousse credited the town with had been mobilized, but since Vire had become the home of 1,400 refugees from the war frontiers it had the largest population in its history. Its history goes back to Robert the Devil, who was William the Conqueror's father. Some of the refugees had money, and they had rented every available house in town; others, called "official refugees," got ten francs (less than twenty-five cents) a day from the Government. The mayor, a tall, desiccated doctor who looked like an old-fashioned New England practitioner, said, "It isn't much, of course, but they get along." He told me he didn't think much of the refugees. Soldiers' wives who were residents of Vire received only eight francs a day for themselves and four for each child. The wives, however, having roots in the district, usually had unmobilized relatives who gave them milk and butter and vegetables, for Vire lies in the best dairy country in France. It rains two days out of three from October until July, and nobody used to complain, because the rain made the pastures lush. Now that the Germans have taken away the cattle the rain may be resented.

The Paris newspapers had been paying a good deal of attention to events in the United States. The repeal of the Neutrality Act had got them started, and they had sent a number of reporters to the United States who promptly filed staggering stories of the vast American aircraft industry which was rolling fighter planes off assembly lines as fast as Fords. One plant a fellow described, I remember, was within a couple of miles of Hollywood, and all the most beautiful stars of the cinema used to come out in their automobiles of great luxury to watch the new planes taking the air like flocks of birds. I was astonished myself when I got back to New York after the debacle to find that we had been producing less than three hundred planes a month, of all categories, at the period of the *grands reportages.* This sort of thing was to cause a disastrous reaction in the spring, when the ground troops discovered that the flocks of airplanes were a myth.

The press of Vire remained strictly cisatlantic. One of the two weeklies, *Le Bocage,* headed its column of criminal proceedings with the news that butter, jam, cake, and sugar had been stolen from one Madame Grandérie by an eleven-year-old boy from a village called Beauquay who had entered her house by climbing a pear tree and breaking three windowpanes. The next item told of the arrest of Joseph Jegu for mendicancy. "Let us add," said *Le Bocage,* "that the individual had a pocketful of money."

When I got to Vire I went to my old hotel, the Cheval Blanc, but found it had changed proprietors. The new man was not nearly as good a cook as the old, who had gone to Angers and taken over a larger hotel also called the Cheval Blanc, but food was as plentiful as before. Outside the grocery stores hung rows of silvery herrings, each with a nail through its tail; the grocers' windows were full of the black smoked sausages called *andouilles de Vire;* the cabbages and onions grew with tropical eagerness in the kitchen gardens even in November. All the local sauces were based on cream and butter and apple brandy—it was a fat country. I wonder how the Virois eat now.

I asked a postman, whom I saw in the café of the hotel, whether old M. Hédouin, the librarian, was still alive, and he said he wasn't.

The economic pulse was steady, I soon found. The farmers were selling beef cattle and horses to the Army at a fixed price which was not a bad one, and there was a new, mysterious war factory among the *vaux*, a mile or two above the town. The countryside reminded me again of southern New England, with rolling hills, birch and holly, elm and oak, except that in the *Bocage* the people had used granite for building houses and barns instead of walls between fields; they marked their boundaries with bands of standing birch and poplar trees. The wet climate has made the Virois quieter than Frenchmen who live in the sun—and harder drinkers. Apple brandy is their regional tipple, and all apple brandy in France is called Calvados in honor of the department in which Vire lies. All over France men had called on the name of this department at marble-topped tables and zinc-topped bars, twenty-four hours a day almost, counting the Paris marketmen who work all night and are great drinkers. Affectionately they had contracted the name to *Calva,* a beautiful name for a drunkard's girl child if any reader wants a tip.

War was no new or strange word in Vire; the Normans had fought the French there, the French the English, and the Huguenots the Catholics; one wall of a transept of the twelfth-century church was covered with the names of Virois killed in War '14. The mayor, to annoy the curé, always told visitors to Vire that the church dated only from the thirteenth century. He was a Conservative Republican, the mayor, which put him in about the same category as a Republican in Vermont. There were few Marxians in Vire, where they still talked of the French Revolution as a fairly recent event. But they accepted the fact of the Republic as unquestioningly as Vermont farmers do.

Le Bocage had an opposition weekly, *Croix du Bocage,* dedicated to the Catholic point of view. Both papers printed letters from Virois with the Army who said that they were playing with their regimental soccer teams, or wanted sweaters. Both papers published the citation of a lieutenant, the son of a dentist in a neighboring town, who, in one of the skirmishes of outposts in which the armies sometimes indulged, had led a detachment in the capture of a German blockhouse and had operated a machine gun after the death of the gunner. That sort of thing then seemed to an American Homeric.

Headquarters for civilian strategists in Vire was the Café de Paris, where the proprietor, whom I found playing innumerable games of dominoes with all comers, was Maurice Brocco, a man who once enjoyed immense seasonal fame in New York as the little six-day bike rider the crowds at Madison Square Garden liked above all others. Something about him amused the bleary-eyed nocturnal public, and for a long time after he retired Garden fans continued to yell "Come on, Brocco!" when there was a jam.

Brocco is French; he was born near Reims, in the Champagne, which is a flat country favorable to the development of bicyclists. He found, however, that Italian riders were drawing the gate in New York, and since his name sounded Italian he usually rode on the Italian team. It always tickled him when the Italians in the infield yelled, *"Avanti, Brocco!"* In Vire, as might have been expected, Brocco in his cap and sweater was the pattern of dashing cosmopolitanism. I thought that even the mayor, who referred to Brocco as "that good rooster," was a bit jealous of him. With me to bear him out Brocco told the other customers terrible lies about prohibition in America. The lies reconciled them to the wartime prices of *apéritifs.*

On a hill near the town there still stood part of a castle built by Henry Beauclerc, the youngest son of William the Conqueror; and at the foot of the hill the gipsies still camped as they had done seasonally since the tribe came to Europe, snaring rabbits for their food. I came back from the trip feeling pretty good about France.

The through train from Granville to Paris stopped at Vire. When I got aboard I found in the first-class compartment I entered a short, thick-necked, thick-bodied little captain of an Algerian regiment, a fellow with badger-gray hair and clipped mustache who was reading a worn clothbound American edition of *The Man That Corrupted Hadleyburg.* "I reread it often," he said in French, noticing me looking at his book. "It is a taste I took in the Cameroons, where I was in garrison for three years. This volume I acquired on a ship where I was of passage to there. Like so many, I read English but I am afraid to speak it. The book has a theme truly French, and an exquisite 'humor.' "

The little captain's regiment was in the northeast, he said, up beyond the end of the old Maginot Line. He was returning from a visit to two married sisters in Granville. He himself had spent most of his life between wars in the colonies—his regiment belonged to the standing army. "It is a splendid regiment," he said. "No *chichi*

—just Normans and Kabyles. Most of the native non-coms fought in the other war. They are hard, like the old Roman legionaries." In the North the French were building formidable field defenses, he said. The captain, like scores of Frenchmen I used to talk to, said that he had been ashamed of the abandonment of the Little Entente. Daladier, on his way back from Munich to Paris, had correctly anticipated this feeling. The anecdote of how he drove from Le Bourget to the Quai d'Orsay expecting catcalls and was astonished by being cheered instead is by now familiar, like his comment, *"Les cons!"* But the "spontaneous" demonstrators in the streets were the same hirelings who led the February 1934 riots, working for precisely the same employers—the eternal Nazi-lovers of the industrial cartels. Men of the caliber of my little captain never went into the streets to yell their thoughts at passing limousines. Daladier, a good Frenchman though perhaps a weak man, was puzzled; within a short while he knew that his first intuition had been right. He could not have abandoned Poland without provoking the disintegration of France.

"From Czechoslovakia the Czechs and Russians, and we from the headwaters of the Rhine—the movement of the shovel, what could have been more simple!" the little captain said. "But it would have meant giving up the concept of a defensive war behind the Maginot Line," he added. "You do not know what the concept means to us. It means the high wall topped with broken bottles that the provincial bourgeois puts around his garden. Behind it he is secure with his cabbages. He can wear his slippers, live the good life without bothering to button all the buttons of his trousers. Because I have lived so long outside metropolitan France I can see this."

CHAPTER VII

Merry Christmas, Horrid New Year

IF YOU WERE A CORRESPONDENT in France in 1939 and wanted to go up to the French front you addressed a letter to Mr. Maynard Barnes at the United States Embassy, telling your place of birth, your journalistic history, some reference, and your reason for wishing to go. Barnes forwarded your request to the Intelligence Section at General Headquarters, and in a week or so you were usually granted a pink paper called "A Special Mission Accorded by the General Staff for the Purpose of Journalism," which was good for a week or ten days. You picked up the paper at the Intelligence Section bureau in the Hôtel Continental, where Madame Gros-Perrin, a stout imperious woman with a good laugh, gave you instructions for getting to the front. She told you to go to Nancy and to wait at the Hôtel Thiers there for a press officer from the Intelligence Section who would have further instructions for you. She told you to carry a gas mask and a field helmet. I already owned a gas mask the first time I went up, but I borrowed an American helmet from Captain Bob Schow, one of the assistant military attachés at our embassy. The American helmet then looked a bit like the British job; our new helmets resemble the German.

I left Paris on my first "mission" on December 23. I took the noon train to Nancy, which rolled at its peacetime express clip until nightfall, when, because of the dimmed signal lights, it dropped into a cautious crawl. Arriving at Nancy that night, I found the town blacked out completely. Luckily the hotel was directly across the street from the station, so I was able to reach it without any trouble. A woman at the hotel desk told me that the press officer had not arrived yet, but if I cared to step into the *brasserie* of the hotel I would find a number of other American and English correspondents awaiting him. I could immediately distinguish the correspondents in the *brasserie* because their uniforms were much more magnificent than those of the French military at the other tables. A particularly tailored-looking uniform on Pashkoff, a photographer for *Life,* had the French officers gnawing their mustaches with envy. The most lavishly accoutered man I have seen in France turned out to be an employee of the Columbia Broadcasting System. Since I was trying to get by in riding pants and a vaguely brownish topcoat, I felt like the only ship passenger in a lounge suit at the captain's dinner. I was cheered by the costume of a Mr. Browne of the *Christian Science Monitor,* who had come to the war in tweeds. After one look at each other, Browne and I decided to stick together so that we wouldn't feel inferior.

Most of the correspondents, it developed, were planning to go

to a great Christmas Eve midnight Mass in a fortress of the Maginot
Line. Columbia and N.B.C. were to broadcast the Mass, and a
number of the newsreel companies were to film it. Before the press
officer appeared, I was afraid that I would be packed off to the
broadcast with all the others, since the Intelligence Section, I figured, probably thought that all Americans were hysterically fond
of *radiodiffusion*. But the officer gave Browne and me permission
to take a train to Alsace the next afternoon and visit the front there.
An officer would call for us when we arrived at a station the captain
named, and in due time we would be allowed to see the front.

When, early the next afternoon, we got to our station, we could
see we had arrived at the war, because there were no women in
sight. Here, against a background of brown, frozen earth and sleety
roads, of trees covered with rime, and of the ugly, amorphous buildings of a railway-junction town, there were only soldiers. Most of
the men on our train were *permissionnaires* returning from furlough. They lingered around the railroad station unhappily, like
students returning from a holiday, then moved off in the direction
of their cantonments. Browne and I didn't bother to look for our
officer; we were so incongruous in that crowd that he couldn't
possibly miss us. After we had waited awhile, an officer stopped in
front of us. He had a square jaw and high Celtic cheekbones, and
was about as big as a Brooklyn baseball pitcher. "Lieutenant Sauvageon," he announced as he saluted, "aviation officer of the Divisional Staff." Sauvageon stepped aside, and we could see another
officer behind him, a slight, smiling man who carried a bamboo
cane and maintained a monocle in his right eye. Introducing him
to us, Sauvageon said, "Captain de Cholet is one of the few cavalry-
men in our sector. He is on the staff also." "I have a horse," the
captain said, "but he is in Paris."

A soldier came up, took the one valise in which Browne and I
had concentrated our possessions, and carried it to a 1936 Citroën
that had a red-and-white-striped pennon on the forward end of the
left mudguard. *"Fanion du général,"* the soldier volunteered pleasantly, pointing to the pennon. The soldier's name, we learned, was
Siegfried. It was a standing joke with the captain and the lieutenant
that Siegfried, who was an Alsatian, had constructed the Siegfried
Line. Browne and I rode in the rear with the captain between us,
and the lieutenant sat in front with Siegfried, who drove. It was

about three o'clock in the afternoon. The road was glassy and the mist was very heavy. "Evidently it is not a good day for observation," said the captain. "Moreover, we are sufficiently distant from anything to observe. Therefore, Lieutenant, where can we buy a drink?" "Siegfried," said the lieutenant, "can you discover the mess of the balloonists?" Siegfried did not answer, but after ten minutes of blind navigation he landed us in front of a shuttered tavern.

We all walked into the taproom, which was decorated with a green tile stove, a Christmas tree, and enough antlers to fit out a small museum. At a heavy, bare table a half-dozen soldiers of the Balloon Corps sat with anilin-dyed apéritifs, wrangling over a card game. A young lieutenant got up from among them to greet us. The officers' mess was upstairs, he explained, but he was the only officer in the house, so he had come down to the bar for company. We invited the lieutenant to join us, and Siegfried took his hand at the card table. We all ordered hot grog, and the drink stimulated Browne to ask the balloonist if he had seen anything of a war which, according to the people in the United States, was at that moment in progress between France and Germany. The lieutenant, it seemed, had actually been under fire. The company had an observation balloon at a near-by field, and twice, when it was up, Messerschmitts had come after it. Both times the ground crew had pulled the bag down safely. Lieutenant Sauvageon said that several German machines had come down in the sector. "Curiously," he added, "three of them were undamaged. The pilots said they were airsick. We reported them as shot down because we did not want their families to have any trouble in Germany."

After talking awhile, we said good-by to the balloonist, wished him a merry Christmas, and went out to the Citroën. By now we might as well have been in somebody's pocket for all we could see, but Siegfried, who knew the terrain, was able to feel his way. "It is now evidently quite impracticable even to try to observe," the captain said, "so we will take you to the fort where you are to lodge tonight. It is an old German fort, one they built after they took Alsace from us. It is not a very good fort, but is comfortable, and when we get there the colonel will buy us a drink." Sauvageon, still seated in front, turned around and said, "We picked this colonel specially for you because he is having a big Christmas party and he will have the best oysters and *foie gras* in the sector, better even than the general's. He is a Parisian and he likes to talk to visitors because he has been in the fort now for four months."

It took a long time to reach the fort, and when we arrived we had to cross a drawbridge spanning a moat to get to it. The forts the Germans built after '71 have the pseudomedieval quality of the National Guard armories in New York City. We entered by a wide, high portal and found ourselves in a thoroughly non-functional place of echoing corridors and vaulted ceilings. It seemed to have been built by people who enjoyed playing soldier. I couldn't help asking the first man to introduce himself to us, an artillery lieutenant, whether the fort had any defensive value against modern ordnance, since Siegfried had informed me we were only about five kilometers from the Rhine. "It would stand up to machine guns and field artillery," he said, "but a heavy shell hitting squarely would go right through the roof to the powder vaults, where there isn't any powder now anyhow. But we wouldn't use the fort to fight from. The regiment is scattered all over this part of the sector by batteries. All we have here is a headquarters company, a medical unit, a telephone central, and a guardhouse."

We all went into the mess hall to wait for the colonel, which, we were told, was the warmest place in the fort. There were two clusters of German lances on the wall, left behind by the Imperial Army when the French occupied Alsace. Captain de Cholet looked at them tenderly and said, "I left for the last war carrying a lance. I even managed once to stick a German with one, but later war ceased to be fresh and joyful." Sauvageon nodded sympathetically. Before long the colonel walked in. He was tall, straight, and consciously picturesque. He wore a brown beret which was barely balanced on the side of his head, like Rodolfo's in *La Bohème*. His cheeks were old rose and his eyes cobalt blue, and his long white mustaches did not droop, but descended in a powerful, rhythmic sweep, like the horns of a musk ox. He was an excellent colonel, we had been informed; he had commanded a large part of the heavy artillery in the campaign around Salonika twenty years ago. Between wars he was a banker in Paris.

"Gentlemen," the colonel said, after we were introduced, "I welcome you to the humble barrack of a sick old man. It is not the Meurice. It is not the Plaza Athénée. The fare is not that of Au Cabaret or the Berkeley." We assured him that his fort would do us

49

very well. A soldier then wheeled over a tea wagon holding about twenty bottles—scotch, port, sherry, and various apéritifs. The colonel took an obvious pride in his gamut of alcohols; it proved he could "defend himself." The verb *"se défendre"* had acquired a very broad meaning in the French Army; it signified "getting along." An officer pulled a pair of old socks over his shoes so that he would not slip on the ice; a private met a stray hen and wrung her neck because otherwise she might fly into Germany; soldiers going on patrol in wooded parts of no man's land set rabbit snares so that on their way back they might pick up a tasty breakfast—all these expedients were part of the French concept of self-defense. It followed logically that a colonel defended himself on a grander scale than a subordinate.

De Cholet and Sauvageon took their leave. The staff, they said, had to accompany the general to midnight Mass. It would not be precisely gay; the general was a great friend of the bishop's. They promised to call for Browne and me early in the morning. As we talked to the colonel, most of the officers of his mess joined us around the tea wagon.

Shortly afterward the officers took their places around a large mess table for dinner. Browne and I were invited to sit flanking the colonel. I had on my right a fair-haired, blue-eyed captain, a Jew from Strasbourg. He said that two uncles and an elder brother of his had deserted from the German Army at the beginning of the war in 1914 and had fought with the French. Being only thirteen years old at the time, he had remained at home. In 1918 he had been conscripted into the German Army and had been stationed in that very fort. In civil life he was an industrial engineer. Most of the officers, he said, were, like himself, reservists, but a number of men from "the active" had been inducted into the regiment at the beginning of the war to set the pace for them. The soldiers were young reservists in the later twenties, and three quarters of them were Alsatians or Lorrainers. "This is a regiment that must be mobilized on the spot at the beginning of a war, because Germany is just across the river," he explained.

Before the dinner could begin, the *popotier,* or mess officer, had to make what I was told was a traditional address. In this particular mess, the popotier was a round, embarrassed little man with bulging eyes. He was an *adjudant* and the only member of the mess who wasn't a fully commissioned officer. "My colonel and gentle-men," he began, standing before his plate at the foot of the table, "I have the pleasure to announce——" He was interrupted by shouts of indignation and, correcting himself, said, "The *honor* and the pleasure to announce to you that the menu tonight, the twenty-fourth of December, will consist of soup of leeks and potatoes (a few scattered shouts of "That's what we had the day before yester-day!"), cauliflower au gratin ("O miserable popotier, without imagination!"), salad, cheese, fruits, and, as wine, Châteauneuf-du-Pape." "Thank you, popotier," the colonel said solemnly, "pro-vided only that the Châteauneuf is tolerable."

The dinner was polished off with businesslike haste because there was a full evening ahead of us. After coffee and armagnac, a Christ-mas mood began to seem more attainable. We all walked along a corridor and down a flight of stairs to an unused powder vault which the soldiers had turned into a *salle de théâtre*. The walls of the vault had been painted to give a three-dimensional illusion of draperies, and at one end of the room there was a real curtain of the same color as the painted ones.

To one side of the curtain stood a great Christmas tree decorated with lighted candles. An orchestra, made up of a violin, saxophone, and piano, played what most Europeans think is the American anthem, "The Stars and Stripes Forever." There were about two hundred soldiers in the vault, wearing ugly, solid shoes and long khaki overcoats that looked like horse blankets. The men were in a state of juvenile excitement. An evening of amateur entertainment was a great event. The leader of the orchestra was a tall, flat-chested fellow with shiny hair and a receding chin. The surgeon major told me that the man was a Berliner who had acquired French citizenship by serving in the Foreign Legion.

After a long overture, a master of ceremonies appeared before the curtain wearing a Prince Albert coat. "Our first number," he announced, "will be a song by our Alsatian chorus—*Rose des Landes.*" The chorus was made up of eleven artillerymen, each standing with feet wide apart and thumbs in his belt. "*Röslein, Röslein, Röslein rot, Röslein auf der Heide,*" they sang. The non-Alsatian officers and men applauded mightily. As an encore, the chorus sang a marching song which began, "*O Strassburg, O Strassburg, du wunderschöne Stadt.*" Then the choirmaster sang a long folk song about the character of the Alsatian people. I remember only one line: "A donkey is no hummingbird." The blond Jewish captain from Strasbourg said to me, "That is the Alsatian situation in one line. We refuse to be what we are not." Soldiers from Brittany and the Midi sang next, and a Parisian corporal delighted all the provincials by losing his nerve completely and breaking down in the middle of a line, belying the metropolitan reputation for nonchalance.

After the last turn there was a rough-and-tumble drawing of Christmas presents. Then the colonel made a speech. The merriest soldier was the best soldier, he said, but the poor, forlorn fellow on outpost duty on the bluffs rising from the Rhine must not be forgotten. He said he was sure every man there would gladly be killed rather than let the Boches pass. "It is very necessary for us to win this war," he added. I think everybody there agreed with him. "There will be a midnight Mass in our new chapel," he announced, "for those who care to attend. This is a free country." I noticed that almost everyone did go to chapel, including those who didn't cross themselves.

After Mass the officers went back to the mess hall for supper. They were in high spirits because they felt that their men had enjoyed the evening's entertainment. In that phase of the war one of the officers' hardest tasks was to keep their men from getting bored. Now the officers had a chance to enjoy themselves, and they were in such good humor that the popotier got through his ritual speech unheckled. There was a slight commotion among the diners, however, when the mess attendants served the consommé in soup plates. "There is a curse upon the mess!" grumbled the surgeon major. "There are no cups for the consommé!" After oysters and some *foie gras de Strasbourg au Porto,* we all began to drink champagne.

We had been sitting at the table for some time when suddenly the colonel shouted, "The battery departs! At a walk!" Immediately the officers began rapping their knuckles on the table, to produce the effect of horses walking. "At a trot!" the colonel ordered. The tempo of the rapping increased. "At a gallop!" The rapping grew faster. "Halt!" There was a second of silence, and the colonel shouted, "First gun—fire!" All the men brought their right fists crashing down on the table. "Second gun—fire!" "Third gun—fire!" "Fourth gun—fire!" After each "Fire!" the table took a sterner thump. After the fourth gun, the officers began to grin shyly, like small boys anticipating the point of a familiar joke. "Fifth gun!" ordered the colonel. That was the cue for the senior captain to speak up, with considerable gravity. "There isn't any, my colonel." (There are only four guns in a French battery.) The colonel appeared dumfounded. Then he recovered. "That doesn't matter!" he shouted. "Fire!" The officers hit the table with both fists. A glass broke, a bottle rolled onto the floor, one dignified-looking captain, overcome with laughter, fell on the neck of the surgeon major.

The party broke up at five o'clock in the morning. The only officer who seemed mildly unhappy was a gangling, thin-lipped captain, a transfer from the regular army, who said to the colonel doubtfully, "This is all very well, my colonel, but it isn't really war." The colonel, whose chest was covered with campaign ribbons and decorations from 1914–18, stopped chuckling and looked at the captain steadily. "Sometime you may look back on this evening," he said, "and you will say, 'The days at the fort were the good ones.' What the devil! A fellow has to defend himself."

I suppose they have looked back upon that evening infinitely often since the Armistice, when practically all of them became prisoners of war. As far as I could ever learn, the regiment was pulled back from the Rhine in early June of 1940, when the Germans had gotten behind the eastern defenses at both the northern and southern ends. Some of them got back into the Vosges, because Sauvageon the aviator, who was himself transferred from that area before the debacle and so did not become a prisoner, wrote to me that one officer I knew had been killed at Hohwald, a summer resort in the mountains fifty miles from Strasbourg. Long before the war I had stayed at Hohwald and walked over the hills to the monastery of St. Odile to drink the white wine called Lacrimae Sanctae Odiliae.

CHAPTER VIII

Colonel Albatross

BROWNE AND I SLEPT BRIEFLY, in a kind of dungeon where the stone walls sweated icicles, after the Christmas Eve celebration. Then Sauvageon and De Cholet arrived to take us to see the Germans.

The bridge across the Rhine between Kehl and Strasbourg remained intact, although for reasons easy to understand traffic over it had been light since the first of September. The mist on the river Christmas morning was so heavy that the French soldiers in the little redoubt on the Strasbourg side were hampered in their game of trying to see Germans through their machine-gun sights. They were not often allowed to shoot, mist or no mist, but at any rate they could look, and the Germans played the same game and sometimes talked to the French in French with a public-address system. The bridge was perhaps eight hundred feet long, and between the French and German redoubts at either end were elaborate festoons of barbed wire, which, when coated with white frost, produced a fine decorative effect.

It was cold on Christmas, and fog had covered the hard earth with a thin glaze of ice. The French soldiers holding the bridgehead were well pleased with themselves, for a young corporal from Lunéville had made his way across the bridge during the night and had stolen a Christmas tree which the Germans had set up in their barbed wire. He had also collected a few German newspapers he found lying about in front of the enemy redoubt, and the tree, decorated with strips of the newspapers, now surmounted the French post. All the company officers, from the captain to the tall, red-bearded second lieutenant who *dans la civile* had been a Protestant pastor, had formally scolded the corporal and then shaken his hand. The corporal, a nineteen-year-old volunteer, said, "What tickles me is that now they'll court-martial the sentinel over there. Those sentinels think they're wise guys, bawling us out with their loud-speaker." The troops did not shoot except when they lost their

54

tempers badly, for they realized that shooting would only increase their common discomfort, but the lull had if anything increased the antipathy between the two forces. When I heard how seldom anybody fired I said I wanted to look over the parapet at the Germans, but the captain at the bridgehead made me take off my American helmet first. "If they think you are an Englishman they may fire," he said. "They have never seen any Englishmen down here, so we cannot say what the result would be." I looked over bareheaded and cannot truthfully say that I observed anybody.

A couple of months later when Sauvageon was in Paris on a ten-day leave he told me of a curious incident in this sector. There were two casemates that faced each other like these, but across an even narrower unbridged stretch of the Rhine. A German colonel, a nasty-looking fellow, used to come out of the German redoubt every evening to smoke a cigar by the water's edge and cock a snook at the French. One evening he started to *pipi* in the river, the better to mark his contempt. A French lieutenant on the left bank stepped to the loud-speaker and said, "You exaggerate. Get away from there or I shoot." The colonel cocked another snook and the lieutenant cut loose on him with a machine gun. The colonel fell on his back, Sauvageon said, his cigar flew out of his mouth, he was dead. Then the German loud-speaker was heard. The Germans said they were coming out to get the colonel's body; they had no hard feelings against anybody but the lieutenant, they said, but if the French fired on the men coming out for the body they would make it a general feud. The French in the casemate were angry at the lieutenant; they considered him in the light of the man who had shot the albatross that shielded them from harm. They did not fire on the Germans again, and they made life so miserable for the lieutenant during the succeeding weeks that he had to ask to be transferred to another casemate. Sauvageon said that he considered this an unhealthy *état d'esprit*. So did I.

The holiday season afforded a precious chance to break the monotony of the long pause, and the army in Alsace was taking full advantage of it. Hunting, for some ridiculous reason, was against the law in wartime even for soldiers, but that did not affect the supply of venison at the front. As one commandant blandly put it, "If deer insist on strangling themselves on the barbed wire, what can one do?" His explanation of the pheasant served at his mess was equally ingenuous. "The battalion medical officer runs over a dozen whenever he goes cycling," he said. "As he is not a veterinary he is unable to save their lives. So we eat them."

General Pichon, the *divisionnaire* at whose mess we stopped for Christmas supper, told us how he had visited a dugout in a forest and found a soldier skinning three rabbits he had illegally snared. "Sir," said the startled soldier, "I had just withdrawn my rifle from the loophole when in jumped these poor rabbits, one after another, and died of fear." "The poor unfortunates," the general had replied, turning to go out and continue his rounds. "Nature is cruel."

In some regiments in the sector eighty per cent of the men were Alsatians. Some had all their possessions locked away in apartments in Strasbourg, whence their families had been removed to Périgord. Strasbourg, through which our guides had Siegfried drive us, was incredibly sad. Ruins are something anyone can understand; but Strasbourg had simply been emptied of life; the stage and all the properties remained. Hats remained in modistes' windows, and beer glasses still stood on café tables where the drinkers had left them the day the war started. In the Place Kleber, where in other years one of the world's finest municipal Christmas trees had always stood, there was a tiny balsam surrounded by bread crumbs; it was a Christmas tree put up by the military police for the abandoned pigeons of the cathedral. With the Corps Franc in Tunisia long afterward I met a towheaded, blue-eyed sixteen-year-old volunteer. "What are you?" I asked him, because the Corps Franc has many German and Austrian and Dutch refugees in it. "French," the boy said. "What city in France?" "Strasbourg," he said, "the most beautiful." It was more than two years since Goebbels had announced the "incorporation" of Alsace-Lorraine in the Reich—like a louse on a man announcing he had now "incorporated" his host.

After Strasbourg, Nancy seemed feverishly gay. The cafés closed at eight-thirty, the blackouts were much blacker than the Paris kind, but there were still women to see and there was even an English correspondent's mess in the Hôtel Thiers, where, by special dispensation of the police, a visitor might stay up and drink as late as twelve o'clock if the lone, crusty old waiter didn't take it into his head to go home before that.

I spent the next couple of days on a conducted tour of a couple of Maginot Line fortifications near St. Avold in Lorraine. They seemed to me excellently contrived, like all the Maginot forts shown to correspondents. They contained mortars and anti-tank cannon but no heavy artillery. The heavy artillery, my conducting officer explained, was several miles back of the Maginot forts proper. This was so that the big guns might be shifted about on the "interior lines" beloved of military writers. Unfortunately interior lines by definition have to be inside something, and the exterior line of fortifications did not exist from Montmédy to the sea. The Germans were to push through unfortified space until they had got behind the left shoulder of the permanent Maginot Line and take it in reverse. As they approached each fort from the left rear, the heavy artillery would have to be pulled out from behind it. That would have left the men in the fort exposed to continual heavy artillery fire without hope of counter-battery. The fort on the extreme left end of the line was taken in this way. It held out through one hundred hours of continuous shelling. No troops came out alive. I heard about it on June 6 from Meyer Handler of the United Press, who had just returned from that sector. Most of the rest of the line was abandoned without fighting.

I returned to Paris on an express train that still had fine, crowded *wagons-restaurants*. These express trains were reserved for officers and civilians. Across the table from me I had a tall, earnest young lieutenant of an infantry regiment that had distinguished itself in the early fall fighting around Forbach. "There are only two armies in the world," he told me with assurance. "Us and them."

CHAPTER IX

Sample Supermen

A FEW WEEKS after I came back from the Maginot Line I went into Lorraine again to see some Germans in a prison camp.

The staff officer who accompanied me seemed embarrassed because there were no large groups of prisoners to see, as there would have been in the last war. "Unfortunately," he said as we set out from Paris, "we have taken few prisoners—perhaps a couple of hundred since the beginning of the war. It's the same with the Germans, of course. We have only the fellows that we bag on patrols between the lines, and the aviators who are shot down in our territory. You can't get many aviators at a time, though."

My guide had served as an artilleryman at the front from 1914 to 1918; now he had an office in the Ministry of War and spent much of his time journeying about to inspect his customers, as he called the prisoners, and to prepare for the reception of more. The camp we were going to was situated in a small city some fifty miles on the French side of the Maginot Line. In our railroad compartment, as we journeyed, the staff officer told me a good deal about prisoners of war. They are supposed to be treated, he said, in accordance with an international agreement signed at Geneva ten years ago, and since prisoners are, in a way, hostages, the three belligerents on the western front respected its terms. Germany did not show the same consideration for Polish prisoners, of whom there were thousands, he said, her official reason being that she did not recognize the Polish Government-in-exile. The real reason, naturally, was that no Germans were being held prisoner by the Poles. German prisoners who felt they were being abused might appeal to the Reich's "protecting power," which, in the case of France, was Sweden. France's protecting power in Germany was, at the time of my trip, the United States. Moreover, the International Red Cross inspected the camps of both sides, so all in all a reasonably close check was kept on the prison officials of the belligerents, he thought.

According to the Geneva agreement, prisoners of war are entitled to living conditions as good as those enjoyed by the garrison troops of the army that has captured them. The troops guarding the prison camps provide a practical measuring stick in this matter: prisoners have a right to the same rations and the same amount of space per man in their dormitories as their guards, and their beds must be as comfortable. They even receive from their captors the same pay as soldiers of equivalent rank in the army that has made prisoners of them. At the end of the war each side will be expected to reimburse the other for this pay. The scheme had worked out well enough so far between France and Germany, although there had been occasional grumbling among the prisoners themselves. The French at home are normally better fed than the Germans, and the Germans are better housed than the French. The men were sensitive to these differences, and to others which similarly upset their habits. The German prisoners, for example, got a ration of wine they couldn't appreciate, French prisoners got beer they didn't like, and neither French nor German can tolerate the other's smoking tobacco.

What I thought of most, going up on the train, was that I was at last to see some Nazis. I had not been in Germany since 1927, and it had been hard for me to understand how the uncertain-looking people I remembered from that trip had become so formidable. I wondered if I would see anybody resembling the thick-legged, bull-necked Storm Troopers in the cartoons left-wing magazines used to publish before the Reich-Soviet pact, or if there would be any of those German idealists you heard about who would say that Nazism was hollow and false. I asked the staff officer if he had heard of such a case of regeneration in any of the camps, and he looked at me as if he thought me remarkably silly. "No," he said. "Even if a prisoner were against Hitler he wouldn't say so, because he is still under the orders of whatever German noncommissioned officers are also at the camp." Commissioned officers were not quartered with the noncommissioned officers and the rank-and-file prisoners. "Anyway," my guide went on, "most prisoners have families in Germany. None of them argue about politics among themselves, except for some Austrians we have in another camp. They seem to think they would not be in this trouble if it were not for the other Germans, and a while back there was a bit of a row about that. Those Austrians are quite a problem. On the other hand, you will find this lot of prisoners we are going to see a very well-disciplined troop. There is an unusually high ratio of noncommissioned officers to men in this camp—about two to five. That is because many of them are aviation prisoners, and only officers and noncommissioned officers fly." I asked what would happen to a German soldier if, regarding the war as over so far as he was concerned, he told one of his German superiors in prison where to get off. The staff officer looked shocked. "We'd put the soldier in the guardhouse," he said. "It would be insubordination."

An army automobile was waiting when we arrived. It was only a five-minute drive out to the prison, a group of buildings which, I was told, had once been a factory. They were arranged in a rectangle, with a yard in the center and a gate at one end. Most of them had slanting glass roofs and were at least thirty feet high, with concrete floors and no upper stories. Halfway up on their walls were rows of enormous windows. The administration offices were near the gate, in what had been the offices of the firm which occupied the factory. We found the commanding officer waiting for us; he had not yet had enough visitors to be bored by them, and he seemed glad of a break in routine. He was a paternal, red-faced captain who appeared capable of taking a sympathetic view of the plight of a prisoner. Beside him was a tall, kind-looking old major, with a pink, bald head and gold-rimmed spectacles, who was introduced to me as an interpreter. The major said he had lived in Germany a long time and thought he understood the German mentality, although he did not approve of it.

The prisoners, it turned out, were in the section of the factory farthest from the gate, and on our way to see them we—the captain, the staff officer, the major, and I—had a chance to look over much of the plant. As we went from one unit to another we passed guards —men of forty or older, selected from a regiment of reserves. The Quartermaster Corps had fitted them out with antique uniforms of horizon blue, and for hats they had old Tank Corps helmets. Almost all looked like peasants, with long arms and hard muscles, and since all had fought in the last war, they handled their rifles with assurance. The guards saluted dutifully as we passed, and that reminded the captain of something. "Wait till you see the Germans," he said, a trifle apologetically. "They *like* to salute." He showed me the guards' bunkhouse so that I could compare their quarters with those of the prisoners later on. The guards had two tiers of fairly wide bunks with metal frames and straw-filled mattresses; the only other furniture was a row of lockers. We walked on through a series of rooms which had been prepared for the reception of prisoners not yet captured. Barbed-wire fences had been rigged up inside all along the walls to keep prisoners away from the windows.

As we approached the occupied unit I heard a man shouting, and by the time we got inside, the prisoners there had quickly formed a double rank in the center of the room. A young German at the head of the platoon was bawling happily the Teutonic equivalents of "Eyes left! Eyes right! Right dress! Attention!" Spines snapped back convulsively, chins jerked up as if each of the Germans in line had received an invisible uppercut. They seemed to enjoy this rigmarole. Their leader turned to the captain with a magnificent salute, as if he had just performed a difficult trick and expected the captain to throw him a bouquet. The captain said hurriedly, "At ease," and looked flustered by so much attention. The German noncom turned on his men. "At ease," he said in a disappointed voice. The men relaxed, appearing depressed at not being asked to do more tricks. The captain said to me, in the tone of a curator explaining an unusual exhibit, "You see? It is their particular mentality."

I walked around the room, an immense one with a concrete floor and brick walls. There was no barbed wire in this unit; the windows were smaller and placed higher than in most parts of the plant. The Germans evidently spent most of their time in the part of the room nearest the door, to be close to the coal stoves which heated the place. The men's cots were arranged head to head in two long rows; they were not double-deckers, like the bunks of the guards, but had the same sort of frames and mattresses. Beyond the cots were a row of rough tables and several long benches. There were books on some of the beds, on which the Germans had evidently been reclining before we came in, and there were chess sets and playing cards on the tables. These little luxuries, I was told, had been sent to the men by their families, who are allowed to send letters and packages, but not newspapers, to the prison. A narrow shelf, with things on it like tooth powder and combs, ran along part of one wall. Each prisoner had a section of the shelf for his possessions and had written his name under it—Hoffmann, Betz, Keil, Muller E., Muller J. were some I noticed. I also noticed a portrait of Goering, torn out of a German magazine; above the portrait was a chunk of wood with a swastika burned into it. There was another picture, also from a magazine, showing tugboats and ice floes in the harbor of Bremen. Near it was a pencil drawing labeled *"Morgenstund,"* which showed a snub-nosed prisoner, stripped to the waist, brushing his teeth in front of a troughlike sink, with a mustachioed sentry, helmeted and carrying a rifle with fixed bayonet, standing vigilantly in the background.

The Germans, eighty or ninety of them, remained standing at ease. With few exceptions they appeared to be between twenty and thirty years old. Most of them still wore the uniforms in which they had been captured, with the addition, in some cases, of a sweater.

61

A couple of men whose clothes, I suppose, had been in particularly bad condition when they arrived were togged out in French tunics and trousers formerly of horizon blue and now dyed a sickly green. Many of the Germans wore smart-looking knee boots, and their forage caps resembled those of the British Royal Air Force. Their uniforms, those that had survived, were decently tailored and made of good cloth; apparently the ersatz fabrics of which one heard so much in France were for civilians.

I noted a variety of coloration and facial types among the men —more dark hair than blond, about as many round heads as long ones, sometimes slant Mongoloid eyes above a red Celtic beard. Regarded as crusaders for race purity, they seemed a mongrel lot. They were not big. The staff officer noticed this, too. "It's a curious thing," he said. "In the last war the prisoners we took at the beginning were almost all huskies." I suspected that the underfeeding of German children during the last war and in the postwar years might have had something to do with it.

The major was chatting with the noncommissioned officer who had been giving orders, and I joined them. This German, a sergeant pilot, was of medium size but athletic-looking and well fed. He was a classic Saxon type—wavy blond hair, blue eyes, and a complexion like boiled ham. He had been piloting a single-seater Messerschmitt pursuit plane when it was shot down with eight other machines in an air battle in November, and upon arriving at camp he had taken command because he was the senior noncommissioned officer. The pilot said he was twenty-eight years old, came from Leipzig, where he had been graduated from the gymnasium, and had served in Spain and Poland. The Air Force obviously was his career, so there was no reason to ask how he felt about Hitler, who created the Air Force. It was a bore being a prisoner, he said; he found the lack of exercise hardest to bear and complained that there was no sports field for the prisoners. Unlike most of his comrades, he enjoyed wine, having acquired a taste for it in Spain; the food, he said, was all right, but there wasn't enough of it. He certainly did not look thin after five months of prison rations. The major said he thought the pilot only imagined he was hungry because the food was strange; Germans, he explained, are used to dark bread, boiled potatoes, cabbage, and fat, overcooked meats, but in French prisons they get white bread, fried potatoes, leeks, and lean red beef. The pilot did not seem convinced by the explanation.

We started back to the office, where, the captain said, I would find it easier to talk at some length to a couple of the prisoners.

A few minutes after we got there the first prisoner chosen for an interview was brought in. "The pilot was a good example of a reliable Nazi," the major said. "Now take a look at this fellow." The prisoner, who came from Berlin, was one of the bloodless industrial-worker type which the postwar years produced in Central Europe. He was an ugly man with a rueful, conciliatory grin, and he looked middle-aged, although he said he was only thirty. He had worked in a hat factory until he was mobilized on the twenty-eighth of August 1939. He had previously served eight weeks in the army back in 1935, when compulsory service was revived in Germany, and that was all the military training he had had before the war. He had been undramatically captured in the Saarland early in September, when he and some other soldiers were sent out on bicycles to lay small mines. He had had more to carry than the others and, on the return trip, had fallen behind. Taking a wrong turn, he had run smack into a French patrol. That was all. Looking at him, I felt sure he had had just such luck all his life.

The major asked the man what he thought the war was about, and he immediately became voluble. As long as there was capitalism, he said, there would be wars. Capitalistic states had to make ammunition to cure unemployment, and then they had to use the ammunition. It was inevitable. I asked him what he thought of Hitler's Germany, and he said emphatically that he considered it a capitalistic state the same as all the others. Russia, he said, was only another dictatorship; she had made the alliance with Germany so that Germany would feel she could safely fight England; Russia hoped that both England and Germany would become exhausted, and then she would rule the world.

The major asked the prisoner what he thought of the showing the Finnish Army had made against the Russian troops. The man said he didn't believe the Finns had won any battles at all. "In Berlin we used to hear also about the big Red victories in Spain," he said, "but it wasn't true. It wasn't true about Finland, either." We asked him whether he knew that British planes had flown over Berlin, and he grinned incredulously, telling us that the German

Air Force was the strongest in the world. "One thing I must say," he went on, as if he believed it. "The English have too many colonies. If they would give some to Germany, maybe even with Hitler I could make a living for my family." After he had left, the major said, "He is a Communist." I wondered what he really was.

The next prisoner to enter was another Berliner, who, like so many of his townsmen, had a Polish name. He was a well-set-up youth, thin but with good shoulders, and he still looked smart in his cap and uniform. He had high cheekbones, an aquiline nose, a thin mouth, which he kept drawn tight in an effort at self-control, and baffled green eyes. He was twenty-seven. Once, he said, he had been a tanner's apprentice, more recently he had become a white-collar worker, and just before the mobilization he had been working as an adding-machine operator. He had been captured while doing patrol duty between the lines. I was astonished to hear that he, too, had had only eight weeks of military training—in 1935. "It's nothing unusual," the major said. "At the beginning of this war the Germans had four eight-week classes in their army—all the men from twenty-seven to thirty—and they had no trained reserves at all between the ages of thirty and forty. It is apparently a very spotty army, with all its strength concentrated in certain *corps d'élite* like the motorized divisions and the aviation. They have worked hard in the last seven months, of course, but so have we."

While we talked in French, the prisoner, tense and frightened, stood watching. He was not a Nazi party member, he told us when we asked him; he had never bothered with politics. He had once belonged to Workman's Sport, an affiliate of the old Socialist party, but that was just for the swimming and water-polo privileges of the organization; he had never been a Marxist. The pact between Germany and Russia didn't bother him. He said it was just for business, and anyway the Russians were all right. He had been in Moscow for four weeks in 1938 with a workmen's swimming team. The major asked him why Germany had gone to war. "Because of poverty," the former adding-machine operator almost shouted. "Germany has been poor all my life because we lost the last war." The major looked at him over his gold-rimmed glasses, like a blasé probation officer questioning an incorrigible. "You think war will cure poverty?" he asked. "What else?" said the puzzled soldier. "If we lose this war, it is the end of Germany. We will be Bolsheviks unless

64

the English give us colonies. Colonies we must have or we will be Bolsheviks." The major interrupted him. "Don't you think," he asked, "that wars always bring poverty, even when you win?" Either this was beyond the prisoner's understanding or he was afraid to consider the question; at any rate, he just shrugged. Perhaps he didn't want to have his last hope destroyed until the slogan-makers had time to offer him another.

I would have liked to listen to more political thought from these men, but the staff officer, who had organized our trip as carefully as an offensive, told me that we had forty-two minutes before the next train back to Paris and that consequently we had thirty-seven minutes left in which to visit the German commissioned officers. I wasn't as interested in them, because aviation lieutenants and infantry subalterns at the beginning of a war are almost certain to be enthusiastic, no matter what army they belong to. If the officer comes from a rich family, he considers the war a lark; if from a poor one, he thinks being an officer is a fine job. The German officers I saw lived up to this rule. They were lodged in what, before the war, had been the city jail. The cell doors were solid, not made of bars like those in an American jail, and the cells were about as large as bedrooms in an average modern apartment house. I don't know what kind of prisoners they had been designed for, but they even had wallpaper.

The pleasantest of the officers I met was a Rhinelander, a tall, blond subaltern who reminded me of the young Germans who used to play deck sports on liners, laughing too loudly and trying with a grim will to win. This man was an artillerist who had had the unfortunate inspiration of going on patrol with the infantry. He was reading a book about golf when we came in. He received a salary of seven hundred francs a month from the French Government, which was the pay of a French second lieutenant "absent from duty." This was not as much as the same French officer would get in active service. The officers were charged three hundred francs a month for their food, so, even if they managed to buy a few incidentals from their guards, they probably saved more than half their pay. The notion of getting rich in prison amused the Rhinelander. "I can't get out to spend it, you know," he said in English.

I next met four aviators who shared a common living room during the day. All had shaved their skulls and grown long, brown beards. When I asked one where he came from he said, "Germany. There are no more Prussians or Bavarians or Saxons. We are all Germans." He said he was a German who happened to live in Berlin, and that was all I could get out of him. Of the others, one said he had been shot down by six Spitfires, another by seven Hurricanes, and a third by a dozen Curtisses. I had never heard such a concerted tribute to Allied superiority in the air; listening to them, I marveled that a Messerschmitt could find its way through the traffic. They were lying, of course.

"You remarked the fellow who said there were no Prussians, no Bavarians, et cetera, the most Nazi of them all, to hear him speak?" the captain said after we had left them; "He came down in an open field behind our lines because of engine trouble, he said, but none of our mechanics could find anything the matter with the plane. Naturally he has to put up a big bluff here or he would be under suspicion. If he sounded lukewarm the other prisoners might suspect the truth and send him to Coventry, or conceivably smuggle into their letters somehow a hint of his treachery and then his family in Germany would lose its pay allotment. But there are also fellows like the sergeant pilot who are really Nazi *cent pour cent;* two classes of cocky prisoners, *les vrais durs* and *les faux durs,* the true hard ones and the fake hard ones."

The proportion of *vrais durs* to *faux durs* among German prisoners in successive phases of the war, I have thought since, is the only significant index to the morale of the German Army. The circumstances of a man's capture are more significant than his tone of voice in replying to the interrogating officer. It is to a prisoner's interest to be cocky, after capture, for he is under the surveillance of his fellows and the governance of superiors whose Naziness is likely to be in proportion with their rank. The Geneva Convention was never drawn up to cover an ideological war; there is no inducement for the German prisoner who is democratic or just anti-war to let anybody know what is on his mind. Vanity also counts in the prisoner's attitude. He likes to think of himself as a Teutonic hero even when he knows he has quit cold.

A friend of mine, a lieutenant colonel with the Eighth Army, once interrogated three German prisoners after the Battle of Akarit in the African campaign, and when he had finished, one of the

Germans, drawing himself up to their cataleptic version of attention, asked, "But do you not think we are fine soldiers?" The lieutenant colonel said, "Not especially." He said the Germans looked as if he had hit them with an elephant-hide whip. By this time they have probably complained against him for violation of the Geneva Convention against torture.

CHAPTER X

The Knockdown: Paris Postscript

THE NEW PHASE of the Second World War began for Paris at daybreak on Friday, May 10, 1940. People had gone to bed Thursday night in their habitual state of uncertainty; the governmental crisis in London which was bringing Winston Churchill to power was still the chief subject of preoccupation. With dawn came the air-raid sirens, startling a city that had heard no *alerte* during the daytime since the first weeks of the war. At once the little Square Louvois in front of my window took on the aspect of an Elizabethan theater, with tiers of spectators framed in the opened windows of every building. Instead of looking down at a stage, however, they all looked up. All wore nightshirts, which, since the prosperity of tenants in a walk-up is in inverse ratio to their altitude, appeared considerably dingier on the sixth and seventh floors than on the second and third.

The anti-aircraft guns were intoning such an impressive overture that startled birds flew out of the trees in at least one of the squares and circled nervously in squadrons over the roofs. As they did so, a large, formless woman in a gray nightshirt, making her *entrée* at a top-floor window, waved her right arm toward them and shouted *"Confiance!"*—putting all her neighbors in hilarious good humor.

The guns kept up their racket, and a number of tracer shells lit up the early morning sky. The noise of the airplane motors was distinctly audible, but in those pre-blitz days we could not distinguish between the sound made by bombers and that of French pursuit planes looking for Germans. At last one airplane appeared, flying so high that it looked like a charm-bracelet toy, and as it passed overhead there seemed to be a deliberate lull in the firing. People stared uneasily at the plane, as they would at a stinging insect near a ceiling, but it went away harmlessly enough, and then the guns opened up again.

The morning air was chilly, so most of the spectators soon closed their windows and went back to bed. In the Square Louvois the neighborhood milkman, with his wagon drawn by two enormous old gray stallions, came along a few minutes after the plane, and the crash of his cans on the cobbles brought a few nervous folk back to their windows under the impression that bombing had begun.

The episode differed so from previous alarms, in which no planes were seen, that nobody seemed astonished to learn from newspapers consisting mostly of headlines that the real war—the war on the western front—had begun. *"Finie la drôle de guerre,"* people said to each other with a kind of relief. Even the *guerre* in Norway had seemed *drôle,* because it was so remote. The rush to news kiosks was such that policemen had to shepherd would-be purchasers into queues, which in some cases were half a block long.

I had a letter from Jean, Henri's son, a corporal in one of the two French armored divisions which were created after the Polish campaign. They were good divisions, and Jean had no way of knowing that the Germans had six times as many. "The real roughhouse is about to begin," he wrote. "So much the better! It will be like bursting an abscess." Jean, whose parents were my oldest friends in France, was a strong, quiet boy who in civil life had been a draftsman in an automobile factory. He liked to play ice hockey and collect marine algae. He had not wanted a soft job in a factory during the war because he did not want to be considered a coward.

On the same morning I had a telephone conversation with another friend of mine, Captain de Cholet, who had just arrived from Alsace on furlough. Upon reaching the Gare de l'Est, he had learned that all furloughs were canceled, so he was going back by the next train. He called me up to say that he wouldn't be able to go to the races at Auteuil with me, as he had planned. "It's good that it's starting at last," he said. "We can beat the Boches and have it over with by autumn."

In the afternoon I went to Auteuil alone. I watched a horse belonging to Senator Hennessy, the cognac man, win the Prix Wild

Monarch for three-year-old hurdlers. The track was crowded with people whose main preoccupations seemed to be the new three-year-olds and the new fashions being worn by the women. That day the Germans were taking Arnhem and Maastricht in Holland and attacking Rotterdam with parachutists. Nobody worried much. Everyone was eager principally to know whether French troops had yet made contact with the enemy. "The Boches have business with somebody their own size now!" they said pugnaciously. "They will see we are not Poles or Norwegians!" It was conceivable, of course, that the Germans would win a few victories, but it would be a long war, like the last one. All France, hypnotized by 1918, still thought in terms of concentrated artillery preparations, followed by short advances and then, probably, by counterattacks. Even if the Allied troops should fail to save Holland, they would join the Belgians in holding the supposedly magnificent fortified line of the Albert Canal. At worst, the armies could fall back to the Franco-Belgian frontier, where, the newspapers had been proclaiming since September, there was a defensive system practically as strong as the Maginot Line. Confidence was a duty. The advertising department of the *Magasins du Louvre* had discovered another duty for France. The store's slogan was "Madame, it is your duty to be elegant!" "They shall not pass" was considered *vieux jeu* and hysterical. The optimistic do-nothingism of the Chamberlain and Daladier regimes was, for millions of people, the new patriotism. Ten days before the war began in May, Alfred Duff Cooper told the Paris American Club, "We have found a new way to make war—without sacrificing human lives."

The news of the break-through at Sedan, which reached Paris on the fifth day of the offensive, was, for a few Parisians who were both pessimistic and analytical, the beginning of fear. But it happened so quickly, so casually, as presented in the communiqués, that the unreflective didn't take it seriously. The Belgian refugees began to arrive in Paris a few days after the fighting started. The great, sleek cars of the de-luxe refugees came first. The bicycle refugees arrived soon after. Slick-haired, sullen young men wearing pullover sweaters shot out of the darkness with terrifying, silent speed. They had the air of conquerors rather than of fugitives. Many of them must have been German spies. Ordinary destitute refugees arrived later by train and as extra riders on trucks. Nothing else happened at first to change the daily life of the town.

Tuesday evening, May 14, I climbed the hill of Montmartre to the Rue Gabrielle to visit Jean's parents. Henri, Jean's father, had long limbs and sad eyes; he combined the frame of a high jumper and the mustaches of a Napoleonic grenadier. He was a good Catholic, and by birth and training he belonged to the wealthier bourgeoisie. By temperament, which he had never been allowed to indulge, he was a bohemian. A long struggle to succeed in business, which he secretly detested, had ended in a defeat just short of total. When war was declared, he was working for a firm of textile stylists whose customers were chiefly foreign mills. Since September, business had fallen off drastically and Henri had had nothing to do except drop in once in a while to keep up the firm's desultory correspondence. Henri spoke English, German, and Dutch in addition to French, and sometimes sang in a deep voice which sounded like a good but slightly flawed 'cello. He often said that he was happy to be living, at last, high on Montmartre, just under Sacré-Coeur. His wife, Eglée, would never have permitted him to live there for any reason less compelling than poverty. Eglée, before her marriage to Henri, had been a buyer in a department store. Recently she had devised a muslin money belt for soldiers to wear under their shirts. She worked an average of sixteen hours a day, making the belts with a frantic dexterity, but about once a fortnight she got so exhausted that she had to stay in bed for two or three days. She had placed the belts in several of the department stores, but her profit was small. Eglée and Henri were both about sixty years old. For thirty-five years Henri had pretended to like trade in order to hold his wife's respect, and Eglée had pretended to loathe trade in order to hold Henri's affection. Neither had succeeded in deceiving the other. He brooded, she scolded, he drank a little, they quarreled incessantly, and they loved each other more than any two people I have ever known.

As I came into their apartment Tuesday night, Eglée was saying she felt sure Jean was dead. Henri said that was nonsense. She said he was an unfeeling parent. Henri became angry and silent. Then he said that often, when he was at Verdun, Eglée had not heard from him for a week at a time. She said that Henri was always talking about Verdun and belittling "Jean's war." "To think that after these years of preparing to avoid the old mistakes," Henri said, "the Germans are now eighty miles from us. If they get to Paris, it's all over." Eglée said he was a defeatist to mention such an eventuality. He said, "I am not a defeatist. I am an old soldier and also an old traveling man, and I know how near they are to Paris." I tried to console him by saying that the Dutch, at any rate, were fighting better than anyone had expected. Henri had cousins in Holland. Eglée said the Dutch were Boches and would before long prove it.

The next morning there was a radio announcement that the Dutch had surrendered in Europe but were going to continue the war in the East Indies. In the afternoon some of the American correspondents, including myself, went to the Netherlands Legation to meet Mynheer Van Kleffens, the Netherlands Minister for Foreign Affairs, who had arrived from London to explain the Dutch decision. Van Kleffens, accompanied by the Netherlands minister to France and the Netherlands Minister for National Defense, received us and the journalists of other neutral countries in the Legation garden. While we were talking, sadly and quietly, among the trees, the French were losing the war. On that Wednesday, May 15, the Germans made the deep incision which a few days later was to split the Allied armies.

The Foreign Minister, a blond, long-faced man, had a pet phrase which he repeated many times, as a man does when he is too tired to think of new forms for his thought. "The Germans tried this," he would say, recounting some particular method of the German attack, and then he would add, "It failed." "It failed," he would say, and again, "It failed"—until you thought he was talking of a long, victorious Dutch resistance—and then finally, "But to fight longer was hopeless." "We will fight on" was another recurrent phrase. When we asked him whether the Dutch had any planes left to fight with, he said, "No. We had fifty bombers. The last one flew off and dropped its last bomb and never returned."

Holland, with one tenth the population of Germany but with several times the wealth per capita, had presented fifty bombers against five thousand. It had been comfortable to believe in neutrality, and cheap. Norway, with the fourth largest merchant marine in the world, had not built the few good light cruisers and destroyers which might have barred the weak German Navy from its ports. France herself had economized on the Maginot Line, had

71

decided it was too expensive to extend the fortifications from Luxembourg to the sea. The democracies had all been comfortable and fond of money. Thinking of the United States, I was uneasy. I suspected that in proportion to our wealth we were the nakedest of them all.

The first panic of the war hit Paris Thursday, May 16. It affected, however, only the most highly sensitized layers of the population: the correspondents, the American and British war-charity workers, and the French politicians. In Paris, because of censorship, news of disaster always arrived unofficially and twenty-four hours late. On the evening of the catastrophic May 15, even the neurotic clientele of the Ritz and Crillon bars had been calm. But on Thursday people began telling you about Germans at Meaux and south of Soissons, points the Germans didn't actually reach until more than three weeks later. There was a run on the Paris branch of the Guaranty Trust Company by American depositors. I lunched in a little restaurant I frequently went to on the Rue Sainte-Anne, and after the meal, M. Bisque, the proprietor, suggested that we go to the Gare du Nord to see the refugees. M. Bisque cried easily. Like most fine cooks, he was emotional and a heavy drinker. He had a long nose like a woodcock and a mustache which had been steamed over cookpots until it hung lifeless from his lip. Since my arrival in France in October he had taken me periodically on his buying trips to the markets so that I could see the Germans weren't starving Paris. On these trips we would carry a number of baskets and, as we filled one after another with oysters, artichokes, or pheasants, we would leave them at a series of bars where we stopped for a drink of apple brandy. The theory was that when we had completed our round of the markets we would circle back on our course, picking up the baskets, and thus avoid a lot of useless carrying. It worked all right when we could remember the bars where we had left the various things, but sometimes we couldn't, and on such occasions M. Bisque would cry that *restauration* was a cursed *métier,* and that if the Government would permit he would take up his old rifle and leave for the front. But they would have to let him wear horizon blue; he could not stand the sight of khaki because it reminded him of the English. "They say the English are very brave at sea," he would say, winking slowly, "but who knows? We don't see them, eh?"

The trip to the Gare du Nord was solemn. M. Bisque dragged me to see various mothers sitting on rolls of bedding and surrounded by miauling children; his eyes would water, and he would offer a child a two-franc piece and then haul me to the buffet, where he would fortify himself with a glass of Beaujolais. At the buffet I remember meeting a red-bearded gnome of a colonial soldier who kept referring to himself as "a real porpoise." "Porpoise" was the traditional army term for a colonial infantryman. "A real porpoise," the soldier repeated dreamily, "an old porpoise, and believe me, monsieur, the Germans need somebody to bust their snouts for them." He had two complete sets of decorations, one from the old war and one from the new. He was going north to rejoin his regiment, and he was full of fight and red wine.

Saturday morning I had another note from Jean. He enclosed a bit of steel from a Dornier shot down near him. "How I am still alive I have not time to write to you," he said, "but chance sometimes manages things well." The letter produced the same effect on me as news of a great victory. I called up Henri. He and Eglée had had a letter too.

On Saturday, May 18, I went to a press conference held by the Ministry of Information, which had just organized an Anglo-American press section, with quarters in a vast, rococo ballroom at the Hôtel Continental called the Salle des Fêtes. Pierre Comert, chief of the section, held conferences for the correspondents at six every evening, when he would discuss the day's developments from the Government's point of view. This evening he announced that Paul Reynaud had taken over the Ministry of National Defense. He also announced that Reynaud had recalled Marshal Pétain from Spain to advise him. General Weygand had already arrived from Syria, and it was understood that he would take over the high command in a few days. The two great names, in conjunction, were expected to raise national morale. The two old men, however, were military opposites. Pétain, cautious at sixty, when he had defended Verdun, was at eighty-four incapable of conceiving any operation bolder than an orderly retreat. Weygand believed in unremitting attack. One staff officer later told me, "Weygand's ideas are so old-fashioned that they have become modern again. He is just what we need." Strategically, the two men canceled each other, but politically they were a perfect team. Both were clericals, royalists, and anti-parliamentarians. There is something about very old soldiers like Hindenburg and Pétain that makes democrats trust them. But Pétain was to serve Laval's purpose as Hindenburg had served Hitler's. However, we were cheerful on the evening we heard about the appointments. The German advance was apparently slowing down, and all of us thought that Weygand might arrange a counterattack soon. A week earlier we had been expecting victories. Now we were cheered by a slightly slower tempo of disaster.

There was a hot, heavy pause the next few days. I took long walks on the boulevards and up and down dull, deserted business streets. The wartime population of Paris had slowly increased from late November until April, as evacuated families returned from the provinces, but since the beginning of the offensive the population had again decreased. All the people who had remained in town seemed to concentrate on the boulevards. It gave them comfort to look at one another. They were not yet consciously afraid, however. There were long queues in front of the movie houses, especially those that showed double features. You could get a table at a sidewalk café only with difficulty, and the ones that had girl orchestras did particularly well. One girl orchestra, at the Grande Maxeville, was called the Joyous Wings, and its bandstand and instruments had been decorated with blue airplanes. There were no young soldiers in the streets, because no furloughs were being issued.

It is simple now to say, "The war on the Continent was lost on May 15." But as the days in May passed, people in Paris only gradually came to suspect how disastrous that day had been. There was a time lag between every blow and the effect on public morale. I can't remember exactly when I first became frightened, or when I first began to notice that the shapes of people's faces were changing. There was plenty of food in Paris. People got thin worrying. I think I noticed first the thinning faces of the sporting girls in the cafés. Since the same girls came to the same cafés every night, it was easy to keep track. Then I became aware that the cheekbones, the noses, and the jaws of all Paris were becoming more prominent.

There was no immediate danger in Paris unless the Germans bombed it, and when the news was in any degree encouraging I did not think of bombing at all. When the news was bad I thought of bombing with apprehension. It helped me understand why troops in a winning army are frequently brave and on the losing side aren't. We heard anti-aircraft fire every night now, but there were no air-raid alarms, because the planes the guns were firing at were reconnaissance planes. The heaviest shooting would begin in the gray period just before dawn. You wouldn't really settle down to sleep until the morning shooting was over, and you wouldn't wake up until noon.

On the night of May 21, after Paul Reynaud announced to the Senate that the Germans were at Arras and that France was in danger, I had a *frousse*—a scare—of such extreme character that it amounted to *le trac,* which means a complete funk. It was an oppressively hot night, with thunder as well as anti-aircraft fire, interspersed with noises which sounded like the detonations of bombs in the suburbs. When I lay on my bed face down, I couldn't help thinking of a slave turning his back to the lash, and when I lay on my back I was afraid of seeing the ceiling fall on me. Afterward I talked to dozens of other people about that night, and they all said they'd suffered from the same funk. The next morning's papers carried Weygand's opinion that the situation was not hopeless. This cheered everybody. It has since been revealed that May 21, the day of the great *frousse,* was the day set for the counterattack which might have cracked the Germans. It never came, and by May 22, when we were all beginning to feel encouraged, the opportunity had been missed.

Later that day word got around among the correspondents that negotiations were already on for a separate peace and that if the French didn't sign it the Germans might arrive in Paris in a few days. This counteracted the effect of the Weygand message. Still later I felt encouraged again as I watched a city gardener weed a bed of petunias in the Square Louvois, the tiny park under my hotel window. Surely, I thought, if the old man believed the Germans were coming in he would not be bothering with the petunias.

The greatest encouragement I got during those sad weeks came from Jean. Shortly after the Reynaud speech I went up the hill to Montmartre to take some flowers to Jean's mother. For once, Henri and Eglée were smiling at the same time. "You should have been here early this morning for a good surprise!" Henri shouted. "At five there was a knock at our door." "And who do you suppose it was?" his wife cried, taking over the narrative. "Suzette?" I de-

75

manded, naming their married daughter, who lived in Grenoble. I was sure that it had been Jean, but I wanted to prolong Eglée's pleasure. "No," Eglée announced happily. "It was Jean. He was magnificent. He looked like a cowboy." "He came with his *adjudant*," Henri broke in, "to get engine parts they needed for tanks. The boy has no rest, you know," he said proudly. "When the division goes into action he fights. When they are in reserve and the other fellows rest, he is head of a repair section. He is a magician with engines. And his morale is good! He says that the first days were hard, but that now they know they can beat the Boche." "On the first day of the battle, Jean's general was arrested," Eglée said, with a sort of pride. "What *canaille!* Jean said it was fantastic what a traitor the general turned out to be. And there were German spies in French officers' uniforms!" "They met a regiment of artillery without officers," Henri said, "but completely! 'So much the better,' the artillerists said. 'They were traitors anyway. But where in the name of God are we supposed to go?' Fifteen German bombers appeared over Jean's unit. 'We're in for it,' he said to himself. But the boy was lucky. The Germans had dropped their bombs elsewhere. Then Jean's unit met German tanks. He says our fellows rode right over them. 'There may be a great many of them,' he said, 'but we are better than they are. Our guns penetrate them, but they do not penetrate us. As for the spy problem, we have solved that. We simply shoot all officers we do not know.' Jean and the *adjudant* stayed for breakfast. Then they had to go away."

Although I knew that an individual soldier had no chance to understand a military situation as a whole, Jean's optimism raised my spirits considerably. I believed fully the details of the encounter with the German tanks. Jean was of that peculiar race of engine-lovers who cannot lie about the performance of a mechanical thing.

When I returned to my hotel I passed along Jean's confident report to Toutou, the hotel's cashier, with whom I often discussed the war. She was a patriot but a congenital pessimist. All the employees slept on the top floor of the hotel, and as soon as Toutou had read of the German parachutists in Holland she had bought a revolver and cartridges. "If one lands on the roof, I'll pop him!" she had said. "Or perhaps as he descends past my window!"

THE WORLD KNOCKED DOWN

In each week of disaster there was an Indian summer of optimism. On the third Sunday after the offensive started, I had dinner with Henri and Eglée. We teased one another about our forebodings a fortnight earlier. "Do you remember how sure you were that the Germans would be here momentarily?" Eglée said to me. "And how you were certain that Jean was no longer alive?" Henri asked Eglée. "It seems a year ago," I said sincerely. "I must admit that the French had their heart well hooked on. Any other people would have caved in after such a blow. I wonder where Weygand will make the counterattack." "In Luxembourg, in my opinion," Henri said. "If he made the counterattack too far to the west he would not catch enough Boches. A good wide turning movement, and you will see—the whole band of them will have to scramble off. They will be on the other side of the Albert Canal again in a week."

We talked and listened to the radio, and, as usual, I stayed for tea, then for supper, and then for the final news-bulletin broadcast at eleven-thirty. The bulletins earlier in the day had been dull. But something in the speaker's voice this time warned us, as soon as he commenced, that the news was bad. We began to get sad before he had said anything important. Then he said, "Whatever the result of the battle in Flanders, the high command has made provision that the enemy will not profit strategically by its result." "What can he mean?" Eglée asked. "He means that they are preparing to embark that army for England," Henri said. "Unless the enemy captures the army, his victory is tactical but not strategical." "But why must they embark?" Eglée asked. "I do not know," Henri said almost savagely. That was the day—though none of us knew it—that King Leopold told his ministers he was going to give up. Eglée began to cry. "Now they are coming to Paris," she said, "now they are coming to Paris."

As late as Monday, May 27, people in Paris still believed that the Allies stood a chance of closing the gap between their southern and northern armies. That evening, Pierre Comert, chief of the Anglo-American section of the Ministry of Information, announced at a press conference I went to that operations in the north were "proceeding normally" and that the high command expected the Battle of Flanders to last at least another two weeks. I slept well that night, awakened only a few times by moderate anti-aircraft fire. In the morning Toutou, the cashier at my hotel, stopped me as I was going out and said, "Did you hear Reynaud on the radio? The King of the Belgians has surrendered his army." She had been crying.

I walked about the streets stupidly the rest of the morning. I had the map well in mind. The Belgians, by their surrender, had laid bare the left flank of the Franco-British armies in Flanders, and I thought the armies would soon be surrounded. Perhaps the French and British in the north would become demoralized and surrender. If they had been seeking an excuse to quit, they had a good one now. People on the streets were saying to each other, "And that isn't the worst of it. All the refugees probably are spies." They did not seem depressed. A fellow wheeling a pushcart loaded with wood stopped and shouted to a colleague on the other side of the street, "Say, old fellow, did you hear the news? Ain't we just taking it on the potato!" In his voice was a note of pride.

I walked around the Place Vendôme a couple of times; the luxury-shop windows had for me a reassuring association of tourists and normal times. Charvet was showing summer ties. I bought a couple from an elegant and hollow-chested salesman. I didn't want to talk to him about the war, because he looked sad enough already, but he began to talk about it himself. "We are an indolent people, monsieur," he said pleasantly. "We need occurrences like this to wake us up." Paris reminded me of that conversational commonplace you hear when someone has died: "Why, I saw him a couple of days ago and he looked perfectly well." Paris looked perfectly well, but I wondered if it might not be better for a city in such danger to show some agitation. Perhaps Paris was dying.

That night, when the shock of the Belgian surrender had begun to wear off, I had a late dinner with two American friends in a little Marseillais restaurant on the Rue Montmartre. We were the only customers. We had Mediterranean rouget burned in brandy over twigs of fennel. Although all three of us knew that the war was lost, we could not believe it. The rouget tasted too much as good rouget always had; the black-browed proprietor was too normally solicitous; even in the full bosom and strong legs of the waitress there was the assurance that this life in Paris would never end. Faith in France was now purely a *mystique;* a good dinner was our profane form of communion.

THE WORLD KNOCKED DOWN

Incredibly, beginning the day after the Belgian surrender, there was a great wave of exhilaration, based on the heroic action of the British and French armies fighting their way out of Flanders. People with relatives in the northern armies had, when they heard of the capitulation, resigned themselves to the capture or death of the trapped men. The German Government, in radio broadcasts, had threatened that even if the Allies were able to make a stand at Dunkirk the Germans would sink every boat that tried to embark troops. It was one German threat that didn't come off. People in Paris began to receive telegrams from relatives who had safely arrived in England. Several of my acquaintances received such messages, so we assumed that the number of troops saved was very large.

My old friends Henri and Eglée had not worried about their son Jean, because, having seen him on leave since the Germans drove the wedge between the Allied armies, they knew he was south of the Somme. But Henri's brother Paul, who at fifty had been called back into service as a lieutenant of artillery, was with the army in Flanders. One evening shortly after the Belgian surrender I climbed up to the Rue Gabrielle, just under the crest of Montmartre, to visit Henri and Eglée, and found them in a happy mood, because Paul had reached England. I tried to talk to Eglée about what she and her husband would do if the Germans turned toward Paris after they finished the Dunkirk job. Her answer was simply that she had an order from the Galeries Lafayette for five dozen of the soldiers' muslin money belts she manufactured at home and that after she completed the order she would have to wait eight days for payment, so how could she think of leaving Paris? As for Henri, he said he now constituted the whole office force of the textile-design company he worked for and couldn't leave without giving a month's notice. Peacetime thought patterns were mercifully persistent.

Everyone now was doing his best to forget that the Allied forces had had too few tanks and guns to begin with, and that now the evacuated armies had lost what little they had. We consoled ourselves with stories of individual heroism and with the thought that the Allies, after all, controlled the sea. Only when the evacuation was completed did the enthusiastic French suddenly take cognizance of the fact that there were no more British troops on their side of the Channel. As if spontaneously, the German gibe, "England will fight to the last Frenchman," swam into the popular consciousness and began to seem a portent.

Two kinds of person are consoling in a dangerous time: those who are completely courageous, and those who are more frightened than you are. Fernand, the night porter at my hotel, was completely courageous. "Well, what do you know?" he would ask me when I came home at night. Before I answered, he would say, "We will have them yet, the camels. It takes a few defeats to get our blood up. They poison our lives by provoking the anti-aircraft into making a noise at night. A surprise is preparing itself for those cocos!" It was a pleasure to see him during the frequent early-morning *alertes*. Hearing the sirens, he would go out into the small park in front of the hotel and, shielding his eyes with his hands, search the sky for airplanes. Seeing none, he would shake his head disgustedly and shout up to the female guests at the windows of the hotel, "Do not derange yourselves, mesdames, it is for nothing again!"

The most frightened man I saw in France was a certain well-known French journalist who wrote under various names in a dozen Parisian newspapers of varying political color. He had a broad, paraffin-textured face which, when he was alarmed, appeared to be on the point of melting. Long before the offensive began in May, he had tried to explain to me why Laval, the appeaser, and Paul Faure, the left-of-Blum Socialist, together with Georges Bonnet, representative of the great banking house of Lazard Frères, were all planning a move to get rid of Paul Reynaud in order to liquidate the war as quickly as possible. They wanted to put Daladier back in Reynaud's place because they knew that as long as Daladier headed the Government there would be no effectual war—that eventually the war would die of dry rot, which was what ninety per cent of the French politicians and all the French Communists, along with the Germans, wanted. I had asked naïvely why Laval didn't try to become premier himself. "Because, of course," my journalist friend had said impatiently, "then everybody would *know* he was going to make peace. Then there would be mutiny in the Army." Personally, he used to say, he was a decided partisan of both Reynaud, who wanted to fight, and of Laval, who wanted to make peace. You were always running up against things like that in French politics.

When I met my journalist at lunch one day the first week of June, he was in as spectacular a funk as I have ever observed. "What a terrible mistake to have provoked those people, my dear!" he shrieked. "What madness to concern ourselves with Poland! Laval was so right to have wished to conciliate Mussolini. I am going to give my dog a lethal injection. He could never stand the nervous shock of those bombs that whistle. Working people are so insouciant. They know they have us in their power. I cannot get a man to dig a trench in my garden for me until tomorrow afternoon, and the bombers may be here any minute!" As he stuffed asparagus into his mouth, large tears welled out of his eyes. "Peace, quickly, quickly!" he shouted, after swallowing the asparagus.

Sunday, June 2, I visited the country home of a French newspaper publisher who lived with his large, intelligent family near the town of Melun, thirty miles south of Paris. The countryside, hot and rich and somnolent, and the family, sitting on the lawn after a chicken dinner, made me think of Sundays on Long Island. It was as if no war had ever been. We sat around in lawn chairs, fighting against drowsiness, talking unintently, resisting the efforts of one woman to get up a game like charades. We spoke with no originality whatever of all the mistakes all the appeasers in the world had made, beginning with Ethiopia. We repeated to one another how Italy could have been squelched in 1935, how a friendly Spanish government could have been maintained in power in 1936, how the Germans could have been prevented from fortifying the Rhineland in the same year. We talked of the Skoda tanks, built according to French designs in Czechoslovakia, that were now ripping the French Army apart. The Germans had never known how to build good tanks until Chamberlain and Daladier presented them with the Skoda plant. These matters had become for every European capable of thought a sort of litany, to be recited almost automatically over and over again.

Women in the train which took me back to town that evening were talking about the leaflets German planes had dropped, promising to bombard Paris the next day. The word "bombardment" had a terrible sound, evoking pictures of Warsaw and Rotterdam. In the dimly lighted, carefully curtained compartments of the local train, the women looked tired and anxious rather than refreshed. Boarding the train at a tiny station, they would exchange the usual flippancies with the people they had been staying with. "Thanks for the peonies. I'll put them right in water when I get home," one of them might say, but her voice would be strained. Some of them must have been going back to jobs at the great Citroën plant on the Quai de Javel, where hundreds of women punched out parts of machines and sprayed paint. The train arrived at the Gare de Lyon after eleven. There were no taxis. In the last month they had become increasingly scarce even in the daytime; the drivers simply refused to risk their necks in the pitch-black streets at night. I could not distinguish one street from another. There was a cluster of dim, moving lights at a distance, like a luminous jellyfish seen by another fish at the bottom of the sea. I started toward the lights and tripped over a plank, skinning my knee. When I reached them I found that they came from the electric lanterns of a group of policemen who were stopping pedestrians and examining their papers. They were polite and quiet. One of them told me how to get to my hotel, which took me almost an hour.

Monday was hot, lovely, and until one o'clock, tranquil. People going out to lunch were just beginning to smile knowingly and to say to each other, "See, it was just another bluff," when the air-raid sirens sounded. At that hour I was of course in a bar, that of the Hôtel Lotti near the Continental, for the *apéritif*. It was a "day without hard liquor," so the apéritif was champagne. The waiters lowered the metal shutters. The bombardment was preceded by a tremendous noise of motors in airplanes too high to be seen, and by the angry hammering of anti-aircraft guns. It was as always hard to distinguish the sound of the bombs from these enfolding noises. After forty-five minutes, the roar of the planes stopped, but the shooting continued awhile, and then the sirens gave the all-clear signal. Everybody I met in the street afterward seemed to know exactly where the bombs had fallen. A taxi driver took me straight to the neighborhood bombed. Some six-story apartment houses in Passy had been shaved down to the first floor, as if by the diagonal sweep of a giant razor. The streets there were covered with broken glass, since every window for nearly a mile around was out, and housewives, not hurt but angry, were already out on the sidewalks

82

sweeping up the glass with brooms. Of two large cafés at an inter-section, one had been pretty well outed by a bomb, but the terrace of the other, twenty minutes after the all-clear, was doing a record business with clients who wanted to *"discuter le coup."*

Technically, I was later given to understand, it had been, from the German standpoint, a very good bombardment. Two hundred and fifty planes participated, the largest number that had been assembled for a single operation in the war until then. The bomb-ing, considering the height at which the planes flew—twenty thou-sand feet—was commendably accurate. However, the results looked nothing like the photographs of Warsaw and Rotterdam, because Paris was reasonably well defended. "The anti-aircraft fire was well nourished," the French said, "so the bombers stayed high." The pursuit squadrons, although they failed to intercept the bombers on their way to Paris, were on their tails so closely that the Ger-mans dropped their bombs quickly and left. If there had been no defending batteries or planes, as at Rotterdam, the bombers would have loafed along a few hundred feet above the main thoroughfares and dropped their high explosives like roach powder. The bombs hit the huge Citroën factory on the Quai de Javel and knocked down a few scattered apartment houses, but the total effect on public morale was tonic. Forty-eight hours after the bombardment, M. Dautry, the Minister of War Industry, took a group of cor-respondents through the Citroën plant, which had been the chief German objective. There we found a smell of burnt paint, and a great deal of broken glass on the floor, but no serious damage to the great automobile-assembly lines or the part of the plant where shells were made. The women making shells worked on as calmly as girls in an American candy factory.

The day we visited the factory, June 5, was also the day the Germans began their second attack, the push southward across the Somme that was to carry them to the Spanish frontier. "It is the beginning of the second round," Pierre Comert announced at the press conference that evening. None of us could admit to our-selves that the war in France might be a two-round knockout. The French would surely be dislodged from the Somme-Aisne line, we conceded, but it would take weeks to do it. Then they would de-fend Paris and the line of the Seine, then the line of the Loire. By that time, perhaps, the British would be able to do something.

Even the United States might begin to understand what was at stake and give a pledge which would put new heart in the defenders. But this fight was not to have even a decent second round. The rest after the first round had not been long enough; the French were still out on their feet. Unarmed and outnumbered, they were led by two old men who were at loggerheads. As for Reynaud, he had called into his government Ybarnegaray and Marin, two reactionaries whose only surface virtue was a blustering show of war spirit. Raised to power by Socialist votes, Reynaud had turned toward men whom he trusted because they were of his own Rightist background—Pétain, Mandel, Ybarnegaray, Marin. All his Rightist friends except Mandel joined in smothering him. They felt that by making war against Hitler he was betraying his own class.

After the bombardment the Government began an intensive, almost convulsive effort to get the United States Government to send over some fighter planes and, Reynaud may even have hoped, some pilots under the same sort of arrangement by which German pilots had gone to Franco or the American Volunteer group to China. Perhaps the French Government itself may have been deceived about the number of fighter planes finished or in construction in the United States. A red-haired Jewish captain in the Armée de l'Air, an ace in the other war but now a staff man, took me out to see a pursuit group in the field and show me how badly planes were needed.

CHAPTER XI

Who Do Not Fight, But Run Away

"THE SITUATION IS VERY BAD," said the captain, as we drove into the country, "but it is not hopeless, because it could still be corrected so easily. We don't need anything like magic."

The captain did not appear to be much interested in the fumbling remarks I made about the machinery of Congress and the mysteries of public opinion in the United States. Every Frenchman with an American acquaintance had heard all that before. Over and over again, Americans tried to explain such things, but their voices lacked conviction, and they wondered as they talked whether their words had any real meaning and whether the Danish politicians talked any differently before they rolled over and died.

My companion said he thought we'd be able to get a good lunch in a town along the way. The day was hot and beautiful, and the land seemed very peaceful as our Renault limousine raced smoothly along over some of the world's best roads. "It is a very comfortable automobile," the captain said wryly. "It used to be employed to take deputies on tours of observation at the front. They invariably found everything perfect."

Driving across the plains of Brie and Champagne, we saw peasants working with their chunky horses in the rich, unfenced fields; from time to time we passed canals in which boys were taking bellywhoppers, and occasionally we came upon a young woman pedaling along on a bicycle and smiling good-naturedly at the shouts of the soldiers in the camions. We had a magnificent lunch consisting of cheese tartlets, brook trout *amandine,* gigot, asparagus, cheese, cherries, and coffee, with a good bottle of still champagne, the local wine—all for slightly less than a dollar apiece. Our chauffeur ate with us. Most of the other lunchers were medical officers from a near-by hospital, who succeeded no better than such officers usually do in looking really martial, despite their fiercely scarlet kepis. After our meal we drove on a few miles and came to a town on which the Germans had dropped incendiary bombs early in their offensive. The bombs had ruined the stores and little houses and churches in about four blocks some distance from the town's main thoroughfare; driving straight through the center of the community, you would never know anything had happened.

We drove well on beyond the town and finally turned off the highway onto a dirt road where another Air Force car, a small, camouflaged Citroën, was waiting for us. It led the way for our shiny black limousine. We went down the side road for a mile or so until we came to a small house on the edge of a meadow. This, it turned out, was our destination—the post of command of a group of pursuit fliers. There were no runways or hangars or wind socks anywhere in sight, pursuit groups went about their business incognito. In back of the house was an automobile trailer equipped as a radio station, and stretched out on poles in the meadow were a number of brown canvas awnings, each of them concealing a pursuit plane, and, I was told, practically impossible to spot from the sky. "They bombed this field once," the captain said, "but they didn't hit anything. Sometimes they fly down with machine guns, hoping to shoot our planes on the ground, but our machine gunners drive them off before they are able to find what they are looking for."

An officer came back from the Citroën, presented himself, and then took us into the post of command. The commandant's office and his bedroom occupied the ground floor. On the wall of the office I noticed a bulletin board divided into five columns marked "Ready for Instant Departure," "Quick Departure," "Reserve," "On Mission," and "Out of Service," and hanging on nails under each heading were some tin markers shaped like airplanes. It was the sort of thing you might expect to find in the office of an up-to-date taxi company. To me, the number of markers, even including those under "Out of Service," seemed terrifyingly small. The commandant, a man in his late thirties, I should say, was a dark, good-looking fellow—a bit underweight and obviously tired, but there was something about him that suggested the taut ruggedness of an airplane strut. He was polite enough, but appeared skeptical about American journalists, of whom he had seen several since May 10, when, as he put it, the war began. His name was Murtin; I've since met him in Algiers under circumstances considerably happier.

The two escadrilles in the group and practically every pilot belonging to it, I was told, had been cited and decorated since the beginning of the offensive; for the haggard fellows who had lived around that meadow during the past four weeks, the war had been an alternation of death and felicitations. "In four weeks the group has shot down eighty-eight enemy planes," the commandant said, "but to be honest, we have lost thirty-five. Our losses include machines grounded in our own territory—technically not defeats, you know, but what's the difference, once they're out of commission? Well, you may say, eighty-eight planes shot down is very good. Unfortunately, it's not good enough. The way the Germans keep sending out new ones is unbelievable. To cut down their margin of superiority in numbers appreciably, we would have to shoot down six for one. To hold our own, we must down five for one."

He said that the pursuit force, to hold its own until production picked up, should have just double its present number of planes, a matter of several hundred. "But why talk of Utopia?" he said. "At the beginning of the offensive, we were lucky. A big shipment must have arrived from America just in time; at any rate, I got eight new Curtisses in a batch. Imagine! Eight Curtisses! I have never before or since seen so many new machines all at once. It was the riches of Peru!"

I shook hands with the commandant and went out to the field with the captain and a tall, pleasant second lieutenant who couldn't have been more than twenty and had shot down eight planes. "You mustn't mind the boss," the lieutenant said apologetically. "He just lost a good man for a couple of months. An explosive bullet drove isinglass splinters from the windbreak into the man's face, and he can't see. The boss takes things like that to heart." We walked out across that meadow dotted with canopies, and the boy said, "It is peaceful here in the country. The local people like us very much because they are sure that, with the pursuit group here, they are safe from bombing planes. They say, 'Now we can sleep on both ears.' They don't know that we may attract more bombers, and what's the good of telling them? Might as well let them be happy."

It was about a five-minute walk over to a frame pavilion where the pilots on duty await orders to take the planes up. The building was on a ridge, surrounded by tall beech trees, and its unpainted boards smelled good in the heat. There were several fliers on hand, among them a Czech who was playing the "New World Symphony" on a phonograph. He looked sheepish when he was introduced to me. He felt ashamed, his friends explained, because on his first patrol with their group he had got into a fight with a Messerschmitt and had had to bail out in a parachute. The other aviators had tried to tell him that that didn't matter, that it happened to everybody at one time or another, but the Czech still felt bad. There were a number of Czechs in the group, the lieutenant said, and a couple of them were among the best combat pilots he'd seen.

The senior officer on duty was a first lieutenant, who introduced himself as "Marin." He was Marin de la Meslée, destined to finish that phase of the war as the leading French fighter pilot, with twenty victories, and later resume in North Africa. He wore his flying suit, and his plane was on the field; in an emergency he could be in the air in less than two minutes. He was long-limbed, with an aquiline Yankee face, and he had a stoop which he had probably acquired from squeezing into cockpits. Several of us walked together over to a great, shallow gravel pit where most of the Curtisses were cached, concealed only by the awnings which, in addition to camouflaging them, served as a protection against stones that might be kicked up by a bomb falling in the middle of the pit. "This gravel is ideal as a cushion for bombs," Marin said, "and there is water not far below the surface, which doesn't help the incendiary ones any. They just drop in here, churn up a little gravel, and expire."

We looked at the Curtisses—small, unimpressive things. The total equipment of an escadrille, including thirty planes, probably cost less than two million dollars. One of the fliers pointed out the difference between the Curtisses available when the war started, which had four machine guns, and the improved ones, which had six—two in each wing and two over the propeller. "The new ones are a little faster, too," he said, "but essentially they're the same. We need a model with eight or ten machine guns, because it takes an average of three thousand bullets to bring down a bomber. Most of all, though, we need more speed. These are good old girls, but they drag their feet—three hundred and twenty-five miles an hour doesn't amount to much any more. You see, you used to be able to come at a Heinkel from the tail end and shoot it down. That was all there was to it. Easy. But now they have put machine guns in the tails of the Heinkels, and these make it very disagreeable. The best way to catch a Heinkel now is to go around it and attack it head on, and for that you need a fast plane. Ah, if I only had one of those English planes with fifty miles more an hour and plenty of machine guns!" He spoke as though he were wishing for a fourteen-room suite on top of the Ritz or a date with his favorite cinema actress.

"Some of the German pilots are good, but most not so good," the flier continued. "Nearly all the planes are good, though, and since the man in the plane you're after may by chance be one of the good pilots, you cannot afford to take anything for granted. The German pilots are very wrought up, too, and when we shoot them down, if they land alive, they continue to yell 'Heil Hitler!' One parachuted into the top of a tree, and when our fellows climbed up to help him descend, he shot at them with a revolver." Marin came over then and said, "The situation until the end of July will be very difficult because the Germans are so reckless and have so many airplanes. It is like a parachute jump. If we come out of it, all right."

When I got back to my hotel that night, tired and discouraged, Fernand the porter, looking radiant, said to me, "What they must be digesting now, the Boches!" He showed me a copy of *Le Temps*, which said the German losses were stupefying. All the attacks had been "contained," but the French Army had executed a slight retreat in good order.

By now there were perceptible changes in the daily life of Paris. There was no telephone service in the hotels, so you had to make a special trip afoot every time you wanted to tell somebody something. Taxis were harder than ever to find. My hotel, which was typical, had six floors. At the beginning of the war in September the proprietor had closed the fourth, fifth, and sixth floors. Now I was the only guest on the second floor, and there were perhaps a half-dozen on the first. The staff, naturally, dwindled like the clientele. Every day somebody said good-by to me. One by one the waiters left, and then it was the headwaiter, who had been kept on after all of his subordinates had been dismissed. The next day it was Toutou, who left the bookkeeping to the housekeeper. A couple of days later, the housekeeper herself left. Finally there were only a porter and one chambermaid in the daytime, and Fernand at night. "Perhaps, if the line holds, there will be an upturn in business," the proprietor said.

It was at about this time that my restaurateur friend, M. Bisque, with whom I used to make the rounds of the markets, decided to close his restaurant. It was not that the Germans worried him, he explained to me, but there were no more customers, and also his wine dealer was pressing him to pay his bill. M. Bisque and his wife, who kept the books, and his daughter Yvette, who possessed the *tour de main* for making a soufflé stand up on a flat plate, and his son, who had been an apprentice in the kitchen of the Café de Paris, and Marie-Louise, the waitress, were all leaving the city to run the canteen in a munitions factory south of Fontainebleau. I wished them Godspeed.

For a few days I had lacked the heart to visit Henri and Eglée. Then Henri had come to my hotel to tell me joyfully they had had

89

another letter from Jean, who said he had been working twenty-one hours a day repairing tanks for his division. On Sunday, June 9, which was a warm and drowsy day, I returned Henri's call. On the way I stopped at a florist's shop and bought some fine pink roses. The woman in the shop said that shipments from the provinces were irregular, but that fortunately the crisis came at a season when the Paris suburbs were producing plenty of flowers. "We have more goods than purchasers," she said, laughing. When I arrived at the apartment I found Eglée busy making her muslin money belts. Henri was amusing himself by reading a 1906 edition of the Encyclopaedia Britannica, one of his favorite possessions, and drinking a *vin ordinaire* in which he professed to find a slight resemblance to Ermitage. "This time I think the line will hold," Henri said. "I served under Pétain at Verdun. He will know how to stop them. Only I don't like the talk of infiltration near Forges-les-Eaux."

"Infiltration" was a grim word in this war. The communiqué never admitted that the Germans had pierced the French line, but invariably announced, "Motorized elements have made an infiltration. They have been surrounded and will be destroyed." Two days later the "infiltration" became a salient, from which new infiltrations radiated. When I left the apartment Henri walked down as far as the Place des Abbesses with me. He wanted to buy a newspaper. As we stood saying good-by we heard a series of reports, too loud and too widely spaced for anti-aircraft. "Those sound like naval guns mounted on railroad cars," Henri said. "The Boches can't be so far away, then." That was the last time I saw Henri. I had a letter from Suzette a year later, telling me he had died in February 1941.

At six o'clock that evening I went to another Anglo-American press conference at the Hôtel Continental. We were told that the Ministry of Information was planning to provide us with safe-conduct passes to use in case we left Paris. That made us suspect that the Government would move very soon. Then M. Comert told us that Jean Provoust, who had just been appointed Minister of Information, wanted to talk to all the American correspondents. M. Provoust, the dynamic publisher of *Paris-Soir*, received us in his office with the factitious cordiality of a newspaper owner about to ask his staff to take a pay cut. He said that he didn't want the United States to think the situation was hopeless. "From a military

90

standpoint," he said, "it is improving steadily. Disregard reports of the Government quitting Paris. We will have many more chats in this room." John Lloyd, of the Associated Press, who was president of the Anglo-American Press Association, waited to see Provoust after the talk and invited him to be guest of honor at a luncheon the correspondents were having the next Wednesday. The Minister said he would be charmed, and then hurried away.

On my way home I saw a number of garbage trucks parked in the middle of the streets to balk airplane landings. Evidently Paris would be defended. I didn't think, after Provoust's talk, that I would have to leave Paris immediately, but the situation looked so bad that I decided to begin getting my passport in order.

Early the next morning, Monday, June 10, I set out in a taxi— which the porter had taken two hours to find for me—to go to the Spanish Consulate General to obtain a transit visa. This was easy to get if you already had the Portuguese visa, and luckily I had one which was good for a year. My taxi driver came from Lorraine, where, he said, people knew what patriotism meant. He had fought the other war, four years of it. The country needed men like Poincaré, a Lorrainer, now. "The politicians have sold us out," he said. "And that Leopold," he shouted, "there is a fellow they should have got onto long ago!" Now, he expected, the Germans would come to Paris. But it would be defended, like Madrid. "They will come here, the dirty birds," he said, "but they will leave plenty of feathers! Imagine a tank trying to upset the building of the Crédit Lyonnais! Big buildings are the best defense against those machines." He did not know that the real-estate men would never encourage such an unprofitable use of their property. "Even ten centimes on the franc is something," the rich men were already telling one another, "when one has a great many francs."

From the Spanish Consulate I went to the Préfecture of Police, where I asked for a visa which would permit me to leave France. A woman police official, a sort of chief clerk, said, "Leave your passport and come back for it in not less than four days." "But by that time, madame," I said, "the Germans may be here and the Préfecture may not exist." Naturally, I didn't leave the passport, but I was foolish to question the permanency of the Préfecture. The French civil servants are the one class unaffected by revolution or conquest. The Germans were to come, as it turned out, but the

Préfecture was to stay open, its personnel and routine unchanged. Its great accumulation of information about individual Frenchmen, so useful for the apprehension of patriots and the blackmailing of politicians, was to be at the disposal of the Germans as it had been at Philippe-Egalité's and Napoleon the Little's and Stavisky's. The well-fed young *agents* were to continue on the same beats, unaffected by the end of the war they had never had to fight in. Yesterday the Préfecture had obeyed the orders of M. Mandel, who hated Germans. Now it would obey Herr Abetz, who hated Jews. Change of administration. *Tant pis.*

Afterward I stopped at the Crillon bar, where I met a Canadian general I knew. "The French still have a fine chance," he said. "I am leaving for Tours as soon as I finish this sandwich." I walked over to the Continental to see if M. Comert had any fresh news. As I arrived at the foot of the staircase leading to Comert's office, I met another correspondent on his way out. "If you're going up to the Ministry," he said, "don't bother. The Government left Paris this morning." Then he began to chuckle. "You remember when John Lloyd stopped Provoust last night and invited him to the Wednesday luncheon?" he asked. Yes, I remembered. "Well," he said, "Provoust was in a hurry because he was leaving for Tours in a few minutes." I said maybe we had better leave too, and we did.

CHAPTER XII

A Man Falling Downstairs

A PROVINCIAL CITY which becomes overnight the capital of a great nation is not like a boom town, because it has no ebullience. People arrive dead tired after a night spent in an automobile or by the side of a road and pass their first hours in town looking for a bed. Finding one is a brief triumph. After a few hours of heavy sleep the new arrival goes out, depressed, to look for other equally sad people whom he has known in the abandoned capital city. With Waverley Root, the correspondent whom I had encountered on the Ministry of Information steps, I entered and left two temporary capitals of France within five days after quitting Paris. Tours was the first.

Root had an old Citroën with a motor that made a noise like anti-aircraft fire and was responsible for a few minor panics during our journey, but it stood up through the constant starting and stopping on the one vehicle-choked road the military authorities permitted civilians to travel south on. John Elliott of the *Herald Tribune* rode with us. He had one of his ankles in a plaster cast; it had been broken when an automobile in which he was returning to Paris from the front had hit a truck in a blackout.

The last impression of Paris we carried with us was of deserted streets everywhere except around the railroad stations, where the crowds were so big that they overflowed all the surrounding sidewalks and partly blocked automobile traffic. About everybody who had any means of transportation, except certain special groups like munitions workers and hospital staffs, whose last-minute evacuation had been guaranteed by the Government, left the city on Monday evening, the tenth of June, or Tuesday, the eleventh. It was exactly a month after the beginning of the attack on the Low Countries. Those who left on Tuesday and re-encountered us at Tours reported a great cloud of black smoke over the city, caused, they thought, by burning villages and farms that had been used one after another as points of support in the retreating battle against the Germans. It seems more probable now that the smoke was a smudge the Germans used to conceal their crossing of the Seine below the city and that was carried on into town by the wind.

The roads leading south from Paris were gorged with what was possibly the strangest assortment of vehicles in history. No smaller city could have produced such a gamut of conveyances, from fiacres of the Second Empire to a farm tractor hitched to a vast trailer displaying the American flag and a sign saying "This trailer is the property of an American citizen." A few men rode horses along the grassy edge of the road, making better progress than the automobiles. During the first few kilometers cars stood still for from five minutes to an hour at a time, moving forward only a few yards to stop again with grinding brakes, a procedure which eventually proved fatal to hundreds of old and overburdened vehicles. The Paris autobuses, requisitioned for the occasion, carried the personnel of government offices and major industrial establishments, and on each bus was a sign saying *"Complet."* Some of the girl stenographers and clerks appeared to be enjoying the excursion.

Although the road originally had been set aside for civilian traffic, we soon met soldiers moving north to Paris as everybody else moved south. They seemed content with what they were doing. There were infantrymen in camions and motorcyclists on their machines, and their faces were strong and untroubled.

Once you have started to leave a place, you become apprehensive. When we were held up in suburban traffic jams we noticed everybody around us looking up at the sky, probably remembering the machine-gunning of civilians on Belgian and Polish roads. But the only planes overhead were French. Not even a German reconnaissance plane appeared.

About twenty-five miles out of Paris the crowds thinned, and the surviving automobiles made pretty good time the rest of the way. Inhabitants of the towns through which the unending caravan passed lined the sidewalks of the long main streets, curious and quiet, probably wondering if they too would have to be on their way soon. In the cities south of Paris where the migrants began to stop at dark, restaurants and hotels were overwhelmed by a rush of business that brought no joy to proprietors who, while they sold much of what they had on hand, thought that in a few days they might have to abandon their establishments. On the first evening we had a late dinner at the Jeanne d'Arc restaurant in Orléans, where an R.A.F. mess was established. The British ate placidly and without apparent pleasure, preparing to quit France with about as much emotion as if it had been Burma. We three Americans were leaving without even having fought. France still hoped for an effectual gesture from our country, so we benefited by a last shred of popularity. Knowing how little the United States was likely to do, however, I wondered whether we should ever to be able to go back to Paris with our heads up.

There wasn't even a vacant sleeping space on the benches of a *brasserie* at Orléans. Remembering old traveling-salesman stories, we thought of going to local bordelloes for the night. But all the bordelloes were full of earlier arrivals from Paris. "They are so tired," the *sous-maîtresse* of one place, who came to the door, said to me compassionately, "that some of them are actually sleeping." So we had to pass the night in the Citroën.

THE WORLD KNOCKED DOWN

The selection of Tours appeared to have been a mistake. It was too small and too near Paris. The Government had just begun to arrive there when it became evident that it would have to move again in a couple of days. A direct move to Bordeaux or even better to Biarritz, where there were great hotels that could have been requisitioned for the Government, would have been better psychologically and every other way. The hunted, pillar-to-post feeling that legislators get when they are evacuated twice in one week is an invitation to panic. From an administrative point of view Tours had such limited facilities that the offices of government had to be scattered over twenty square miles of villages, occupying town halls and schoolhouses. Publishing the addresses of government bureaus in the local newspapers was not permitted, on the theory that German agents might get hold of the papers and tip off the Luftwaffe. So much of the time in the new capital was spent in a sort of furious hide-and-seek, trying to find the functionaries with whom one had business. The ministers themselves, arriving from Paris with their flustered and indignant mistresses who put the blame for the whole inconvenience upon them, were unable to find their ministries in some cases. The mistresses occasioned a great deal of trouble; there were not enough suites at the Hôtel de l'Univers to go around. Some of the women had to choose between putting up with a room and bath or going to a second-rate hotel. Naturally they made things unpleasant for the protectors who had subjected them to such a humiliation.

Most of the minor officials of the Government and the inhabitants of Tours as well as all the civilian refugees expected Paris to be defended. When it became plain that it would not be, a great wave of defeatism swept the stop-off capital. The people of the city, unused to air raids and anti-aircraft fire, were hospitable but uneasy. They were also overworked, doing their best to take care of their unprecedentedly numerous friends and customers. Garage proprietors, for example, had to listen to scores of appeals every day from refugees whose automobiles had broken down anywhere within a radius of fifteen miles of Tours, and who begged the garagemen to haul in the cars and repair them. I heard a *garagiste* try to turn down a man from Boulogne-sur-Seine who said he had a wife, an old mother, and a couple of children in his car, with all their possessions. The garagiste, whose best employees had been called up for the army months before this great rush of work, finally agreed to take on one more job. He was already working day and night, like a surgeon in a field hospital during a battle. I talked to an old bookseller, a myopic man who wore a straw boater in his shop. I wanted a book about the period in '70–'71 when the Government had been temporarily at Tours. The old man said he might be able to find such a book for me in a month. "The Germans will not succeed," he said, "because they exaggerate. They lack a sense of measure. All the peoples that lacked a sense of measure perished, monsieur. Look at the Babylonians, the Romans of the late Empire." I left him carefully dusting the backs of an early collected edition of Diderot. The Government remained in Tours for four days, and we followed them out. *"Nous suivons le Gouvernement,"* we always said to the military police who stopped us along the roads. They seldom made us show our papers. It became a refrain. "We follow the Government."

Anthony J. Drexel Biddle, Jr., who had been appointed envoy extraordinary to the Government of France, was following the Government too. Bullitt had remained in Paris, and Biddle, who as ambassador to Poland had followed the Polish Government to France, seemed to be making a career of pursuit diplomacy. Biddle was keeping Washington informed of the progress of the collapse. His dispatches must have read like a play-by-play account of a man falling downstairs. Paul Reynaud himself, who saw clearly what was happening, was beginning to succumb to self-pity. Hélène de Portes, his since-famous mistress, wept continually and urged him to ask terms from the Germans, with whom she had dubious relations. Reynaud, the small man with a big head, had interested me ever since the day I had first seen him at the American Club of Paris. Speaking in English, he had reminded me of an eager terrier struggling against a strange and heavy leash. Shortly after he had become President of the Council, in March, he had sent for General Giraud, commander of one of the armies in the north, and after their conference a rumor spread through Paris that Giraud was to replace Gamelin as army chief. It would have meant Daladier's resignation as Minister of Defense, and that in turn would have brought a vote in the Chamber which Renaud was afraid to dare. Giraud had gone back to his post and was now a German prisoner.

One man only showed any hope in Tours—the long-nosed, stork-legged Brigadier General Charles de Gaulle, Under-Secretary for War, who was there chiefly because the field commanders had refused to have him with them. He had offended both Weygand and Pétain in 1934 by advocating a mechanized army with a core of armored divisions. He had until then been considered in the Army as one of Pétain's personal *protégés*. Conventional army officers considered his stubbornness in this dispute proof of lightness and ingratitude. He had not remained within what poor Gamelin called "the just bounds of intellectual discipline." Weygand during the 1940 campaign had once ordered De Gaulle put under arrest unless he left the front.

The armored-division idea had not, as a matter of probability, offered much hope for France. If two nations go in for mobile armor and one nation has only half the industrial capacity of the other, the larger industrial nation will inevitably produce twice as great an armored force as its rival. Tanks cannot defend against tanks, and on the "tankable" terrain over which any Franco-German war must be fought the larger tank force, the German, would win by a quick knockout every time.

Biddle, who saw De Gaulle often in those days, remembers him as a gaunt watchdog in Reynaud's anteroom, sitting with his long legs stretched out before him and his nose and the visor of his kepi, nearly parallel, pointed at a spot on the floor just in advance of his right big toe. Whenever the advocates of surrender left Reynaud for a minute, De Gaulle would squeeze in and insist that now was the moment to begin a massed assault with the remaining French tanks. Reynaud cried at one point, "De Gaulle has the character of a stubborn pig, but he *has* character." It was more than he could say for the others around him. De Gaulle, in London a year later, told me that he still thought of Reynaud with respect. "He was like a man who knows he must swim a river," De Gaulle said, "and who sees the other bank clear. But he was not strong enough to reach it."

The day came when the Government abandoned Tours, leaving a thin line of impassive Moroccans squatting by their machine guns along the Loire and pretending to ignore their rulers' desertion. The Moroccans stayed and were killed. But we followed the Government.

Bordeaux was the next capital. Reynaud had sent for Biddle

when the move from Tours was decided upon, and asked him as a last favor to take Madame de Portes into the ambassadorial automobile and see that she got safely to the second provisional capital. He feared that if she rode in a French car she might be recognized and attacked. "Without her he couldn't have carried on at all, old boy," Biddle, a friendly and decorative diplomat, says now, "so we took her." All the way to Bordeaux she railed against De Gaulle.

Root and Elliott and I had been living in an idyllic little roadhouse on the left bank of the Loire between Amboise and Tours. It had rose bowers and a garden by the riverside, and the bedrooms were what the French call *coquette*. It must have been a pleasant place of assignation in time of peace, but when the Moroccans set up a machine gun in the rose bower we decided it was time to move. The ride down to Bordeaux was not as bad as the one from Paris to Tours. So many cars had fallen by the way; it was like a grim Grand National. Italy was in the war now, not that it made much difference. There was a persistent rumor that somebody had heard a radio speaker announce that Russia and Turkey had declared war on Germany and Italy, but nobody could confirm it, because it wasn't so.

We drove as far as a town called Barbezieux the first day, where we got a good supper but couldn't find any lodging until I began a conversation with the owner of a garage and automobile-parts store who was standing in front of his shop watching the refugees go by. Elliott had his ankle in a pretty spectacular cast. "It wouldn't matter for one of my colleagues and myself," I told the garageman, "but my other colleague there gravely wounded his leg at the front, and if he is compelled to remain in the automobile overnight in a cramped position the limb may be permanently deformed." The *garagiste* said that his wife would put a mattress on the dining-room floor for John. "And in effect, as long as we deprive you of your dining room, my other colleague and I may as well sleep on the floor alongside him," I said. "Do not derange yourself to find us mattresses." "But why not?" the garagiste said. "There are plenty of mattresses." So we all got into the house on John's bad leg. The people wouldn't take any money.

We had our *café au lait* with a professor of the local lycée in the garden of a restaurant the next morning. None of the little people one met, like the garagiste and the professor, considered that France might drop out of the war altogether or that Germany might win it. They took it for granted the Government would retain the fleet, go on to North Africa and fight from there. We weren't so sure. The little people hadn't seen the ministers and their mistresses. Poor Comert, whom I had seen only briefly in Tours, had said, resentfully, "The leaders are not worthy of their people."

Bordeaux was the worst of all. Day after day the exhausted piano player from Harry's New York bar in Paris slept at a table on the terrace of a café, his head cradled in his arms. He typified all uprooted Paris packed into this city of indecision. While there was still a chance that Reynaud would be able to take the Government to Africa to continue the war, Biddle tried his best to support the Premier's prestige by extraofficial means. France had been our dike as well as England's, and poor Biddle was cast in the role of the State Department's thumb, thrust in to stop a breach that was too big for a fist.

The American managed to be seen often in Reynaud's company, or on the way to the Premier's quarters, or returning from them, as if he were conveying some tangible offer from Washington. He was, however, under the handicap common to all American diplomats then of not being able to offer anything more satisfying than good wishes. When admitted to the Premier's presence, Biddle says, he could say only, *"Bon jour, mon pauvre vieux."* Reynaud would say, *"Bon jour."* Then they would sit in the office together for ten minutes so that people in the anteroom would think they were discussing something, and after that Biddle would return to the United States Consulate, which he was using as temporary embassy.

There was a climate of death in Bordeaux, heavy and unhealthy like the smell of tuberoses. The famous restaurants like the Chapon Fin had never known such business. Men of wealth, heavy-jowled, waxy-faced, wearing an odd expression of relief from fear, waited for a couple of hours for tables and then spent all afternoon over their meals, ordering sequences of famous claret vintages as if they were on a *tour gastronomique* instead of being parties to a catastrophe. I remember particularly the gay hissing dinner party of the Japanese Embassy at the Chapon Fin. They were having a jolly time. I said to Root and Elliott, "The people here look as if they had been let in on a fixed race. France is out of the war now."

It was on the night of June 16 that Reynaud was finally argued into relinquishing his place and putting the country in the hands of its betrayers, the representatives of the great industrialists. He did not give up, however, without one more long wrangle in which he found few supporters of continued resistance among the men he had invited to be his colleagues in the Government. Reynaud sent for Biddle early on the evening of the sixteenth and said to him, "I know you can't do anything tangible for us, but for my sake say you will return at midnight. That will gain six hours for me, during which I may still be able to persuade them to go to Africa." He then appealed to his colleagues to delay their final decision until Biddle had received a message the ambassador expected from Washington. Biddle returned at midnight. The report had got all about the city that he was awaiting word from his Government. Nights, the streets of Bordeaux were full of people; only the wealthiest or luckiest of the refugees could find a bed to sleep in. The rest walked about or sat on the curbstones and talked. As the ambassador's car made its way through the Place de la Comédie on its way to the rendezvous, the crowd packed so closely about it that the chauffeur had to stop for a moment. The people began to cheer. Somebody had started a rumor that the United States had entered the war on the side of the Allies and that that was why Monsieur Biddle was on his way to see Reynaud in the middle of the night. "Old boy, I sat there in that car and I had a lump in my throat," Biddle says now. "Because I knew that we weren't going to do a damn thing."

The men served by Laval, Chautemps, and their team of interchangeable shills and blinds at Bordeaux were the chiefs of heavy industry who since late in 1934 had been working for France's subjection to Germany. They preferred that she be brought into the German orbit as a satellite rather than annexed. They wanted to distribute the patronage, subject to confirmation by Germany, rather than have administrators imposed on them direct. They thought that Hitler would leave them their share of Europe and Africa to run, just as their colleagues the German members of the steel and coal cartels, which long antedated Hitler, had left them their share of the business. Theirs was the really dangerous International.

Those German colleagues had been the best missionaries for the

Nazi state, which guaranteed profits—consider the Goering works, *mon cher!*—eliminated labor unions, and prevented the people from getting any foolish ideas in their heads by simply forbidding them to think. The French are peculiarly susceptible to ideas of justice. The steel masters thought the great stupid mass of Germany was just the anchor the French intelligence needed to keep it below the surface forever. This was the doctrine of the men who paid Laval's bills—heavy ones, but then it pays to patronize the best assassin, like the best dentist, when one has *le fric*.

The army chiefs had provided the defeat; Laval capitalized it for his clients. Laval had been lurking on the fringe of the battle like one of those naked peasants armed with a knife who waited on medieval battlefields until an armored knight was unhorsed and helpless, when they cut his throat. When France was down, Laval's knife flashed.

On Sunday, June 16, while Reynaud was entering his last fight at Bordeaux, Root and I were at St.-Jean-de-Luz, within a few miles of the Spanish frontier, relaxing. His wife and their baby daughter had been living at St. Jean all spring. There wasn't much war feeling there; the hotels were full of Parisians who had come to get as far from the fighting as they could without a passport. It is the kind of place that people who like Provincetown would like, to me vaguely annoying. Early the next morning the radio in my hotel announced that Reynaud had resigned and that a new government had been formed with Laval and Paul Faure, the Socialist collaborationist, in leading places. Shortly afterward, news got around that the Laval-Faure thing had not come off, that there was a Pétain-Weygand government, and that Pétain had appealed to the Germans for honorable terms. It meant that effective resistance was over. If the German authorities had publicly requested terms on November 4, 1918, the German Army would have dissolved before November 11 of that year. Whatever potentialities of resistance remained to the beaten French Army on June 16, there were none on June 23, when the Armistice was actually signed.

The primary reason for the French military defeat as of June 16 is not obscure; it was the disparity of population and industrial capacity between Germany and France. A great part of the reason for the speed and completeness of the defeat lay in the superior use the Germans made of their already superior potentialities.

But there are other reasons not completely apparent even now. It must have been a little like one of those football games in which one team seems certain in advance to beat the other by two or three touchdowns, but in which the inferior team plays far below its form. The worse the poor devils muck things up the more confidently the destined victors play, and the result is an unwarranted score. The French have an excellent word for this kind of losers' dementia. They call it *la pagaille*. After such a game the spectators always think the winning team much stronger than it really is and the losers weaker than they possibly could have been.

The French strategy had been amorphous, the tactics bad, and the material woefully and unexpectedly deficient, for the men had been assured repeatedly that there was enough of everything. This was worse than telling them from the beginning that they would have to fight barehanded. After a football calamity the professional coach, to save his reputation, sometimes implies his players lacked courage. It would not suit Laval's book to have too much of a scandal about war material, because his clients had supplied it. Nor could Pétain, Huntziger, and Weygand afford to disparage generalship, because they had supplied that. And so Pétain started out to spread the libel of decadence against his own countrymen.

The betrayed people were responsible for everything, he implied. Their morals were bad (this attracted to the new regime the support of the Catholic hierarchy). They had been in love with soft living (translate decent wages, hours, and housing). "Look at the Germans," the old marshal cackled—"weren't they wonderful?" (Material and generalship had had nothing to do with it.) "And see how many Germans there were! Be like them, breed!" he adjured his compatriots. People must have some pleasure to keep them from thinking, and that is undoubtedly the cheapest.

I wrote a letter of farewell to Sauvageon, who I knew was now with a fighter group at Marseille, and another to Suzette, Henri's daughter, at Grenoble, since I thought it more likely that she had stayed there than that the old people had remained at Paris. Both letters were full of more optimism than I felt. America would avenge France, I said. Damned if I haven't already seen part of it come true.

Then I took a taxi down to the international bridge at La Hendaye that I had crossed so briskly nine months before, went over to

Irun, and bought a ticket and a sleeping compartment to Lisbon on an express train.

CHAPTER XIII

Once Down Is No Battle

I HAD A FEW HOURS TO SPARE at Irun because the train left in the early evening, so I took a walk about the town, in which the damage done by the Franco people's shells in July 1936 was still unrepaired, and out to Fuenterrabia, an old Gothic town on a hill. A learner was playing a piano inside one of the steep Fuenterrabian houses. The weather, so beautiful all that ghastly spring, was like a false unchanging smile. I walked for the first time in nine months without thinking of France. I became conscious of this and felt guilty, as you do when you walk out of a hospital where your wife is and in a couple of blocks catch yourself whistling.

I had had a fairly adequate lunch, soup and veal, at the hotel in the railroad terminus; the fact that it was possible to get such a meal even at a price far beyond people who lived on Spanish wages appeared to me to mark some kind of advance. In the previous fall it had been impossible to get a satisfying meal at all. When I came back from Fuenterrabia I went into a wine bar on an Irun street for a glass of sherry and got to talking, in English, to a dark and a fair man. The dark man was a Spaniard who had lived in New York; he was rather pleased at what had happened to the French. He made bitter fun of the Italians, though. "The Germans will give them nothing at all," he predicted. The blond fellow was a German who said he had been a merchant seaman for a long time but now had some kind of business in Irun. He said he had been a prisoner in England in the last war. He asked me what I thought would happen next, and I said I didn't know, but that the United States had better get going before the Germans got around to us.

He said, "My dear sir, Hitler has absolutely no designs on Canada or the United States. He is a fair man who wants only his rights." It recalled what the Germans had said before each of their gobbles. I looked at this undistinguished specimen of a people so mean and stupid that they repeated their lies in unison like a marching song, and I thought of the weak bands of wolfish dolts who had drifted across the boundaries of the Roman Empire with protestations of friendship. Once in, they had looked about them like German servants in a Jewish household picking out objects to steal when the Storm Troopers came. The Germans had never been warriors, properly speaking; they had been the scavengers who plucked the eyes out of sick nations. This was their cultural heritage.

Returned to the railroad station, I found two oldish men who were also bound for Lisbon. One, who was indignant because all the first-class sleeping compartments had already been sold, kept waving a card under the nose of the woman Wagons-Lits agent and shouting in French, "I am the Baron Rothschild." The other, who had his accommodations already, was a Sir Charles Something-or-Other from the British Embassy in France, but no stock-company actor would have dared play the role so obviously. I think that his company on the journey down colored all my thinking about Great Britain with pessimism that was to prove unwarranted.

Lisbon was, for the moment, one of the few remaining comfortable cities left in Europe, but it was not easy in its mind. The events in France had placed a certain restraint on the preparations for the dual celebration of the eighth centennial of Portuguese independence and the third centennial of the "liberation from the Spanish yoke" which terminated a temporary union with Portugal's neighbor. The Portuguese, placid as they are, could not avoid the reflection that now there was nothing much to stop the reimposition of a Spanish yoke whenever Franco felt like it, and they hoped he would not take the festivities in ill part.

The regime of Senhor Salazar, the university professor of political economy turned plain-clothes dictator, had kept Portugal solvent, with one of the lowest living standards and highest venereal-disease rates in Europe, but virtually without armament. Fascist Spain, whose financial position was impossible, as any political economist could explain to you in ten minutes, was bristling with expensive ordnance. Senhor Salazar must have hoped that Franco was grateful for favors received during the Spanish Civil War. He was aware that, for the first time since the Peninsular War, the traditional Portuguese alliance with England had become more of a liability than an asset. But it was not the sort of association that even a dictator could end on short notice, for English was the second language of Lisbon, English banks controlled the country's finances, the English for centuries had been the best customers for port, and Portugal knew that if Great Britain was defeated in the war, the victors would confiscate the Portuguese colonies. Italians were not popular in Lisbon, and neither were Germans, of whom there were a good many. Some weeks before my arrival the police had raided the German club and school and uncovered a lot of arms—almost enough for a Portuguese army.

Few residents of Lisbon could forget this political background for long at a time, but outwardly the life of the town and of the crescent-shaped Portuguese Riviera, which begins just north of the capital and follows the shore for thirty miles, went on exactly as it always had. Windows were not darkened at night, some moving-picture shows started at one in the morning, and the Casino in Estoril, the beach resort, began to be gay at about three. British social life in Lisbon had always had the atmosphere of a colonial governor's garden party, and it continued in the same tenor of dropping cards on fellow residents, amateur theatricals (Sir James Barrie and Ian Hay continued to be the favorite playwrights), and mild gambling at the Casino. The Duke of Kent was expected to help open the centennial show, and a special committee of the Royal British Club was proceeding gravely with preparations for his reception, wondering the while whether Germans or Spaniards would arrive before him. The visit was subsequently canceled.

The Pan American Clippers to New York and the boats to South America were then about the only reliable means of leaving the country, and since the demand for passage to South America was not precisely lively, the hotels were full of Americans from France waiting for a place on a Clipper. The total number, perhaps a thousand, was not impressive, but in proportion to the number of passengers a Clipper could carry—twenty-five was about the maximum for the westbound trip—and to the number of good hotel rooms in Lisbon and near-by Estoril, it seemed large. The *New Yorker* had booked my passage already, and I found a good room in the Grand Hotel at Mont-Estoril, so I had no trouble of any kind. I had five or six days to wait for the Clipper, and I employed them in swimming from the beach at Estoril and playing roulette for small sums at the Casino in the evenings. I also visited a British oil company official I knew, an atypical chap because he had had a Spanish mother, spoke Portuguese well, and spent a great deal of time with the Portuguese, a practice disapproved by his peers. They thought it smacked of going native. He was the "number two" in his firm in Lisbon. His chief was a more conventional Briton; he hardly seemed to think that there was anything to worry about. This irritated but in a way reassured me. All of the Lisbon British were packed to move out on twenty-four hours' notice and go aboard British warships, but at the same time the women of the colony were busy taking care of British refugees from France. And, as I have already said, they went on with their amateur theatricals.

The British went about gravely wagging their heads and saying that it was sporting of Churchill to forego recriminations and that, really, what was left of the French Army should have been evacuated to defend the British Isles. The disappearance of that army had altered the position of every nation on the Continent so drastically that people as yet couldn't get used to the idea; it reminded me of the death of the uninsured breadwinner of a large and helpless family.

On the day after I checked into my hotel I went down to the beach to swim. After swimming I sat on the terrace of the bathing pavilion, drinking vermouth and eating remarkably good olives. The vermouth was called the Vermouth of the Good Jesus. (There is a bank in Lisbon called the Bank of the Holy Ghost and of Commerce.) The pavilion people gave you a whole tumblerful of olives with each drink. There were a few German refugee families about, sitting at little tables under beach umbrellas and tremulous with masochistic fear as usual, happily certain that everything was going to turn out for the worst. An Englishman whom I had met at the bar of my hotel sat down next to me, already tight as a tick although it was just midmorning, and began telling me how he personally had piloted the plane that brought Franco from the Canaries to Spain. This broomstick journey must have been a mass enterprise. "Within three years all Democrats will be shot or in prison!" this lovable character told me. There was a public-address system at the bathing pavilion, and the management played phonograph records over it, usually Carmen Miranda. But just as I was sipping the Vermouth of the Good Jesus and wondering whether I ought to knock out the Englishman's brain with an olive pit, adapting the size of the missile to the importance of the target, the phonograph soloist put on a record of Charles Trenet singing "Boum!" The salt water and the sun and the vermouth had put me in a good frame of mind; the happy Parisian tune and the crazy lyric had an exaggerated effect upon me. I looked at the sadist and the masochists and said to myself, "They will both be disappointed." And I remembered something said to me by an old man who had been the last bare-knuckle lightweight champion of the world and had retired undefeated. This old boy was named Jack McAuliffe, and he had told me, "In Cork, where I was born, there was an old saying:

"Once down is no battle."

BOOK II

THE WORLD ON ONE KNEE

CHAPTER I

No Place Like It

WHEN I WAS GETTING ABOARD the Clipper at the mouth of the Tagus to come home I told the radio operator, who was checking off the names on the passenger list, that I had been in France. "Yeah," he said offhandedly, "it looks like we'll have to beat the hell out of those Germans." I began to understand that Hitler would not have us as he had had the Social Democrats, without fighting. It made me feel better. At that time I may have had an exaggerated idea of the boldness of German strategy. I was sure that we had no ground or air forces that could meet a series of quick landings at widely separated parts of our or the Mexican coast. That was a good guess, because when I talked to General Marshall in Washington several weeks later he told me that we had "the possible equivalent of three divisions" of troops ready to fight, and that included the garrisons of the Canal Zone and Hawaii. I was not at all sure that Germany would not offer, and Great Britain accept, terms for a peace that would leave the British Empire temporarily intact and the Reich free to move against the richest, softest, and most inviting target: us. My estimate of Great Britain had been conditioned by ten months in France; like the French, I thought that the British showing had been halfhearted and ineffectual. The British newspapers flown over to Paris even in the last days we were there had been full of racing and cricket. If they were the expression of a nation, England wasn't even interested. It is unnecessary to state that I was wrong about what Great Britain would do, but I had logical reasons for being so, like poor Gamelin. The real wonder of the world, though, is that Japan didn't hop in then. If she had, the nearly disarmed British would have been simply outclassed, no matter how great their determination. Certainly no reasons of conscience deterred the Japanese. The dictatorships were too timid. They had the world on the point of a knockout, but they "lost" it, the way a novice boxer fails to finish another novice after having him groggy.

Getting off the plane and meeting people who had stayed in America was a strange experience, because they hardly seemed to know that anything was wrong. When you started to tell them they said soothingly that probably you had had a lot of painful experiences, and if you just took a few grains of nembutol so you would get one good night's sleep, and then go out to the horse races twice, you would be your old sweet self again. It was like the dream in which you yell at people and they don't hear you. I went down to Washington to do a profile of General Marshall. The War Department took the situation seriously enough, God knows, but when you had got out of the Munitions Building you were in an unconcerned world again. It reminded me of leaving a feverish last rehearsal in a theater and coming out on a sidewalk where few of the passers-by even know there's a show about to open.

After you had been here awhile you began to get stupid too, and more recent arrivals from Europe began to bore you slightly. Dick Boyer came back from Berlin, where he had been as a correspondent for *PM,* and visited me at the *New Yorker* office in October.

It was only the second day after Boyer's return, and he still looked at people with astonishment, because they did not seem worried enough. I, who knew the symptoms, understood the way Boyer felt as soon as I saw him come into the office. We were to have lunch together and talk about Europe and Boyer's experiences as a war correspondent. Boyer was bigger and blonder than ever; he walked with chin and nose pointed upward and talked with wide gestures. He would have a noble and stupid face if it were not for his malicious and intelligent little eyes, which redeem it. Boyer still talked a little too loud, as people do in a foreign country where they assume nobody around understands them. He had arrived by Clipper and so had not had time to change back from his foreign to his domestic personality. When we got into the elevator to go

down to lunch, Boyer began talking about the bombings he had
been in. "The first time they bombed Berlin," he said, "they didn't
do enough damage." The office girls who were jammed into the
elevator all about him, some with their shoulder blades against his
belly and others with their chins against his shoulder blades, looked
up with interest. "The second time they bombed it, they were really
getting somewhere," he said. "It made me feel good down in my
air-raid shelter. Those bastards in Berlin don't like it." When he
said "bastards" the girls looked confused, because he had no right
to say that to them, but they had no right to be listening, either.

I said in a perfunctory way, "The only bombardment I was in
was at Paris." I had said it so often that it didn't even interest me
any longer, and June 3, 1940, seemed as long ago as the Battle of
Hastings. All the girls continued looking at Boyer as if I had not
said anything at all.

The elevator reached the street floor, and Boyer said, "What I
want is a really good meal. With wine. I am used to drinking wine
with my meals." We headed toward Fifth Avenue. Boyer suddenly
stopped and said, "What are we doing about our defenses? I mean,
have we really started or are we still futzing around?" His voice
sounded very anxious.

I remembered when I had felt the same way, coming back from
Lisbon, but just before meeting Boyer for lunch I had been thinking
principally about the heavy overlay against a race horse named
Hash, on which I had failed to bet. Understanding Boyer's anxiety,
I tried to formulate in my mind what I truly believed about defense,
canceling out wishful thinking. "Yeah," I said, "I think we've
started."

Boyer began walking again, looking over the heads of the people
in the street, who were so unworried and foolish. "Well, maybe
we'll be all right then," he said.

We walked uptown without any precise destination, until we
came to the sunken roller-skating rink at Rockefeller Plaza. As
usual, there were a good many people hanging over the railings,
watching the skaters. We joined them. Two professional skaters
were putting on an exhibition. The man wore a blue uniform like
a moving-picture usher's, and the girl short skirts which showed
chunky, chapped legs. They were going through a complicated sort
of waltz to music relayed by a loud-speaker. The trouble was, how-

ever, that while they skated well, they would have danced badly under any circumstances. Several times the girl threw herself sideways through the air, the man holding onto her wrists, and when she landed on her skates with a clacking, mechanical noise, she looked around for approval. There were restaurant tables at either end of the rink and on a level with it.

"This is a pretty good place to eat," I said. "It's nice outdoors today." Boyer thought the place looked all right, too, so we walked down the steps and a maître d'hôtel showed us to a table.

After we had ordered oysters, lobster Thermidor, and a bottle of Pouilly, I asked whether the Germans seemed much bucked up by their victories. Boyer said the army Germans did but the civilians didn't. "But the civilians have nothing to say anyway," he said. "It's just the Army and the Party. The country will never crack until somebody cracks the Army."

"Who?" said I.

We both knew the only possible answer.

Boyer looked gloomily at the people hanging over the railing above the rink and at the skaters. They didn't seem potentially formidable. "It's a wonderful country," he said, "but I think everybody is crazy."

I tried to be funny. "That's just a European frame of mind," I said, imitating the voice of a normal, unfrightened American, like Harold Ross. "You forget about the three thousand miles of ocean and the time Hitler will need to digest all the countries he has already taken."

"People who talk like that give me a pain in the butt," Boyer said.

"I used to be like you myself, old man," I continued, "but now, after a couple of months in a sane atmosphere compounded of Lindbergh's speeches and editorials in the *New Masses,* I see how things really are."

Boyer said, "When you begin to think that sort of stupidity is even funny, you are beginning to go crazy yourself. The first batch of French prisoners I saw, I cried."

I was not listening very intently, because I had said the same things until I had noticed people didn't like to listen to me. Boyer was right, and nobody cared, I thought, and after a while Boyer would understand that without anybody telling him. A waiter served the oysters and poured two glasses of wine, and we began to eat. The beginning of a meal demands concentration, and while we were appraising the oysters and ranking the wine in the scale of all oysters and wine that had gone down our gullets, a tall girl came out of the little skate room under the stairs and began to move about the rink. There is nothing finer to watch than a graceful animal on legs a bit too long for symmetry—a two-year-old thoroughbred, a kudu, or a heron. The girl was leggy, and I thought she was brave to put on skates at all, because her little scut was such a long way from the ground in case she fell. There didn't seem much risk of that, though, the way she moved around. She seldom lifted her skates far off the surface, and she didn't jump up or squat on her haunches and revolve with one foot in the air like the instructress. She just moved well, and her hands made slight, disarticulated motions from the wrist, as if to call attention to the lovely, slow turns she was making.

Boyer had finished his oysters—he always ate with the speed of a small dog consuming meat in the presence of larger dogs of whose forbearance it is not sure—and was beginning to talk of the gray, tasteless fish in Germany and the gray, tasteless people who endured it when he noticed the girl. He said, "It's funny, but when you're terribly worried you're not interested in food. I didn't mind the taste of the stuff. But I wouldn't eat a piece of it now for a buck." The girl was wearing a black skirt and a thin shirtwaist through which the men could see the white, clean straps of her underwear. Boyer's nostrils flared, as if he could smell the faint aroma of laundry soap and ironing board that such underwear should have. If the girl had spoiled this bouquet with a perfume, as she probably had, nobody at that distance could know it.

"I know," I said. "Then, when you're a little less worried, you take an interest in food again, but not in women. When you take an interest in women, you're not worried."

Boyer said, "I don't feel like a man from Mars but like a man from earth who has landed on another planet. Don't the damn fools know what is happening on earth?" But his voice was milder than before, and he watched the girl's thin hips.

The girl summoned a male instructor with one of her small motions, and the two of them skated hand in hand. She was very blonde, with fine, threadlike hair that wouldn't stay up, and she had dark eyebrows and a small, turned-up nose that gave her a silly, friendly look. Boyer and I followed her with our eyes, and both felt angry when she placed the instructor's arm around her, under her right armpit. We were glad she held his hand firmly in hers, so it did not touch her breast.

"That girl skates as if thousands of other girls weren't cold and hungry, or cowering from bombs," Boyer said with a last, feeble effort to appear outraged. But he was obviously more interested in her than in his talk.

"He's beginning to be comfortable," I thought, "and he's ashamed of it." Just then the waiter arrived with the lobster Thermidor. I said, tactfully, "Oh, what the hell! Why don't you tell me all about Europe some other time?"

Boyer looked relieved. "Sure," he said. "That girl looks like somebody I used to know."

CHAPTER II

Rape Is Impossible

THAT KIND OF FEELING was involuntary. It was due to the mental climate. Even actions directly connected with war had an unreal quality when they took place here; I remember the curious feeling I had when I went to register for compulsory service on October 16, 1940, in a schoolhouse where I had to squeeze 215 pounds of me into a child's seat, behind a child's desk, to fill out a blank. The associations evoked were of learning long division and looking forward to recess, rather than of bombed cities. Yet I had seen bombed cities, which none of the other men registering had. After sitting in the small seat for a couple of minutes I began to be overawed by the schoolteacher who was issuing the registration cards. I hoped she wouldn't ask me anything I did not know. I just got into the draft by two days; on October 18 I was going to be thirty-six years old and officially middle-aged. The psychological benefit was not slight; I have thought of myself ever since as a mere kid. I never was destined to fight, though—just get shot at.

116

Remoteness from the war affected everybody, but there were at least two groups in the country that tried consciously to minimize our danger. They were precisely these that had worked to the same end in France—a strong faction of men of wealth and the Communist party. The money people wanted to prove fascism more efficient than democracy, the Communists that democracy offered no protection against fascism. A military victory for the democracies would shatter the pretensions of both.

Pierre-Etienne Flandin, a former premier who has never been rated a revolutionary, gave me last winter a concise account of the way in which the French industrialists arrived at their policy of collaboration. Retrospectively it clarifies for me a great deal of what went on here in 1940–41.

"The great industrialists had never contributed so largely to a national campaign as they did to André Tardieu's group in the general elections of 1932," Flandin said. "Tardieu was badly beaten. So they said, 'What has the Republic come to when you can't even buy an election? Evidently it is time to change the system of government.' Being French, they felt particularly bad because they had wasted so much money. So they began to back the French fascist movements—De la Rocque, Doriot, all that, with Chiappe of course running the show. They mounted the riots of February 1934, expecting to take power by a *coup d'état*. The coup didn't come off. Then they gave up on accomplishing anything from inside France and decided to wait for the arrival of the Germans. The Front Populaire Government, elected in 1936" (of which Flandin had been an active parliamentary opponent), "had nothing to do with their decision. They had made up their minds two years earlier."

The American opposite numbers of the men of the *grands cartels* had been too badly panicked in 1932 to get together then. It was not until after the Roosevelt-Landon campaign of 1936 that they began to despair of democracy and to get vocal about it. The little men in Statler Hotel bars and golf-club locker rooms echoed the official line. What good was a system under which the majority of people voted to protect their own interests? It was damn selfish of working people to vote that way. "As a matter of fact this country was never meant to be a democracy anyway," they would say with the same knowing air with which they knocked a competing line of scrapple when they were out peddling pork products, "it was

meant to be a republic. Get it?" And suffrage in a republic could
be as limited as it was in a stockholder's meeting of Republic Steel.
Money had never articulated its dislike of democracy during the
years when it had been possible to elect McKinleys and Hardings
and Coolidges and Hoovers.

I do not think that the money men who were to turn isolationists
ever backed an American fascist movement on a large scale as the
cartels had in France in 1934; they were not so conscious of what
they wanted or perhaps so cynical as their European counterparts,
and besides they had not completely given up on the ballot box.
In 1940 they applied not only money but advertising techniques.
When the advertising men failed to elect a President, they had to
regretfully inform their clientele that the jig was up. There was no
time to mount a nationalist authoritarian movement. The money
by-passed that step and went in for isolationism, which was a form
of passive aid for the Axis.

I stayed in the United States from July 1940 until July 1941.
An important phase of the war was being waged all around me. It
went well for the ultimate good of the country, but a trifle slowly.
The election in the United States was a defeat for Germany; newspapers there and in Great Britain treated it as such. I had never
been worried about it; the confidence expressed up to the last minute by my little friends who were identified with big business showed
they lacked all sense of reality. The advertising manager of the
Herald Tribune took five to four from me on the eve of the election.
The beating did Willkie good too; it served as a disinfectant bath
to rid him of parasites. He came out of the race minus the most
antisocial elements of his support. When I met him for the first time,
in the following January, he was still astonished by their desertion.
I had imagined him a knave. I found him a naïf.

My most nightmarish memory of the year is of a trip I made to
Chicago to interview the leaders of America First for an article I
had been engaged to write for *McCall's Magazine* on propaganda
in the United States. I was to cover all varieties of propaganda in
two thousand words and make the subject as clear as a dress pattern. I hit Chicago during the debate on the Lease-Lend Bill. The
Chicago *Tribune* carried on its editorial page the day I arrived a
cartoon showing Liberty loaded with chains and being beaten with
a spiked club by a sort of ape-man. The ape-man was labeled not

THE WORLD ON ONE KNEE

"Nazism" or "Fascism" but "New Deal." The president of America First, an ecclesiastical-looking white-haired man rather like Warren Harding or Samuel Seabury, told me in a paternal, authoritative tone that Great Britain was in no danger but that it was no use trying to help her because she was doomed. It would be dangerous to help her while she was still in the war, he continued, but if we permitted her to get knocked out of the war we would be well able to take care of ourselves against any combination of powers that could have whipped her and us combined. I detected a certain confusion, but I was there to report and not to argue, and besides a reedy young man who was publicity-directing for the committee told me that the president knew all about modern war because he had been a Quartermaster General in 1917 and sold several million dollars' worth of sundries by mail catalogue every week. I am not sure yet whether all these people desired an Axis victory consciously, but the irrational stubbornness with which they denied its possibility made you think of certain women who continually and compulsively talk about the impossibility of rape. The subject fascinates them. It was a successful article, the editors of *McCall's* said, except that I had mentioned one America Firster's business connection with the Quaker Oats Company, which was an advertiser. They fixed it to read he was "an official of a cereal company."

Although I believed that in the United States, as in France, the para-Fascists were more dangerous than the Communists, the latter caused me considerably more personal annoyance, because a number of my friends had listened to them. I never expect to see eye to eye with a Ford personnel manager or the vice-president of an advertising agency, and it causes me no anguish at all to find myself in disagreement with a newspaper publisher. But I did hate to drop in on a perfectly good reporter or physician and find myself howling and banging the table because he thought that there was no choice between Churchill and Hitler and demanded who were we to object to the slaughter of a couple of million Jews in Poland when there were resort hotels right here that wouldn't take Jewish guests? Unpeculiarly enough, the two propaganda groups had taken the same line on perfecting the United States before we opposed the Nazis— Robert Maynard Hutchins of the University of Chicago, who was the accredited intellect of the money people, hit exactly the same note on that as *New Masses*.

119

THE ROAD BACK TO PARIS

I think I must say here what I believe myself, because if you are going to see a war through a man's eyes you ought to know what there is behind them. I think democracy a most precious thing, not because any democratic state is perfect, but because it is perfectible. It sounds heartbreakingly banal, but I believe that you cannot even fool most of the people most of the time. They are quite likely to vote in their own interest. I also believe that since a democracy is made up of individual electors, the electors will protect the rights of the individual. A democracy may sometimes grant too little power to its government and at others allow government to infringe on the rights of the individual—Prohibition is example enough— but the vote always offers the means of correcting imbalance, and the repeal of Prohibition is an example of that. Any system that is run by a few, whether they sit in a Fascist Grand Council or at the pinnacle of a pyramid of holding companies, is a damned bad system, and Italy is a fine example of that, but unfortunately we didn't have its finish to point to in 1940–41. And so much for my ideology.

I had thought all along that the Germans would invade Great Britain in the spring or summer of 1941 and that that was the place to be for a *New Yorker* man who wanted to see the war, but I had gotten to fiddle-fluting around with the State Department Passport Bureau about giving me permission to travel on a belligerent ship. I also fiddle-fluted with the British Ministry of Information about getting me a passage either on a freighter in convoy or a bomber, and before I got under way Germany had invaded Russia. That slimmed the prospects of an invasion of England, but I choked back my disappointment and decided to go anyway. June 22, when the news of the invasion of Russia got around in New York, was a hot Sunday. I walked up through Union Square, where the free-style catch-as-catch-can Marxist arguers hang out, and all the boys who two days earlier had been howling for Churchill's blood were now screaming for us to get right into the war. "Well," I thought, "we are on the same side of a question for once, anyway." Somehow, I remembered my old French general who had said to his estranged friend, "I will shake hands, if you have arrived at better sentiments." The reason I had thought all year that we should declare war on the Axis immediately was that I didn't think either the training of our Army or war production could attain even half-speed until the Government had war powers.

CHAPTER III

Destination: United Kingdom

ALONG IN JULY I got my passport and my means of transportation straightened out. I was to go by bomber.

Since fairly early in the war the British had been flying American-built bombers from Canada for immediate incorporation into the R.A.F. The bombers which made these one-way trips were the light types, like Lockheed Hudsons, and after they had been fitted with extra fuel tanks for the long hop, they had little space for freight or passengers. However, during the past few weeks the British Air Ministry had been using a number of the big, long-range, four-engined Consolidated bombers, which had been christened Liberators, in a regular two-way service. On westward trips they brought over groups of small-bomber pilots and occasional voyagers like the Duke of Kent and Prince Bernhard of Lippe. Going east, they carried not only passengers, mostly British subjects on official business, but also light freight, such as engine parts.

The division of the Air Ministry which managed this trans-atlantic service then was known as Atfero, which stood for Atlantic Ferry. An Atfero man at a Montreal airport put a tag on my suitcase which read "Destination: United Kingdom," and in approximately sixteen hours, which included four hours of loafing at an air base in Newfoundland, I reached my destination. The actual flying time was less than half that of the Pan American Clippers between New York and Lisbon. A loaded Liberator is only about half as heavy as a Clipper, but it has four fifths as much power in its engines. Its published top speed is three hundred miles an hour and a Clipper's is a hundred and ninety, but the published top speed of a military airplane is likely to be an underestimate. A secondary advantage of travel by Atfero was that it spared you from the bleak scorn of the Lisbon hotelkeepers, all of whose rooms, I heard, had been full since the fall of France. The principal reason more Americans did not go by Atfero is that passengers had to wangle both an invitation from the British authorities and permission from our own State Department.

On the morning before my plane was scheduled to leave Montreal, I reported to the Atfero office in a large office building in the city. The manager, a Mr. Jackson, received me with all the excitement a Long Island Railroad conductor displays at the sight of a commuter. After looking at my credentials, he turned me over to a Mr. Hart, who gave me a slip of pink paper which said, in effect, that I had been accorded a trip to the United Kingdom in a bomber but if I broke my neck it was my own fault. Hart assured me that this was just a matter of form. He gave me, in addition to my ticket, two pages of mimeographed instructions to passengers. One instruction read, "The following subjects should not be referred to within the hearing of any unauthorized persons: airports of departure and arrival; departure and arrival times of aircraft; details of armament, supply, storage, and the performance of aircraft, engines, and other war material. Particular discretion should be exercised in speaking with representatives of the press, whose object it is to extract the maximum amount of information and who often collaborate and piece together the scraps of information they collect individually." There were also instructions for the use of oxygen equipment. For example: "On the flight it may be necessary to use oxygen owing to the height at which the aircraft may have to fly. Oxygen masks are provided for each person on board. They will be found already connected to the oxygen supply. Please use great care in the handling of the masks, as they are quite fragile and will break easily if mishandled."

"It gets pretty cold above twenty thousand feet," Hart told me, "and I advise you to buy one of the flying suits that Atfero sells for seventeen dollars. I'll bring the suit to the field for you." I gave him seventeen dollars and then went out to stroll around the grounds of McGill University, where I had once taken a summer course shortly after the other great war, when Canadians and Americans were still slapping each other on the back because Those People had been put in their places forever. The grounds were full of Royal Canadian Air Force cadets, marching smartly and self-consciously between classrooms, where they were studying the theory of flight. I then went into the quiet tavern of the Prince of Wales Hotel, on McGill Street, the place where I had first tasted ale, and polished off a couple of reminiscent pints. Then I walked back to the Mount Royal, where I was stopping. A car was to pick me up in front of the hotel early the next morning and take me to the airport.

As I stepped into the elevator with my bag the next morning, I met Jackson, the Atfero man. He said he usually stayed at the hotel when he had a batch of planes to send off. Four more men with bags, a couple of them carrying flying suits, were already standing outside the hotel when we got to the sidewalk, and I judged, correctly, that they were to be my shipmates. Jackson introduced me to two of the men, a brisk, sandy-haired Lancashireman named Steadman, evidently in his forties, who had been in the United States on some business for the British Government, and a tall, sallow young Hollander named Van Der Schrieck, who carried a small canvas sack in his left hand. It was a diplomatic pouch, he explained. He had been out in the East Indies for the Dutch Government. The other two fellows stood a little apart. They were both very young, perhaps eighteen or nineteen, and they wore Texas-style sombreros and fancy, high-heeled cowboy boots. "They are a couple of kids who are going out as transport pilots to fly planes from factories to flying fields in England," Jackson said. "They haven't had enough experience to take bombers across, so they are going over as passengers."

Steadman, Van Der Schrieck, and I got into an automobile with Jackson, and the two kids got into another car, along with most of the baggage. When they climbed out at the airport, they looked more at home than they had at the hotel. They began walking about the nearest plane and talking like a couple of horse fanciers around a nag. I guess they liked the plane all right. It was the four-engined one in which we were to make the journey, and it was a mottled tan and green. The silvery Pan American Clippers have always looked to me like something a giant built with a Meccano set. This thing looked like a big, ill-tempered insect. I went over and introduced myself to the two kids in the cowboy hats. They shook my hand with fervor. "It certainly is mighty good to meet someone from the States," one of them said. "We been up here nearly a week." "You from Texas?" I asked, looking right at the hats. "How did you guess?" the other kid asked with obvious admiration. "Yes, sir, and it's far away now."

While we waited beside our plane, one of its sister ships came in from England. The kids were frankly critical of the pilot's landing. "Landed with his brakes on," one of them said. Jackson came over with two men wearing blue uniforms and visored caps. Each wore three rings of gold braid on his sleeve, indicating that he was a captain of a British air line. Jackson introduced the older of the two men as the captain of our plane and the other as Jimmy, a colleague who was going to cross as co-pilot with us because he felt a bit under the weather and didn't want the full responsibility of a ship this trip. Our captain was a round-faced, pink-fleshed man of about forty with a voice something like Charles Laughton's. Jimmy, who might have been about thirty-five, was tall, broad-shouldered, and apologetic. "Tonsillitis, you know," he whispered. "Going up to London and have my tonsils out. Do you suppose it's frightfully painful?"

Hart, Jackson's assistant, delivered my flying suit. It was a big brown affair, like a sleeping suit, and had a hood. "You won't need it until you leave Newfoundland," Hart told me. "He won't really go up until then." By this time somebody had let down a flap in the Liberator's belly. There were a couple of steps on the upper surface of this flap, and one by one we boosted ourselves inside. Our captain and Jimmy went up into the insect's head, where they could look out, but the rest of us remained, undigested, in its windowless thorax. The forward end of this thorax, the deepest part of the ship, was divided into two decks. A radio man, facing his instruments, had the upper deck all to himself. A big, red-haired chap, munching an apple, he sat there like a professor on a dais. The aft end of the thorax was not decked, but had two fairly wide shelves along the sides, and a passageway about the width of one of the shelves between them.

The engines began to turn over, and a man who we had been told was our flight engineer appeared from up forward. He was a tow-haired, wild-eyed young man who galloped about the ship as if he had passed his boyhood running on the tops of picket fences. He motioned us to get down into the bomb bay, under the radio man's feet; the captain, it turned out, wanted our weight in that part of the ship. We scuttled obediently into the bomb bay, a dark and miniature hold, where packing cases were stowed. The cargo was heavy rather than bulky, so we had plenty of room, and the Atfero people had spread mattresses over the crates. The engine noise increased, and we could feel the plane start to move in a series of quick, gentle lifts, as if somebody were pushing against our diaphragms with the heel of his hand. Then she steadied and we knew we were up. One of the kids from Texas waved both hands, palms upward, and grinned.

The flight engineer, who had disappeared forward, came tearing back again and made signs that we could come out from under, so we moved into the space aft of the radio man. A glorious and welcome light was coming through eight little windows and a sort of skylight known as an astrodome. We could move still farther aft into the tail of the ship, clear back to the glass-enclosed perch that the rear gunner occupies when the plane is on a bombing mission. In a short while we distributed ourselves about the ship according to our various temperaments. The two kids scrambled all over like monkeys. Steadman went back to the rear gunner's seat and looked out, perhaps trying to identify landmarks. Van Der Schrieck stretched out on one of the shelves under the astrodome and started to read *Berlin Diary*. I lay down on the other shelf and did nothing at all. It was possible to talk above the noise of the four 1,200-horsepower engines, but sustained conversation would have been difficult. If you yield to the noise, the way a fighter rolls with a punch, it is soothing. The plane rode more smoothly than any other I had ever been in. Once I made motions with my lips at the radio man: "How high?" He understood and held up ten fingers, then waved his hands and held up two fingers more—twelve thousand feet. The sky, through the astrodome, was blue, and the sun was brilliant.

We had a couple of dozen thermos bottles of hot tea, coffee, and cocoa aboard, stowed in the forward part of the tail, and a stack of lunchboxes from the Mount Royal, but as we were going to make a stop in Newfoundland for lunch there was not much reason to eat now. Jackson had told us that we would arrive at the base there in four hours; it was approximately nine hundred miles from Montreal. My reflections, as I lay on my shelf, were not entirely happy, despite the ideal flying conditions. I began to worry about my oxygen mask and how I should use it. I noticed several petcocks marked "Oxygen" at intervals along the side walls. Still, I felt like a city fellow who sees a cow but doesn't know how to get milk from it. Besides, I had read somewhere that at thirty-five thousand feet there is a constant temperature of sixty-seven degrees below zero, and I hoped that the captain would not go *too* high even though I had a flying suit. These thoughts were interrupted when the plane began to descend toward the Newfoundland airport. Looking out through the windows, we could see what appeared to be an enormous bare spot in the middle of an infinite green forest. As we circled lower we could make out a great airfield, its runways dotted with planes and protected by machine-gun pillboxes. The captain put the big Liberator on the ground as lightly as a dragon fly alighting on a leaf. I looked at the two boys from Texas. Their faces were ecstatic. When the plane came to a stop, the boys opened the hole in her belly and we all crawled out.

A slender, grinning young officer in some sort of khaki uniform was waiting beside the plane to greet us. We couldn't hear what he said, but when he turned and marched off across the runways we followed him. We learned afterward that he was a member of the Newfoundland Ranger Force, which polices the airport. He led us to a big, square frame building which bore a sign saying "Eastbound Inn." It was like a very large and unpretentious summer resort hotel. It houses the airport personnel and aviators and passengers who for one reason or another are lying over at this way station. We had lunch there: steak-and-kidney pie, stewed pears, and tea. As our deafness wore off, we began to talk a bit. Presently the radio man came in and sat down at our table. He was a Lowland Scot named Mitchell, and he said that this was his eleventh ferry crossing. Nothing serious had ever happened to him, he told us. "This is one of the largest military airfields in the world," he added, "and it's all been hacked out of the scrub since the beginning of the war. It's many hours' travel by land to a railroad or a town." He said he had been grounded there by a blizzard last March and had not been able to get away for three weeks. "It was very quiet," he remarked.

Our captain and Jimmy had stayed inside the plane. Now they came in to lunch, and the captain stopped by our table to say that we would have a four-hour wait. "I don't want to get in before dawn," he said. "Nothing to be gained by it." I went for a long walk in the sun with Steadman. Then I came back to the inn and sat around with Van Der Schrieck. We talked about the ninth-century Middle Kingdom of Lothaire, which had included the Low Coun-

THE WORLD ON ONE KNEE

tries, Alsace-Lorraine, and what is now Switzerland. Finally I went
into the recreation room and watched the Texas boys play table
tennis. By the time a Ranger came to summon us to our plane, we
were bored with Newfoundland.

When we got aboard the Liberator again we put on our flying
suits and ate a large number of sandwiches, although it was only
a few hours after lunchtime. The two shelves along the sides of the
part of the ship we passengers chose had hinged longitudinal leaves,
which, when raised and fastened together, formed a continuous
deck on which to spread our sleeping things. We decided we would
be better off there than down in the bomb bay, which was very
drafty and where there were no windows from which to watch the
sunset or dawn, so we dragged three mattresses up from the bay
and spread them athwartship on our newly created deck. Our deck
was slightly lower than the radio man's. We had a few light
blankets, and we hung one over the aperture between us and the
bay to shut off any draft. The radio man stayed at his instruments,
wearing his headphones and munching another of what appeared
to be an endless series of apples. He would be up all night, of course.
We closed the door that led into the tail of the ship, and then the
five of us lay down on the mattresses across-ship, forming an intri-
cate mosaic of legs and arms. My feet were at the right of the Hollander's head, and his were next to my right ear. The arrangement
proved fairly comfortable, but whenever somebody had to go out to
make use of the toilet facilities, which were aft, it meant untying
the human knot, opening the door, banging it several times to close
it, and then reversing the whole operation on the return trip. The
larder was also in the tail of the ship, and it seemed that as the air
grew colder we thought more of food, so there were constant trips
for thermos bottles and sandwiches. I realized after a few minutes
that the plane had been badly tailored for me. It was about three
inches too narrow. In order to lie down I had to bend either my neck
or my knees just enough to develop a kink. Van Der Schrieck was
a couple of inches taller, and the taller of the Texan boys was in as
bad a plight. Steadman and the smaller Texan fitted all right. It
was cold, but not as cold as I had expected, and to my great satisfaction I was breathing easily at the altitude, whatever it was. I
dozed, for exactly how long I did not know, and saw a raspberry-

pink glow through the windows when I awoke. I wondered whether it was the late American sunset or the early European dawn, but soon the sky grew dark and I knew.

I awoke again in the night, chilled and stiff. All of us seemed to awake at about the same time. Maybe one of us, in turning, had joggled the others. Mitchell sat there unblinking, the dimmed bulb on his table the only illumination in the place. The small Texan stumbled out to the larder and came back with three lunchboxes and a thermos of hot tea. We all shared the tea and grabbed things out of the lunchboxes. I got a ham sandwich as stiff and chilly as a slab of ice cream. I took a cold, rigid piece of ham out of the sandwich and held it in my palm, inside my flying suit, until it got at least as warm as I was. Then I ate it and went to sleep again. The next time I opened my eyes it was to a new quality of twilight. I knew it must be daybreak. We all got up and began to stretch, stamp, and look out of the windows, but we could as yet see only clouds. After a short while we sighted land far under us—Scotland or Ireland, I guessed. We grew restless. It's like getting into Grand Central on a train; the minutes after 125th Street seem the longest. We packed our mattresses back into the bomb bay, climbed out of our flying suits, and began to exchange our English addresses. The captain made another good landing, and we crawled out of the plane for the second time. We saw, rather than heard, a brisk R.A.F. officer, waiting outside, say, "Good morning." A friendly bull terrier with one pink eye thrust his muzzle against my hand. Then we got into a couple of ancient Rolls-Royces and were trundled over to the officers' club at the edge of the flying field for a wash and breakfast. There was an immigration man with a couple of perfunctory questions to ask the aliens on the plane, who of course included me. By the time I got to the dining room for breakfast, our captain and Jimmy had established themselves at a table with Van Der Schrieck. I sat down with them, and we all had bacon, tomato, and sausage. The bacon was excellent, but the sausage contained, I was told, sixty-five per cent bread, which made it taste like a hot dog with the roll inside the frankfurter casing.

I complimented the captain on our fine crossing and then said, because I was a little curious, "We didn't have to use oxygen at all. Don't you usually fly higher than that?"

"Oh yes," the captain replied brightly, as he poured milk in his tea. "But I just kept her at thirteen thousand last night. Didn't want to aggravate Jimmy's tonsillitis."

CHAPTER IV

Non Angeli Sed Angli

I SPENT THE NIGHT of my arrival in Britain at the Central Hotel in Glasgow. The Central has an indefinite number of rooms, alcoves, and lounges, all meant to drink in, spread along the sides of a corridor on the first floor. At that date it was still easy to get whisky in any of them early in the evening (by 1942 there was very little of it). At eleven o'clock service ceased except in a lounge marked "For use of residents only." This was in deference to the eleven-o'clock closing law in public drinking places. If you are living in a hotel it counts as your home. Everybody from the other rooms moved into this lounge and continued to drink, but at midnight a lame waiter whom any ex-Walter Scott fan could identify instantly as a crusty old servitor, announced that drinks would be sold only to *actual* residents of the hotel. After he had weeded out small tippers and Englishmen whose faces he did not like he waved the survivors, mostly Scotsmen, Norwegians, Americans, and trulls, into another, more exclusive lounge. He applied the fine comb again at one o'clock and again we moved, to a lounge for *bona-fide* residents of the hotel. At four in the morning I found myself in what I thought was my eleventh drinking nook of the night, together with a major in kilts, a lieutenant in kilts, and a merchant-navy skipper. The major spoke a trifle brusquely to the waiter, and the waiter said, "Major, you've had enough. Go to bed now." The major sulked for a couple of minutes and then went, for he knew the waiter was the only man in Glasgow who could give him a drink. The merchant-navy man had been glaring at the lieutenant disapprovingly, and now he said, "It amuses me to see you wearing the kilt when I have better Highland blood than you." This sounded like a quotation from a Waverly novel, but I could not identify it.

The lieutenant said, "I have just come from a place called Crrete.

Have you heard of it? I am a MacInnes of Skye." The merchant-navy man said, "I never cared for Skye." The lieutenant said, "That is no' imporrtant." The seafarer said, "I am a MacNeill of Barra." The lieutenant said, "You lie. You have not the faceel appearrance of a MacNeill of Barra." The crusty old servitor got between them and said, "Gentlemen, you've a wee thingie on both. There'll be no more drink tonight." I went to bed still trying to figure whether they had framed me with some amateur theatricals. But it had all been on the level. The first fact one must accept about Britain is that all British literature, no matter how improbably it reads, is realistic. You meet its most outrageous models everywhere you turn, because Britain is full of improbable people, behaving in what an American or a Frenchman wrongly suspects is a fictitious manner. Before coming to Britain I had intended to write about it from an American point of view, but the project reminded me of one Sam Langford once described. "It would be like a man who only under-stand Italian trying to teach French to a man who do not under-stand Italian either." The essential point in writing about Britain is never to try to explain it, and, in talking to Britons, never to try to make them explain themselves.

When I went down to my train the next day I was pleasurably impressed to find nearly all the seats in the first-class carriages occu-pied by private soldiers and aircraftsmen. The head porter of the hotel had sent a lad along half an hour ahead of time to get a place for me. I decided that the British social revolution, of which we had heard a good deal in America, had at last arrived. One minute before train time all the "other ranks" yielded their seats to officers and got out. They were batmen who had been sent to hold the places. "Obviously," I thought to myself, "in this country it is un-wise to jump to conclusions."

The young man who had taken the seat opposite me in my com-partment was a subaltern in a regiment identified for initiates but not for me by a pair of bronze pretzels on his lapels. They were, I was to learn later, representations of Staffordshire knots, and his regiment was the South Staffords. He was about six feet tall and rugged, but apparently suffering from concussion of the brain or an extraordinary hangover. I had a Penguin book that I had bought at a station newsstand in a hurry; it was the second volume of Robert Graves's *I, Claudius*. I had meant to buy the first volume.

The subaltern slept for a while with mouth open; after we had ridden for half an hour he began to stir. In another half-hour he said,
"Intrsting?" I said, "Yes, but I got the second volume by mistake
and I haven't read the first volume." Half an hour later he said,
"I think it's prefrable to begin reading early on in a book. Don't
you agree?" I asked him if he cared to read a newspaper, and he
declined on the grounds of ill-health. "Just finished a physical-
training course, you know," he said, "and I felt so nauseously fit I
went on a frightful beano." I suggested that we might get a drink
in the restaurant car, and a little color came back into his face,
elevating the tint to a dead white. "Would've never have had the
courage to go of my own accord," he said. "Thanks immensely for
moral support." We got the drink—that was the golden age when
there were still restaurant cars and they still had a bit of drink to
sell on British railways—and then we got another. Peter, the name
the subaltern answered to when he had drunk himself back to semi-
consciousness, said the waitress looked *enfilable;* a part of his boyhood had been spent at a school in France. He had been tossed out
of Oxford during his first year, he said—not the intellectual type.
He regretted it, because he had hoped for a boxing blue if he had
remained. What really "intrsted" him was driving racing automobiles. He had enlisted as a private in the Brigade of Guards at the
beginning of the war and had worked his way up to a commission
in the less exalted South Staffords. "I attribute my success to working jolly hard," he said. He was such a congenial type that I con-
sulted him about setting up my London life. I said I didn't want
to go to the Savoy, which had from reports become a transatlantic
succursale of the Stork Club, and which was the only London hotel
I had ever heard of. Peter said he knew three really British hotels,
one in St. James's Place, one on Dover Street—"that's where my
parents always put up when they come up to town," he said—and
a third on Half Moon Street. The parents put me off the Dover
Street place. When we got to Euston Station, Peter led me out into
London to find a lodging. We got in a taxi and had the cabbie drive
us to St. James's Place, but that hotel had been blitzed. "Awfully
sorry," Peter said, "I haven't been up to London in a couple of
months, you know." We tried the one on Half Moon Street next.
By that time our drunk was beginning to run down on us and we
were in desperate need of drinks to keep it going, so I hardly looked

around me before I registered. As I rushed out into the London blackout with Peter, I retained only a vague impression of a room with heavy yellow damask draperies. We got into a place called the Lansdowne soon after that and had some drinks with a boxer named Jackie Kid Berg whom Ray Arcel in New York used to train, and then into the Hungaria, where we were told we had to order dinner with our drinks because it was after eleven o'clock. "We have an extension until half-past twelve," they said, "but only for diners." So we ordered up a couple of redundant meals, which would have seemed to me curious in a country where food was rationed if I had not quite resigned myself to being Through the Looking Glass. After the Hungaria closed we went to a thing Peter knew called a bottle club, which was exactly like a 1924 New York clip joint with a cockney accent. For all I could tell they had imported it stone by stone, as Hearst used to buy himself knocked-down monasteries. This place had a dance floor as big as a copy desk, four colored musicians, a social secretary who was under indictment for crimes against nature, and the most terrible liquor in the world. It also had hostesses to help you drink this stuff. Everything was on a membership basis, cards and all; I wept joyous tears of recognition.

A couple of girls came over and sat with us; one was not making too much sense. "They laid the bodies on the dance floor," she would say. She'd had a lot. I gathered at last that a bomb had dropped next door during a blitz and the rescue people had really brought the dead and nearly-dead into the club and laid them out there. "Why don't you get out of this bloody awful London?" she said encouragingly. "Every time the blitz came I'd get blind drunk," she said, "and then I wouldn't mind it so, but next afternoon when I got up I'd have an awful hangover. Then the blitz would begin again and I'd get blind again. I thought I'd go mad." There hadn't been a blitz for nearly two months, but people were still edgy. I paid for one bottle of whisky—the legal theory was that it was your whisky and you just came there to drink it and bought chasers, so you couldn't ever order less than a bottle at a time. Peter paid for another and then, when I began to think of going home, I looked around and he wasn't there. I ran out into Denman Street, which was as black as deep mourning, and shouted "Peter! Peter!" but I never saw him again. Pamela, the blitz-batty hostess, got a cab and saw me home.

THE WORLD ON ONE KNEE

I put up at the hotel in Half Moon Street for six months following that and came back to it when I returned to England in 1942.

The hotel when I came there was governed by a board of directors largely composed of marquises, viscounts, and bart.'s—their
names were printed on the stationery, which left so little room for
correspondence that it was necessary to use two sheets of note-
paper where one would ordinarily serve. None of these notables
came in to operate the lift or the telephone switchboard, however,
and the hotel, which has about forty rooms, was as short of help
as it was long on directors. The rooms, even those that are technically on the same floors, are all on slightly different levels, as in the
country houses most prized by Englishmen, and are always entered
by falling down one step, tripping over three steps, or marching up
a hall with a floor at a twenty-five-degree angle. The concierge by
day was a magnificently pink, pompous, and sly Devon man known
as Roberts either because that was his name or because he used to
refer to the days when he had been Lord Roberts' batman. He wore
a beautiful red-and-green-striped waistcoat that made his belly look
like a beetle's back, with wide gold buttons and a watch chain over
his paunch that you could have hung an anchor on, and he used to
have a fairly good thing of pressing my trousers on an ironing board
that he had rigged behind the desk. There was no valet *en titre,* but
I always felt that a crease good enough for Lord Roberts was good
enough for me. The concierge was respectful, pleasant-spoken, a
man who had obviously understood how to limit his ambitions and
adjust to his world.

The night porter, whom I knew only as Mac, was gaunt, yellow-
toothed, limber, and rebellious. He was part Irish, part Canadian,
and all cockney; he played the races, horse and dog, every day and
usually came on duty tight but conscious and self-controlled. He
had been a noncom in India and had a cigarette case that the Duke
of Windsor, then Prince of Wales, had sent him for being one of a
guard of honor at New Delhi, of which he took an un-Kiplingesque
view. The clientele of the hotel alternately irritated and amused
him, but he could put on as soldierly a show of respect to an arriving leftenant-colonel as would merit a half-crown from any decent
lush. Once he had graded the tipping proclivities of the colonel he
would cool off. Mac played darts on the team representing the Rule
Britannia pub, Allen Street, Kensington, in the "News of the

World" tournament. The team had got to the finals one year, but the cup had been dashed from the lip, as in most of Mac's enterprises. He swam in the Serpentine every morning before going home from work. Mac's domestic affairs, from the fragmentary references that he made to them in our conversations, which usually occurred in the early morning before I went to bed, must have been fairly involved. He was finally sacked for threatening to bash the French chef in the nose; he said he could never stomach bloody foreigners.

The clientele of the hotel in the summer of 1941, when London was just beginning to fill up again after the blitz, consisted partly of people, mostly old, whom Roberts liked to refer to as "county." The typical dinner party in the restaurant—where the hors d'oeuvre invariably consisted of vegetable marrow, beetroot, celery, and one sardine—was made up of an old deaf gentleman, three deaf old ladies (presumably his wife and two of her or his sisters), four girls with buck teeth and large feet, and one elegant subaltern or sublieutenant, the heir and pride of the family. The dowdy girls would look adoringly at the young man, who had come up to London on leave; the family had come up to meet him. His problem was to be sufficiently agreeable to the old people to borrow money, without spending so much time in their company that the leave and the borrowed money would do him no good. After he had left, the old people would converse in well-bred howls, because of their deafness, their comments on their acquaintances resounding to the furthest corner of what they always called the "restaraw." I remember one old Galsworthy type shouting that "Lady Viola must be eighty." "EIGHTY!" his *commère* shrieked back to him, "Why, she's older than I am!"

The cellar then was one of the best that survived in London, because young people never came to the place unless they could help it, and the old people's doctors did not allow them to drink much. Cerutti, the old Italian wine waiter, one of Thackeray's own illustrations, was a shabby but a proud man then. A year later, when the restaurant had become one of the gayest and most constantly crowded-out in London, I was to see him resplendent in a new long-tailed coat and a sommelier's glittering chain, but cringing because he knew that there was nothing left in the house fit to drink.

Outside the window drapes that veiled this inner nodule of British propriety there resounded pretty continually the cheerful click of the Piccadilly tarts' high heels. Half Moon and Clarges streets, which are traverses between Piccadilly and Curzon Street, are important trade routes of summer evenings. The Piccadilly packets, having picked up cargoes, convey them back to their Curzon Street and Shepherds' Market home ports. They come back up Clarges Street light, chattering happily. The police, except for enforcing certain trade agreements, deal with the girls in the same spirit of comradely venality as cops in any other country. The fine aroma of larceny in the air makes a New Yorker feel at home. If the British were half as stuffy as they like to think they are, nobody could live with them.

They are, for example, the only nation in the world that habitually boasts of its own modesty. It is commonplace to read in a London leader or letter to the editor, "It is perhaps our fault as a nation that we do not speak sufficiently often of our own achievements." Really, it is one fault of which not even the Irish would accuse them. The Noel Coward kind of underemphasis is as glaring an affectation as a Von Stroheim strut, but happily no Briton can maintain it beyond the second drink. Drink, by the way, may have represented the difference in the resistant qualities of British and French statesmen. Hitler, whenever he denounces the British Prime Minister as "that drunkard," betrays his puzzlement at something Sam Langford understood. "You can sweat oat beer," Sam used to say, "and you can sweat oat whisky. But you can't sweat oat women."

On my second evening in London, just at the official blackout time, I saw a light showing through the interstice between a window shade and sash in a basement window. A man in front of a house diagonally across the street from it shouted, "Put out that bloody light!" and then walked over and kicked in the windowpane. There were still a good many people sleeping in bunks in the tube stations, and blitz reminiscences were not entirely out of fashion. In the early morning hours of July 27 there was a raid, which I waited out in my hotel bedroom. I thought that when it got really bad I would go downstairs, but it never got as bad as I expected, and then the all-clear sounded. When the guns first awoke me I thought for a minute that I was a fool for not having stayed home, but the feeling soon wore off. A couple of days later I was at the great

plant of the London Gas, Light and Coke Company, talking to some
workmen, because I had brought from America the idea of writing
a profile of a typical British workingman. I never found one who
was typical of all; it was presumptuous of me to have supposed I
would. But at the gas works that day I met a mechanic from Poplar,
a district in the East End of London, who told me that in his immediate neighborhood the July raid had been one of the worst ever.
A heavy bomb had fallen in a court in the center of three or four
old riverside warehouses belonging to a dog-biscuit manufacturer
that served the people as shelters. The warehouses had caved in,
and about seventy persons had been killed and a couple of hundred
injured. "Lucky as 'ow less and less is sleepin' in the shelters every
night," the Poplar man said. "A month ago a big one in the sime
spot would 'ave killed five 'undred. But they cawn't beat Poplar.
One old woman about itey-one years of ige, when they dug 'er out
of the debbris, she let out a cry, 'Bloody 'itler cawn't kill me!' Why,
when the moanin' Lizzies started up that night it was like old times,
and the barridges and all. But what was unfortunate, the pubs,
what we could a done with that time of night, was closed, so we
couldn't get the old darlin' a bottle of Guinness."

The mechanic, a "welder and burner," who earned between seven
and eight pounds a week—twenty-eight to thirty-two dollars, and
excellent pay by English standards—was not much like an American workman of the same grade. He was dressed like a caricature
of a coster, with cap and neckerchief—again that disquieting resemblance to a "literary" concept—and he was apparently quite
willing to live in a slum, because he had long possessed enough
money to move out of it if he had wished. But he had a heart as
big as a melon. "In Poplar we're cool, calm, and collective," he said.
"And we're determined to defeat this bloody 'itler and 'e *will* be
defeated and all, there's no doubt about that, because we're not
'aving any."

"Any what?" I asked.

"Any dictytor," he said, and with a sudden burst of eloquence,
as if to make it all clear:

"Once a Britisher 'as put 'is back to the wall and 'e says, 'I am
not going to 'ave it'—then 'e's not going to 'ave it. Because 'e's *determined* not to 'ave it. And consequently—'E WILL NOT 'AVE
IT."

Poplar and a thousand places like it, I understood, formed the wall against which Churchill had put *his* back. They also, quite without enthusiasm on their own part, form a protective wall around Mayfair.

CHAPTER V

It Showed Nice Instincts

THE WAR, IN THE SUMMER OF 1941, had hit a dead level. All through 1940 and the first half of 1941 the Germans had knocked the world about. They had occupied France and western Europe and then bombed England and after that taken over the Balkans, but now to a fellow in London it looked like anybody's fight, or a deadlock. The Germans had gone into Russia and taken their bombers with them; Britain was getting stronger by the minute, with the German grip off her collar. It already began to be plain that the German victories in Russia had less significance than victories in western Europe. No way was apparent for Great Britain and Russia to win the war unless the United States came in, but it began to seem improbable they could lose it. And since American entry into the war was a good possibility, while Germany had no equal good fortune to anticipate, a betting man would have had to lay slight odds against the Axis. I tried to fight off undue optimism, but I couldn't help thinking that any side which had come so near winning and failed was not going to win at all. It was so irresistibly reminiscent of the first time Germany had tried. The Punic Wars were not decided by a rubber, best two out of three. The same side won the First, Second, *and* Third, and I had a hunch that the German Wars would be the same, except that no Third might be necessary. Cannae, of which the Germans had always talked so much, had been the winning battle of a losing army. In their souls they identified themselves with Carthage that had been beaten and Siegfried that had been murdered. Behind their arrogance they were full of self-pity. Poplar had a better ticker than Potsdam, but I didn't see how you could make a man quit by putting your own back to a wall. It was better to push him up to a wall and then knock his head against it. The power for the push would have to come from the United States, as it had the last time. In the meantime the only active warfare based on Britain was being carried on by the R.A.F., which had gained a distinct edge on the Luftwaffe. So I asked permission to visit a fighter field.

I could not help thinking that morning of the trip I had made to St. Dizier in June 1940, when the French pilots were outnumbered twenty to one by the enemy. Now, a year and a bit later, I was riding in an English train to an English flying field, and the offensive in the air war in the West had passed to the British. As in 1940, belligerent pilots were flying over France, but now it was the Germans, operating from French airports, who had to maintain the unending patrol against an enemy who could strike at the point and moment he chose.

The road to St. Dizier that June day had been filled with troop-carrying lorries and French tanks and anti-tank guns going up to reinforce the hinge in the new line that Weygand had set himself to defend without any faith in his chances. Moroccan troops stood along the village streets, watching the tanks go by. The Moroccans had been scattered through the countryside to deal with the parachutists, whom, it turned out later, the Germans were not to use in that phase of the war. The weather was beautiful, and there was a feel of death in the air. You wanted to get off the road and lie down under a big oak tree by a canal and forget what was going to happen, but you couldn't. To console yourself, you said, "There are only ninety-nine chances out of a hundred it will happen." That had been optimism.

There was nothing beautiful about the English weather on the morning of the second journey; just a sun the color of lard trying to burn a mist away. During the invasion scare railroad-station signs giving the names of places had been taken down, but not advertising signs, and from the car window I could view a succession of mildly pretty semisuburban towns, all apparently called Mazawattee Tea or Bovril. The names of towns in 1941 were usually marked in small letters on the backs of station benches, and a stranger traveled in a constant state of fear that he had passed his destination.

I had picked this particular field for my visit because there were Polish fighter squadrons there. Poles are not only good fighter pilots but hyperdemonstrative. Underemphasis is probably a sterling virtue, but I sometimes think the English overdo it. An officer I knew who commanded the ground defenses at another English airport had told me, "The Poles knock the Germans out of the air by the dozens, and when they come in from a good fight they land like a swarm of wasps, upwind, downwind, acrosswind, and all over the place. They jump out of their cockpits and kiss one another and they hold up their fingers to show how many Germans they have shot down." It had seemed to me that that would be a cheerful thing to see.

I succeeded in getting off at the right town and walked about half a mile through the streets of a neat, quiet community to the airport. An infantryman and an airman on sentry duty together at the gate inspected my pass from the Air Ministry and waved me on to the station adjutant's office. Soldiers are posted at all British flying fields to guard them against ground-strafing and parachutists, so that the airmen can concentrate on keeping the planes flying. The troops at this field belonged to the Irish Guards. The atmosphere of the place was relaxed. Men were raking and burning leaves along the tree-lined road that led to the administration building, and I suppose it was the smell and the season and the comfortable red-brick architecture which combined to remind me of the opening of a semester at an American university—a co-ed university at that, because there were plenty of girls about. These were Waafs, wearing the gray uniform of the Women's Auxiliary Air Force, with flat, visored caps and commendably short skirts. Naturally enough, few girls with unshapely legs volunteered for this branch of the service, although conscription of women has since brought the standard down, and I never saw more than two together without half expecting them to put their arms on one another's shoulders and dance off into the wings, but what the Waafs really did at the field was the clerical work and a good deal of just plain scrubbing-up around the place.

The station adjutant had been expecting me and had assigned a flying officer, an Irishman with a wide acquaintance among the Poles, to show me around. My guide's regular duty was to work with the Polish intelligence officers, piecing together their accounts of each day's operations. He and I got into a small car and started off toward what he called a squadron dispersal hut. There were three squadrons at the field, and their dispersal huts were widely separated, as were the hangars, workshops, and fuel tanks. Because of this, the flying officer said, the field had made a disappointing target for the Germans, who had never been able to do more than flatten one or two buildings and put a few holes in the runways.

Since a fighter plane has a limited fuel capacity, a sweep seldom lasts more than two hours, including getting out and back. Fliers taking part in the day's operations change into their battle clothes in the dispersal huts and wait there until they go off on their jobs. When they return, they report results at the huts, change to slacks, go over to the mess for tea, and are quite likely to show up for cocktails and dinner in the nearest big town.

As we drove along a road winding among the hangars, the flying officer waved toward a group of Hurricanes whose mottled camouflage was being painted solid black. "The good old Hurricanes are a little slow for day fighting now," he said, "but with some changes in equipment and a new coat of paint they make very useful night fighters." I could not help remembering how a French pilot had said to me in the previous summer, "Ah, if I only had a Hurricane!" We drove a couple of hundred yards farther and then stopped beside a field where half a dozen Spitfires were drawn up in front of a hangar. A man was tinkering under the cowl of one of them. We got out of the car and walked over toward him, and as we did so he straightened up to greet us. He was a blond chap, with a complete set of gold front teeth, and my guide introduced him to me as a Polish officer, an engineer charged with the maintenance of planes. I noticed that the fuselage of the Spitfire he had been working on bore not only the usual emblems but a drawing of the hind end of a kitten with a coquettish red heart on it, and I asked the Pole what that stood for. "Is design peculiar to pilot," he replied. "Without official significance. He is very original *esprit.*" I asked if the original *esprit* was also a successful pilot, and the engineer said, "Moderately, yes. Here he has shot down two, three, *quatre*—yes, I think five *avions*. In Poland, two, I think, or three." The engineer flashed a golden grin. "We move so very much between countries," he said, "I have my Polish forgot, my French forgot, and English I have not yet ever arrived to learn, so sometimes I mix all together."

The engineer said that he, like ninety per cent of the Poles in the R.A.F., had been in the Polish Air Force, in which they all had flown crude Polish-built fighters with French engines. They had started the war with only a couple of hundred such planes and had managed to fly a few to Rumania when it was all over, but most of the pilots had crossed the border on foot. It took some of them months to reach France. There they had been incorporated in the Armée de l'Air and assigned to planes that were inferior even by French standards. "Squadron leader, who is our high man here, flew Caudron 406 in France," the engineer said, with his usual aureate display. "Took half an hour to climb ten thousand feet." He insisted on showing me over the Spitfire, one of the newest types, with two machine guns and a cannon in each wing. "Guns fire individually or all together," he said. "Just press button." He sounded like a very persuasive Manhattan radio salesman. Since arriving at this airfield early last summer, he told me, the three squadrons had shot down forty-five German planes and lost eighteen pilots. "Now, when a pilot is descended," he said, "is usually over France, so is captured. Last year we had many pilots shot down over Britain. They make forced landing or bail out, and next morning they report back to station for another plane."

We took our leave of the engineer and drove on down to the dispersal hut we had set out for, a one-story frame building, with a red-and-white Polish flag drooping from a staff in front of it. The mist had begun to clear, and the flying officer said to me, "I was afraid you had picked a bad day, but it looks as if they'll go up all right. It'll probably be just a sweep over the Channel, maybe over Cherbourg or Le Havre. I don't think they'll find much opposition." When the pilots on a sweep can't get a fight, he said, they sometimes drop low and "beat up" gun positions, airdromes, and anything that looks as if it might be a military objective. "Those two cannons can do real damage," he said, "but the most important thing about ground-strafing is that it keeps our fellows happy. Makes them think they're doing something, you know. The risk isn't great. I've known of only one plane from this station to be lost that way."

The hut was furnished with a double row of cots for the men to rest on and a set of metal lockers for their flying gear. The most prominent decoration was a very large poster of a slinky and altogether attractive female—obviously a spy, if you know your poster types. It bore the legend, "Keep mum. She's not dumb." There

141

was also a chart showing how to inflate and make use of the pneumatic doughnut-shaped dinghies which airmen carry on flights over the Channel. It was like a cartoon strip, with drawings of an airman descending by parachute, landing on the water, climbing into his dinghy, and finally comfortably sitting in it, smiling happily. Someone had cut a cheesecake picture of a Hollywood girl out of a magazine and fitted her into the dinghy beside the airman. "Happy landing!" a young Pole said when he saw me looking at it. There were half a dozen pilots in the place, wearing their battle dress, smoking cigarettes, and chattering in Polish. They illustrated their words with great, full-arm gestures, imitating swoops and sudden banks and climbs; you could follow three or four dogfights at once by watching them. Occasionally some flier would make a clucking noise suggestive of a machine gun, and laugh as if he had told a good joke. Their battle dress had a distinctly Slavic look, consisting of a sort of Russian blouse pulled tight at the waist and baggy, gray woolen trousers stuffed into black boots.

They were all boys in their early twenties, except one tall, hawk-nosed man, who, I was told, used to be a great landowner in Poland. He had been in the Polish Air Force Reserve long before the war began and had returned to the service as a fighter pilot. "He could have a ground job if he wanted it," the flying officer said, "but he prefers to go on sweeps. He's very old for a fighter pilot—thirty-eight."

The hawk-nosed man offered to explain one of the hut's most important features—a large-scale map of the southeast coast of England, the Channel, and the French shore. He pointed to a number of pins stuck into the map here and there within the limits of the Channel and said, "Boats to pick us up if we fall in. If a pilot knows he can't reach the coast—maybe petrol tank punctured —he makes for nearest boat. We carry this map in our heads. Very useful." Next he showed me his Mae West—one of those partially inflated jackets airmen wear, which look like an umpire's chest protector except that there is a rear as well as a front panel. Each Mae West has a pocket with a small container of compressed air in it, so arranged that the pilot can release the air as he bails out, thus fully inflating the contrivance in a few seconds. Another accessory in each jacket is a phial of yellow fluid. The phial breaks as the jacket hits the water, and the yellow stuff forms a large floating patch around the flier, making his whereabouts easy to spot from the air. Still another part of the equipment is a powerful flashlight, with which to attract the attention of passing planes if the flier is unlucky enough to be still in the water after sundown. The Mae West is practically unsinkable, but it will not, of course, protect a man from the Channel's cold waters. That's where the pneumatic dinghy helps; it is attached to the pilot's parachute, and if he can swim to it and get aboard, he probably has a much longer lease on life. One Polish pilot lasted seventy-two hours in a dinghy in mid-Channel, then was picked up, and returned to duty within a week.

The flying officer suggested that we start for the mess, since the pilots would be going out to their planes in a few minutes. "We can have a sherry and then stand on the terrace in front of the mess and see all three squadrons take off," he said. "After that we'll have a spot of lunch, and by the time we're through coffee they'll be back. Then we can stop by here again and see what they did. I don't expect there'll be much, though. A number of bombers from other fields will be going over, and our fellows are supposed to get to the coast just as the bombers reach it on their way back. If there are any Messerschmitts following the bombers, our crowd will tackle them. But I don't expect there'll be any Messerschmitts to get; they seldom come across any more. If the bombers aren't being followed, our fellows will continue on and make a sweep over the Channel, with maybe a look over a corner of France."

We got into the car again and drove to the mess, which was in a large Georgian brick building with a portico. The social room, where we went for our sherry, was full of faded black leather armchairs and settees that reminded me of the lobby of a Y.M.C.A. There were portrait photographs of the royal family scattered about the vaguely green walls, and there were files of half a dozen London newspapers, including the Polish daily and the Polish weekly now published here and *France,* the French-language daily. Most of the men in the place wore either the R.A.F. gray or the khaki battle dress of the Irish Guards, with its neat green-and-white shoulder badge. Irish and Poles were mingling as convivially as if they were all attending Notre Dame. "It is wonderful to have a Pole in our party when we're drinking," my companion observed. "Then, if we have any trouble with a policeman, we all pretend to be Poles.

The real Pole says to the constable, 'I am sorry, officer, my friends don't understand good English. Perhaps you speak also Polish, no?' The copper just waves helplessly and says, 'Oh, go away!' "

When we had finished our sherry we went out onto the terrace. From there we could look down on a wide field where a row of Spitfires was lined up at either end, facing the center, as if for a quadrille. "This station was only built to accommodate two squadrons, or twenty-four planes," the flying officer explained, "and there isn't room for our three squadrons to taxi to the same side of the field and take off; there would be a lag of ten minutes or so. The first two squadrons would be out of sight before the third got into the air, or else they would be circling about, wasting petrol. So we divide the three squadrons into two sets and send them off in opposite directions. First set takes off over the second set's heads, second set takes off almost as the first gets into the air."

A good many of the officers in the mess hall had straggled outside to watch the take-off. I gathered that it was a fixture in their day, like the arrival of the noon train at a rural railroad station. A short, bull-necked pilot wearing flying clothes spoke to my companion. "I was going," he said, "but at eleven o'clock squadron leader changed plan. Where they go today?" "Le Havre, probably," the Irishman said. The Pole looked relieved. "Oh boy, I miss a beautiful useless trip!" he said. "They won't find anything. I was over there the other day—not one little Messerschmitt for shooting down."

A big officer with the chest, the shoulders, and the cheerful pink face of a New York police captain stopped directly in front of me and asked how I liked the place. His sleeves were ringed with the four stripes of a group captain, which is the R.A.F. equivalent of a colonel. "I heard you were coming," he said with a slow wink. "I have my sources of information." The enunciation was old-school-tie, but the tone and the manner were unmistakably Irish. "I am the group captain," he said, "and I have the misfortune to command this odd collection of mad people."

By now the noise of the Spitfires' motors was urgent and impatient, and the line of planes at our left began to move toward the center of the field. They picked up speed and soared like racing pigeons simultaneously released, and they were hardly in the air before the planes on the other side of the field began to advance.

THE WORLD ON ONE KNEE

By the time the first set was a few hundred feet from the ground, the second had taken off. For a moment there seemed to be a single spiral of planes in the air; then the machines split up neatly into three groups and were off.

The planes disappeared in the direction of the Channel, and the group captain and I were turning to go back into the mess when a lone Spitfire started to tear across the field. "And who may that be?" the group captain demanded as the plane left the ground. He sounded startled. "It is the wing commander, sir," said a Pole at his side. "He decided to go too." The group captain kept a straight face until his informant moved away, and then he turned to me with a grin. "You see," he said, "the discipline is not what one would expect of a purely British wing. Only yesterday I was telling that wing commander that he must impress on his men the necessity of sticking to their formations. They leave formation and go out looking for individual fights. Well, if he goes off on his own, what is one to expect of the others?" I could tell by the group captain's tone that he thought the Poles were all right. "Last year, during the battle, we ran a little short of Spitfires at this base," he went on. "That wing commander was a squadron leader then, and his squadron lacked one Spitfire. He was certainly entitled to a fast plane for himself, but he chose to lead that squadron in a Hurricane and let his juniors have the Spitfires. He used to take off a quarter of an hour before the others and tell them to catch up to him over Brest or St. Omer or some such place. When they got there, they would find him in the middle of a dogfight. It was horribly irregular, but it showed nice instincts."

My flying-officer friend having faded discreetly away, the group captain and I lunched together in rather impressive solitude at the head table in the dining hall. The food was depressingly British—thick soup, joint and two veg, and suet pudding—but the group captain's spirits were immune to it. He told me that Poles from this field had brought down a hundred and thirty German planes during the Battle of Britain. At the start there had been some linguistic difficulties. "The most terrifying moment of my life came right out on that terrace last summer," the group captain said. "The first Polish squadron we ever had in the R.A.F. was making its first operational take-off. We had a New Zealand and a Canadian squadron at the field at the same time, and the whole

145

lot were to take off just as you saw it done today. The New Zealanders and Canadians were on one side of the field and the Poles on the other. The officer at the control-room radio said to the Canadian flight leader, 'Lead and go first.' He said to the Pole, 'Lead and go last.' The Pole only understood 'lead,' and the two lines of planes started at the same second. There they were, rushing across the field at each other head on. I couldn't bear to look. Do you know, sir, those planes took off simultaneously, all thirty-six of them, without a single collision. It was just like putting the fingers of one hand between the fingers of the other. The Poles must have thought it was a particularly flashy maneuver."

By the time we had finished lunch and had coffee in the social hall, the group captain said he thought I had better be getting back to the dispersal hut to see the pilots come in, and sent for the flying officer, who again drove me to it. There we found only the squadron intelligence officer, a self-effacing man who had been in the old Polish Air Force since its formation. The three of us talked for a bit, and then we heard the planes and went out in front of the hut to watch them come in. Again they reminded me of pigeons, but this time of pigeons circling and swooping down to their loft as the owner signals with a white cloth on a pole. In a moment they were on the ground, and those from our squadron were jogging along toward the hut, their idly turning propellers high in the air and their noses hiding the pilots in the cockpits. As each plane neared the hut, a dozen Polish aircraftsmen rushed to greet it. Even before the pilots spoke, the men on the field knew there had been no fighting, because the rubber nipples on the muzzles of the planes' guns were unbroken. These nipples are put on to keep dust out of the gun barrels, and when the guns have been fired the rubber hangs in shreds about their mouths.

The Poles climbed out of their planes and walked toward the hut, lighting cigarettes. They were cheerful but not exuberant, because nothing much had happened. They crowded into the hut and gathered around the intelligence officer, who had spread a large map on a table. The squadron leader, a stocky, pugnacious little Slav with light gray eyes and a dented nose, pointed out the course his men had taken, and the intelligence officer marked it on the map with a pencil. The line crossed the English coast southeast of the airfield, zigzagged northeast over the Channel, crossed

146

a corner of France, and came back to England again. One of the pilots said to me, "Nothing. No good. We saw three Messerschmitts, but too high, too far away. They beat it."

As the flying officer and I were taking our leave of the squadron, the tall, hawk-nosed pilot—the "old" one—said to me, "Is funny, no? In two summers, in two countries, we have only couple old planes. Then there come thousands Germans to hunt us from the sky. Now we have very many beautiful planes and we cannot find any Germans to fight with us."

CHAPTER VI

The Long Name for the Lifeboat

LONDON, DURING THAT SUMMER OF 1941 when the tide of war stood still at lowest ebb, just before it started to flow in, was the official capital of eight countries and the unofficial one of France; there were besides the governments of Great Britain, Norway, Poland, Holland, Belgium, Czechoslovakia, Yugoslavia, and Greece, and the Free French, a half-dozen semirecognized national movements, free Danish, free Rumanian, free Bulgarian, and free Austrian. His Royal Highness Prince Hassan, legitimate heir to the throne of Persia—he was a brother of the last shah of the old line and had been acting as regent when Reza Khan took over the power—lived in the room next to mine at the hotel on Half Moon Street and would have been popped back onto a throne when the British and Russians ran Reza Khan out that summer, I think, if Reza's son, the present shah, had not been married to the sister of King Fuad of Egypt. His Highness was a cheerful ovoid little man who touched his heart and brow when he talked and was rather better in French than English. The town was full of intrigue over postwar Europe that began to assume some relation to reality as it became plain that the Reich would not win decisively. As yet, however, the cabals resembled deals in Imperial Russian bonds; even Balkan statesmen felt it silly to become really heated about remote possibilities. The acerbity among the exiled governments increased in proportion to their chances of getting home. In 1941 they resembled cabin passengers on a raft. They got on fairly well together, but as soon as they were rescued they would start jockeying for a stateroom with a bath, and by the time the rescuing ship reached land they would all be scrambling for the same taxicab.

All the governments had their own intelligence services. The prime ministers received exhaustive reports not only on what was happening in their German-occupied countries, where their sources supplemented and sometimes scooped the British Intelligence Service, but on what was happening in London. Ministers got reports on their opposite numbers in half a dozen other governments, and operatives shadowed each other, until lunch at Claridge's or the Ritz Grill resembled a traffic jam of characters out of an Alfred Hitchcock film. Operatives of lower categories and corresponding expense accounts shadowed *their* opposite numbers at the White Tower, the Greek restaurant on Percy Street. Every twenty-four hours there was a general pooling and interchange of information, probably held in Albert Hall or Piccadilly tube station, and then everybody heard the secret information that everybody else had been compiling. London, since Pepys's day and before, has been a gossiping city. The coffeehouses of the eighteenth century flourished with talk as the main attraction; the Englishman in his club is sometimes a marvel of malicious veiled curiosity. There is a fair argument for the thesis that all the careful barriers the Briton builds around privacy—the blackball, the no-trespass, the truth-increases, the libel principle in newspaper law, the mannered reserve, and the choked voice—began simply as precautions against the national weakness for talking too much. The flood of refugee gossip adding to the normally high stream of British indiscretions, the torrent of confidential conversation overflowed its banks and London became the gabbiest city in the world.

My favorites in Babel were the Norwegians and the Poles, I suppose because I am a sucker for extremes. The Norwegians listened and never talked. The Poles talked and never listened.

"Why did Mr. Murrow" (Ed Murrow, the Columbia Broadcasting System announcer) "talk for two hours with Dr. Beneš yesterday?" a member of the Polish Government once asked me at lunch, after receiving a report from one of his agents. The Poles are always worried about the Czechs. "Why he don't talk to me?"

my Polish friend insisted. "Why nobody take us seriously? Because
we laugh, my God?" The Czechs seem to the Poles solid heavy
people like liver dumplings. They used to go about in 1941 impressing visiting members of the Foreign Policy Association and the like.
I tried to reassure my Pole by telling him the bravura of the Polish
pilots had a greater effect on public opinion than any amount of
ponderous talk, but he remained unhappy. "After the war all the
Poles so brave will be dead and the Czechs will own Europe," he
said. A moment later he began to laugh. "The Ministry of Shipping is giving to Polish Government new merchant ship to replace
one we lost," he said. "We are thinking of name for it. I would like
to call *Alma Mater Cracoviensis,* Holy Virgin of Cracow. But this
name is too long to paint on one lifeboat." He emptied his wine-
glass, swallowed a mouthful of vegetable marrow, grimaced, and
then said, in a discouraged tone, "Nobody take us seriously."

I suppose that on a strictly ideological basis I should not have
favored the Poles. A Polish diplomat whom we all called Prince
Tommy once said to me, with a delightful smile, "Poland was a
democracy before the war, but without popular representation."
That sounds like a National Association of Manufacturers' program
for America, but whereas I might have bellowed with rage and
started throwing beer glasses if a Republican had said it in the
Artists' and Writers' Saloon, when Prince Tommy said the same
thing it just sounded amiably ridiculous. Since I didn't work for
the Chicago *Tribune* I wasn't bound to an ideological line anyway.

There was an extravagance about the gestures of the Poles I
knew that would have repelled me if I had encountered it in a
work of fiction, where I can always recognize an implausibility.
What could be more trite than the story of the impoverished noble-
man who borrows his arrears of room rent to save himself from
being dispossessed and who stops on his way home and buys a bottle
of champagne with the money? It sounds like the theme of an inferior *Lettre de Mon Moulin.* Except that I knew the protagonist.
He was the Pole who once told me that he had been faithful all his
life to one woman: "Any fragile blonde with a morbid expression."

There was also the story of Radomski. Radomski was a fighter
pilot. On a sweep over France he broke formation, yielding to the
bad Polish habit, and pursued three Messerschmitts, which when
they had got him away from his comrades turned on him, accord-

ing to the sensible German custom. "Radomski dive to get away," one of his colleagues told me, recounting the adventure, "and then he reach for the clutch to pull out. 'Funny,' he say to himself, 'cannot find clutch.' He reach again. Still cannot find clutch. He say, *'Curieux,'* and he look. Clutch was there, all right, but Radomski's left arm was shot away. He brought plane back across Channel and landed."

One Pole I knew in the Ministry of Finance had remained in Warsaw, where he had been a factory owner, until December of 1940 before he had been able to escape. "Four Schutzstaffel men came to my house a few weeks before Christmas," he said. "They came to pick out presents for their wives. They went through the house, opening closets, dressers, cabinets, to find nice things to steal. I understand German well, naturally, and I could hear what they said to each other. There was one man, the tallest of the four, who was ashamed of himself, but he did not dare say so. Everything that the others proposed to him to steal for his wife, he made an excuse for not accepting. 'These sheets would not fit our bed,' he would say, or, 'Trude does not like that color.' The others got angry with him. One, who was as a corporal, said at last, 'Take these handkerchiefs anyway. I command you.' The tall man took the handkerchiefs. I saw his face when he went out. He looked very crushed, very guilty. Now he was one of the gang. He had shared in the loot. This is the policy all through Germany. The furnishings, the clothes from Polish homes are transported there and distributed among the German civilians. Not to accept marks a family as anti-Nazi, so all accept. Then they are *participes criminis.* 'Stand fast,' the Government tells them, 'because if the Allies come and find the loot, the noose will be about your necks. Stand fast, now we are all gangsters together.' It will not matter, really," he said, smiling, "because we will kill them all." As a British friend once remarked to me, the Poles are great cards.

The points of view that the Allies brought to London were not easy to reconcile, although a number of nice old retired naval officers and brewers' widows were always trying to do it by promoting Allied circles and forums. I remember one gathering at the Hyde Park Hotel where a member of the Polish Government who had resigned because of the 1941 treaty of friendship with Soviets spoke, not on Russia, which would have been too controversial, but on what should be done with Germany after the war. As might be expected, his project resembled a blueprint for an ax murder. Then a Dutch economist got up and said that the future prosperity of Europe depended on the survival of an economically sound Germany. The Pole shouted, "That is the way your countrymen always were at Geneva—on the German side. Traitors!" There is nothing like free discussion for promoting good will. My friend who likes fragile blondes said to me after the row:

"It was so disgusting, so human, so deplorable."

CHAPTER VII

Rosie, You Be'ave Yourself

WHILE STILL HOPEFUL of finding the typical British workingman I walked one summer day down to Bermondsey, where there is at least a homogeneous type known as the Bermondsey man. Bermondsey, across the Thames from the proper East End, is the oldest transpontine borough of London. It is the only district on that side of the river named among the twenty-six wards of London in Thomas Stow's "Survey," where it is called Bridge Ward Without. It is named, according to Stow again, for the monks of the Abbey of St. Bermond's Eye, a redoubtable relic. Despite these Elizabethan and medieval associations, and the street names like Tooley Street and the Old Kent Road that suggest a pleasant antiquity, Bermondsey doesn't look any older than a grim part of Pittsburgh. The architecture is divided between early-nineteenth-century slum residential and late-nineteenth-century ghastly industrial. It was not apparent to me why anybody should love the place, and I don't think that any American workingman could.

But I knew from friends that Bermondsey people bred Bermondsey people who in turn lived and died in Bermondsey. They worked on the Bermondsey docks or in the great jam and pickle factories within the borough—the factories, of course, got all the women— and they had their fun in the Bermondsey pubs and cinemas. "Over the water" in Bermondsey means, not America, but Stepney, the

East End Borough across the river that you can nearly spit across. For Bermondsey it is a foreign land. "Stepney's full of Irish and Chinks and Jews," one of the first Bermondsey men I met said to me. "Here we've only our own people." A moment later he was telling me how Sir Oswald Mosley and his blackshirts had once tried to march through Bermondsey before the war. "We gave them a proper bloody 'iding," he said with pleasure. Bermondsey's thinking is Left Labor, its feeling dominated by xenophobia. In its emotional quality it sometimes reminds me of a compact Brooklyn. Bermondsey constantly sends up to Parliament a local physician who is an avowed pacifist and a prohibitionist, being in direct disagreement with all his constituents on both counts. But he is a Bermondsey man. If the Government should send Anthony Eden down into the borough to contest the seat, I am convinced Eden would get licked. The only non-Bermondsey men with whom Bermondsey people have anything essential to do are owners of housing estates, owners of factories, and German airmen, and they don't like any of them.

Walking down to the Bermondsey Town Hall, I passed the blitz ruins of a great jam, pickle, chutney, and vinegar factory. A rescue worker of the Bermondsey civil defense told me how that had gone. "It was at night," he said, "so fortunately there was nobody in it but the watchmen and nine people in a shelter in the bisement. You should've seen the flimes—and the streets knee-deep in strawberry jam. We went in to dig the people out of the shelter, we could 'ear 'em shouting. We broke through a wall, but we couldn't put in the props to keep it open while we went on. The place was all over jam, sir. The props slipped away in the jam, and one of our chaps was crushed. It was bloody awful to think of, sir, and the smell of vinegar. We 'ad better luck some other times, o' course. Once we got a girl and 'er mother that was buried under twenty feet of debbris. It took sixteen hours. The girl was on top of her mother, and after we'd worked a few hours I got to where I could reach the girl's 'and. I 'eld it for hours to give 'er 'eart, and the old lady underneath was cheerful as a lark. ' 'Old on, Rosie,' I'd say to the girl. Most of us knows one another in Bermondsey. When we got 'em out the old woman, that 'ad been so plucky, went out like that. Dead. And the girl became quite 'ighsterical. 'You be'ave yourself,

Rosie,' I said. 'It won't do, my girl.' It's criminal to lose one after you've dug for 'er so long, sir."

There was another, rougher type of rescue worker there who had more cheerful memories. "It would surprise you 'ow much people can stand, sir," he said. "Once we dug all night and got out a couple of old women weighing sixteen stone apiece. Then there was the old cove a warden found sitting on the kerbstone in front of where a lodging'ouse 'ad been a little before that, only now there was nothing left except a lonely criter. 'Come along with me,' the warden says. 'No,' says the old bloke, 'I've paid my tanner and I want my kip.' 'E meant to say," the rescue worker translated at my request, "that 'e 'ad paid sixpence for 'is bed and 'e was going to stay there until 'e got one or the other. It was like the chap who was in the Dundee Arms when it was 'it and they brought 'im into a first-aid stition with 'is chin split open. 'What 'appened to you?' the doctor says, just to mike conversition, and the chap says, 'What 'appened to me? I was standing at the bar and I 'ad just put down a florin and the guvnor 'ad just put a pint of bitter in front o' me and wallop! I found myself in the cellar without the beer, and I've lost the chinge o' me florin.' "

A mild man, an ambulance driver, told me how he and his mates went into ruins to collect the injured that the rescue men had dug out. "When there's nobody to 'elp sometimes, we go about collectin' the pieces what's left," he said shyly. "I once scriped most of an old lydy off a wall. It does sound a bit ghouly, doesn't it, now? But it 'as to be done."

A still milder man, the chief of the borough mortuary service, said, "We wash every bit with soap, no matter 'ow small, and it would please you to see them, sir. Not a speck of dust on 'em. And they 'ave a coffin and all the rites. Only we can't save their clothes for the relatives. You'll agree with me that when a person gets bombed their clothes is not much good afterward."

I went into the garage that served as headquarters for the civil-defense men and talked to a lot of them, after that. There were twenty-five or thirty about, and they had nothing much to do until the next raid, which, incidentally, was not to come until the spring of 1943, although none of us would have been sufficiently optimistic to suppose so. I had been talking to Joe Blake, the town clerk, who is an intellectual. Joe had been bitter about the lack of free secondary education, or at least the great difficulty of obtaining it. That automatically prevented working-class boys from getting any higher degrees, he said. "Bermondsey has just short of a hundred thousand people in normal times," Joe had said. "Do you know how many Bermondsey boys have gone up to the universities in the last twenty years? Three." But none of the defense workers were indignant about that. In civil life they had been dockers, mechanics' mates, shop assistants, and the like. "I once knew a chap 'oo 'ad been to Oxford," one fellow said. " 'E was a 'surance igent." That evidently settled the question for him.

I asked them what they expected to get out of the war, and most of them said with a puzzled air that they didn't expect to get anything except their old jobs, a vague something that they referred to as "better working conditions," and perhaps better housing, all in Bermondsey. "Of course we *should* get something out of it, shouldn't we?" one fellow said. "If we'd lost, we'd have lost something, wouldn't we? It's like putting up a bet." This seemed to strike most of the others as a heterodox and perhaps dangerous thought. Of the whole group only one had ever considered going to the colonies or America, having as a boy even obtained some free literature put out by a Canadian government bureau in London. But he had given up the thought. Curiously, for me, not one in the lot, although they were all under thirty-five, expected that he as an individual would ever earn twice as much as his best previous salary. Since none of them had ever earned better than six pounds, or $24, before, that meant that out of the thirty men none ever expected to make $48 a week. It seemed to me that of thirty New Yorkers in the same age range at least fifteen would have had sure-fire private schemes to get up in the world and make a lot of money, and most of the rest would have trusted to luck to bring them money too. At least twenty-five of the thirty New Yorkers would have been fooling themselves, I imagined.

CHAPTER VIII
Dev's Double

THE FRENCH IN LONDON had their full share of humanity.

I had first heard the voice of Charles de Gaulle in the lounge of the Grand Hotel do Mont Estoril in Portugal in June 1940. It came over the radio from London: "I, the General de Gaulle" . . . "France has lost a battle, not a war" . . . "I invite to join me" . . . *"Vive la France."* The voice spoke of resistance and hope; it was strong and manly. The half-dozen weeping Frenchwomen huddled about the radio cabinet where they had been listening to the bulletins of defeat and surrender ceased for a moment in their sobbing. Someone had spoken for France; Pétain always seemed to speak *against* her, reproachful with the cruelty of the impotent. When I arrived in London in the following summer I wanted to see General de Gaulle as soon as possible and write a whacking profile about a modern Bertrand du Guesclin. Du Guesclin was the great fourteenth-century guerrilla knight who, anxious only to rid France of the invader (in that war the English), fought tirelessly until he had righted what appeared a hopeless military situation. Like most of my preconceptions, this one was on the romantic side. General de Gaulle, when I met him, was to remind me rather of another tall man whom I had encountered in Redmen's Hall over a cigar store in a shabby quarter of Providence, R.I., in about 1928. That man had been named Eamon de Valera, and at the time I had met him his party had been out of power in Eire and Dev had been barnstorming the United States to get Irish-Americans to sign away their claims to money from Irish Republican bonds. De Gaulle and De Valera both are tall and long-legged and long-nosed and narrow-boned, with long upper lips and the faces of a pair of hidalgos that El Greco might have painted on either side of the crucified Christ. They share the quality of being so long and narrow they appear out of drawing. They share also an Iberian pride, stubbornness, and suspicion of the people around them; there may be actual consanguinity, since De Valera's father was Spanish and De Gaulle comes from the part of France that Spaniards occupied repeatedly during the wars of the sixteenth and seventeenth centuries. Both are great patriots and have had to maintain their faith in causes of which more practical men would have despaired. But neither is easy to live with.

I learned from friends when I first got to London that I could not interview General de Gaulle at once. He was walking about in the streets contiguous to Carlton Gardens, his headquarters, but he was by official decree out of town. De Gaulle had displeased Winston Churchill by something he had said in Brazzaville, where the General had recently been, so neither the French nor British press was allowed to allude to his return to London. Naturally American correspondents couldn't allude to it either. "As soon as he makes it up with the P.M. it will be all right," my British friends told me, "but he has been a very naughty boy."

General de Gaulle's naughtiness in that instance had consisted of giving an interview to George Weller of the Chicago *Daily News* syndicate, in which he had put out a feeler for direct American support. Weller had quoted De Gaulle as offering to the United States bases in the African territories and Pacific islands under Free French control "without demanding destroyers in return." The Free French were keen to get Lend-Lease materials directly, instead of through the British Government. His Majesty's Gov. construed the talk about destroyers as a reflection on His Majesty's Gov. General de Gaulle repudiated the interview, although Weller is a reliable reporter. And shortly after this public expiation the British press acknowledged the General's return from Africa, sometimes spelled Coventry.

This sort of thing contributed to what one of my best-informed and most British friends called De Gaulle's "justified anglophobia," but it did nothing to encourage him in further gestures toward America. De Gaulle is intolerant of restraint, as he proved in the famous armored-division row in the French Army, and his London irritation was increased by the knowledge that Vichy propaganda in France accused him of being under Churchill's thumb. It was natural that he should try to bite a piece out of the thumb occasionally. But Churchill was stuck with De Gaulle almost as firmly as De Gaulle was stuck with Churchill.

If the Prime Minister had forced De Gaulle's permanent retirement to private life he would have confirmed the charge that Great Britain controlled the Free French. He would also have wasted a whole year of advertising De Gaulle's name. De Gaulle had to stay on.

Among the thirty or forty thousand Frenchmen and French-women in England, the General had no great personal support. They consisted of French citizens who had been in England before the fall of France, of refugees who had crossed on the last boats from French ports primarily to get away from the Germans, and only in small minority of young men who had escaped from occu-pied France with the specific purpose of joining De Gaulle. Mem-bers of the first group, the "French of England," found difficulty in comprehending the extent of the French disaster even in 1941. For them France had never ceased to be a great power, French law had never ceased to operate, and De Gaulle was a fantastic, un-authorized intruder on their schizoid dream. Many of the June 1940 refugees, hard fighters themselves, resented De Gaulle's claim to one-man leadership. They said that he had no right to claim a copyright on France, that nobody had elected him, and that even in accordance with military rank he was junior to several other officers who had escaped the debacle, like Catroux, a five-star gen-eral, and Vice-Admiral Muselier. These critics included the men of the Left, who doubted De Gaulle's republicanism, and some others whose Gallic irreverence was outraged by the man's mere aspect. "He looks as if he had swallowed his saber," these latter said. There were very few white men in the Free French "Empire" of Equa-torial Africa. André Labarthe, the founder of the revue, *La France Libre,* once referred to De Gaulle as *"le roi des nègres."* The *mot* made its instant round of the limited French world in London; De Gaulle, who is as serious as a saint, never forgave Labarthe. Labarthe, a scientist, military critic, and editor, whose republican-ism, unlike De Gaulle's, dated from long before the war, had dem-onstrated his practical patriotism by kidnaping a ship loaded with copper from Bordeaux and forcing the skipper to take it to England in the last days before the Armistice of Compiègne. He had also made *La France Libre* the best of anti-collaborationist publications outside France. Labarthe came down to Algiers in the spring of 1943 and was made Minister of Information for the Government of North Africa. But De Gaulle refused to enter into the new combination government later that year until Labarthe had been dismissed. He preferred as Minister of Information a Frenchman of restrained bellicosity, Bonnet, whose name has unfortunate associations, and who had passed his time since the Armistice lecturing in America. It was a similar story with Vice-Admiral Muselier, whom General de Gaulle eliminated first from the Free or Fighting French Committee in London and then from any role in Algiers. Muselier had seized St. Pierre and Miquelon to permit a plebiscite by which the Free French gained those islands; he was perhaps the one man most hated by Vichy admirals like Darlan. Collaborationism was scarcely the basis of De Gaulle's trouble with him.

De Gaulle, however, protected with great obstinacy all through 1941, and may still be protecting, for all I know, a Colonel P———, who was considered a Fascist by every Frenchman and Englishman at all acquainted with the Free French setup whom I ever met. P——— carried stories against other Free Frenchmen; any attack upon him therefore aroused De Gaulle's suspicion—"the others" were trying to deprive him of his faithful watchdog! I was to see General Giraud go through a similar routine in defense of General Bergeret, in Algiers more than a year later. Most reactions of French generals are interchangeable. Again, in the summer of 1942 when I was in London a putty-colored little man of archetypical Mussolini-Mosley mien, one Charles Vallin, who for years had been second in command of the Croix de Feu organization in France, appeared mysteriously in London. This little man, composed entirely of stomach and eyebrows, announced that although he had not changed any of his anti-democratic views he had seen the light (i.e., decided Hitler would lose) and was promptly accepted by De Gaulle as a great anti-German. The General did not proclaim that Vichyites were irredeemable, but that only he had the right to give absolution. A hint of papal infallibility was implicit in his pretention.

De Gaulle's enthusiasm for democracy required considerable prodding during his first year of exile. I can remember the struggle of the British Political Warfare people to induce him to say, "Liberté, Egalité, Fraternité," during the course of a broadcast to France; he balked like a zebra and finally yielded with the air of Henri IV saying "Paris is worth a Mass." His imposition of the

Cross of Lorraine on the Free French version of the tricolor never went down well with the anti-clericals among his compatriots. It left an opening for criticism which not even General Giraud in 1942 was to miss, although Giraud is no adept at controversy.

The politics of "the movement" furnished the subject for endless arguments over the wine-stained tablecloths of the "French pub," the York Minster in Dean Street, where the commonalty crowded in, as over the elegant napery of L'Ecu de France and Prunier's in the West End, where the immediate entourage of the General and the wealthy refugees made *langouste* and partridge serve in place of rationed meat and kept unquivering chins in spite of having to drink minor vintages. It was at the Ecu that the truly chic Free French of London gave a public farewell party for the young bloods leaving on the "secret" expedition to surprise Dakar in September 1940. Madame Prunier has carried on the London restaurant of the firm throughout the war, while Monsieur has continued to conduct the business in Paris. There were Frenchmen in London who were willing to be called "Free French" but not "De Gaullistes," and others who said that just "French" was enough, that a Frenchman was by definition free. One of the great weaknesses of the French community in Britain, considered as a microcosm of France, was that few representatives of labor and none of the peasantry had escaped the debacle. The two largest classes of French society were without expression in the plans for the future of their country. I had a good many friends among the soldiers and intellectuals who had come on to London after the fall of France, and I had, moreover, in a manner that it would be perhaps indiscreet to detail, rediscovered a number of old acquaintances in the British services concerned with work in occupied Europe, so that I found myself in the thick of the arguments. I always maintained the thesis, against Frenchmen who deprecated De Gaulle and Britons who complained of his crankiness, that since he was the only horse they had entered in the race they had better try hard with him. I thought him valuable as a trade-mark and as a person. For stubbornness and a lack of objectivity, in the leader of a forlorn hope, are rather qualities than defects. And I would quote Reynaud, with the addition of a softening *peut-être,* "He has perhaps the character of a stubborn pig—but he *has* character." It is, believe it or not, a great asset.

THE ROAD BACK TO PARIS

The consequence of this overelaborate discussion of every facet of De Gaulle's character was that by the time I interviewed him I was completely insulated against fresh impressions. I was in the frame of mind of a soldier entering a house that he has reason to believe booby-trapped. The General, suspicious by nature, had been made more so by numerous and probably conflicting reports on me, and my first innocent question, designed to stimulate conversation, was a disaster. "When are you coming to America, my general?" I asked him. He immediately had to decide whether I was a scout for the Foreign Office or whether Anthony J. Drexel Biddle, Jr., whom he knew I knew, had sent me over to feel him out with a view to a later official bid from the State Department. "I have not yet been invited," he said after a pause of a couple of minutes, and settled back in his chair as I have seen witnesses in a murder trial momentarily relax after turning a tough question from a cross-examiner.

De Gaulle is decidedly less imposing sitting down than standing up, because the part of him showing above a desk does not suggest a man of extraordinary stature. He is small-boned, with fine, slender hands and no great depth of chest or breadth of shoulder. His height folds up under his desk with his legs. He is consistently pale rather than sallow. It is as difficult to carry on a sequential conversation with De Gaulle as with De Valera. He reacts, but does not respond, to a question by delivering a speech on a tangential subject.

The General said that he was convinced the little people of France, the sailors, the peasants, the factory hands, the barbers, were for him and the rich were for Vichy and against him. I noticed, perhaps frivolously, that he did not say the little were against the rich or the rich against the little, but that he made of the breach between classes a question of reaction to De Gaulle. After the war, he said, a government with "bold ideas," "*des idées hardies*," would be necessary in France. He said that the people of France must determine their own future form of government, under a plebiscite to be called after the reconquest.

I left him without any idea that in the spring of 1942 he was to be canonized alive by the stay-at-home seers of the American press. It is nice to learn, however late, that one has talked with an angel.

CHAPTER IX

They Are Not Gone

THE WORKMAN AND SAILORS of Great Britain made great war in 1941. Opportunities for fighting were limited by circumstance, but the need for war material was limitless, especially after Germany attacked Russia. Not only the great forges and shipyards turned out the stuff; there were hundreds of peacetime plants converted to war industry along the network of roads that radiate from Manchester to the scores of smaller factory towns around, places with names we never hear in America, like Blackburn and Bury and Ramsbottom and Rawtenstall and Eccleston and Rochdale and Warrington. The bare hills north of the city were full of them; the flatlands that stretch westward to Liverpool and south into Cheshire bristled with smoking chimneys. That was where the war was. A Lancashireman working for the Ministry of Labour said to me, "Lancashire people have co-operation in their blood. It's here the trade unions, as well as the factories, started. And the Co-operative Stores, which are the largest medium of distribution in all England now, began at Rochdale, a bit north of Manchester. Why, even the troupes of girls who dance in unison—precision dancers, I think you call them—originated here. The original Tiller Girls were recruited from Manchester."

The engineers were as good as the workpeople they directed, and they used every bit of equipment they had. I remember coming into one Lancashire village and seeing two meticulously beautiful new Bofors gun barrels on a wagon drawn by an aged white horse on the high street, en route from a machinery plant to the railway station. The animal looked as if it might have pulled a field piece at Waterloo. The plant was a hundred and ten years old, with flagstone paving. Most of the lathes dated from the last century. The strong, beefy old man who ran it was boring gun barrels with a tolerance of two ten thousandths of an inch of error with an arrangement of machinery he had improvised himself. Before the war he had made textile printing presses for coloring calicoes. The power for his pet ordnance machine came from a dismounted motorcycle engine; the Archimedes lever with which he met all engineering problems was a bicycle chain. "Anything for war," he told me. "Ah'm 'eart and soul in it." He said, with a juvenile pride, "Ah'm number one wi' Admiralty. They tell me send goon tubes to London by passenger coach, not goods train." Men like him had held the breach while Britain modernized its industrial plant with machine tools from America, but now production had already reached the turn.

The Lancashire lads and the Lancashire ladies were, in their northern phrase, "champion." My favorite town in all England, however, was and is Grimsby, Lincs., which rhymes with "drinks."

In the men's bar of the Ship Hotel at Grimsby, Englishmen speak to other Englishmen after less than five drinks. This is a tribute to Grimsby's genius, which is bacchic and maritime in equal parts. Grimsby sent ships to the fleet of King John and still sends its ships to the wars with Grimsby skippers and Grimsby crews, eked out, it is true, by a supplement of fellows from other parts of England, whom Grimsby men refer to impartially as "they dommed farmers." The farmers drown like the Grimsby men, but they cause them a lot of vexation in the interim. In the Ship bar one may meet fifty-year-old sublieutenants of the Royal Navy (Reserve, naturally) who have tattooed fists and unbutton their unform jackets to allow room for beer. They are not quite gentlemen, of course, any more than middle-aged Lieutenant James Cook was a gentleman when he sailed to find a continent. The gentlemen lose the continents. The sublieutenants come ashore from the mine sweepers and patrol boats that used to be trawlers. Only the very old boats with maimed or ancient skippers fish now. As for the convivial part of the Grimsby tradition, Sir Fretcheville Hollis, a Parliament man for Grimsby, told Samuel Pepys in 1667 that to win an election there he had to spend £352 for beer. Pepys set this down as a "develish lie," but Pepys was no Grimsby man. Under the combined influence of Grimsby beer and Grimsby informality, even pink-cheeked and well-turned-out young officers off destroyers become relatively effusive. They say "Beastly weathah we ah having" to men to whom they have never been introduced. Since ships bigger than destroyers seldom come to Grimsby, the town is relaxingly free of officers of senior grade.

THE WORLD ON ONE KNEE

The highest-ranking officer in the bar as I entered one evening was a lieutenant commander named Armstrong, whom I had met at the naval base, where I had been getting material for a story. He was a big man who looked to be about forty but must have been a good deal older than that, because he had once told me that he had been in sail in 1904. He had fought in the other war and then been a captain in the merchant marine and then retired, and now he was in service again. Armstrong was a kind of patrol-boat admiral. He had under his command at least a dozen converted fishing boats, of about two hundred tons each, carrying crews of thirty men.

Most of the patrons of the Ship get their drinks at the bar and then carry them to the long wooden tables. Armstrong was at a table with a pint of the local brew in front of him, and he motioned me to come and sit beside him. I got my beer and joined him. "One of my fellows had a do with a German plane," he said, by way of beginning. "Plane was attacking some fishing boats, and my fellow went to help. Between all of them they shot the plane down, but they're rowing about who did it. Fishermen say they did; my chaps say they did, naturally. One fishing boat sank. A bomb dropped close to her and she just came apart. My fellow said that the bomb hit the water, and the next thing he thought he heard was a burst of machine-gun fire. 'But it wasn't machine-gun fire,' he said. 'It was her rivets popping out so fast it just sounded like machine-gun fire.' All of her crew were saved. I thought you'd like that description. Same chap once told me he'd seen a trawler bombed, and she went so high he could see the top of a near-by lighthouse under her keel. And two sea gulls over the lighthouse, he said." I said something about wishing the fellow would write a book. Armstrong said, "I once had one chap who did. Well, it wasn't a book exactly, but a diary, anyway." I got up and brought another round of beer.

"You know how it is in our boats," Armstrong said when I had sat down again. "The chap in command gets lonely. When the ship is fishing, most of the space in her hull is used for a fish hold. The men all muck in together, eating and sleeping in the smallest possible space, and the skipper mucks in with everyone else. They don't mind that, because they're on shares, and the more fish they carry the more money they get. But when we take the boat over for the Navy we convert the fish hold into quarters for the crew. The

163

skipper has a cabin forward, and since he's the only commissioned officer aboard, he can't eat with the rest. He has to take his meals alone, and the others say 'Sir' to him. That makes him moody and sometimes inclines him to drink. Spirits are tax-free in the Navy, as you probably know, and that is a temptation. Then he begins to brood about the new chaps in the crew. It would be splendid if we could man our boats a hundred per cent with fishermen, but it's impossible. A fishing boat carries a crew of thirteen, but when she goes to the Navy she needs thirty—gunners and fellows to handle mines and all that. And some of the new men have never been to sea. This chap who wrote the diary didn't drink heavily. The writing was his outlet. I came across it when I was going through his effects, poor chap. He copped it in a fight with some motor torpedo boats. A one-pound shell took half of his head off. I sent the diary, along with the rest of his things, to the widow, but I couldn't help copying a few entries."

Armstrong reached inside his jacket and brought out a typewritten page, which he passed to me. These were the entries:

Dec. 11. Coventry, London. Manchester. Ow I wish I could come up with a Jerry plane. I would show them. Today my steward put my knife spoon and fork in bucket of water to wash then forgot they were there chooked water overboard with them in it. I could of chooked im overboard too.

Dec. 16. I of a fine crew. One chap that worked in sweetshop. One bus conductor. One building workman. Two married men that of never been to sea.

What a bloody sample.

Dec. 21. I told cook to make rice pud. Late in day rice floating on galley floor he put about ½ a stone of rice in boiling water nice pud.

January 6. Today men grappled German mine were bringing it over side but not fast enough. I leaned over side and seized cable to help. Opened my mouth to give order and upper and lower plates fell out.

They are not gone. I know where they are.

"Do you know," Armstrong said, "something about that last entry makes me rather sad. So many Grimsby lads, you know."

"Yes," I said. "I get it. We know where they are."

In November I began to feel more curious about the front in the United States than anxious about Britain. In the United States there was still a great decision to be taken; Britain could do nothing but wait. It seemed to me that the old British official propaganda line, "Give us the tools and we will finish the job," had begun to boomerang. I was certain that the British alone could not do all the fighting that would be required away from the Russian front, and I knew that we would never produce weapons in quantity commensurate with our industrial strength until we were in the war. I was afraid that people at home might be taken in by the official British optimism as they had been by the French. I went home by sea because I wanted to experience what the British press liked to call the Battle of the Atlantic.

CHAPTER X

Westbound Tanker

A TANKER IS A KIND OF SHIP that inspires small affection. It is an oilcan with a Diesel motor to push it through the water, and it looks painfully functional. Its silhouette suggests a monster submarine with two conning towers. A destroyer's clipper-ship ancestry is patent in the lines of its hull, but neither tankers nor submarines betray any origin. They seem to have been improvised simultaneously by some rudely practical person and then put in the water to fight each other. A tanker scores a point when it completes a voyage. When the oil reservoirs of the Allied bases are full, the tankers are beating the submarines. They have been doing that since the beginning of this war, but few people think of a tanker as a fighting ship. When a tanker gets sunk you read about it in the paper, but when it docks safely nobody hangs any flags in the streets.

The *Regnbue,* on which I came home from England to the United States, is a Norwegian tanker. It is not remarkable in any way. Norway had a tanker fleet second only to that of the United States, and Norwegian tankers in 1941 carried fifty per cent of the oil that had gone to Britain since the war began. The *Regnbue—*

the name means "Rainbow," as you may have surmised—was built at Gothenburg, Sweden, in 1930. She displaces nine thousand tons, a good, middling tanker size, and can do eleven knots loaded, a fair, medium speed. Her lead-gray hull was streaked with rust, and her masts and funnel and deckhouses showed only a trace of paint the first time I saw her. A grimy Norwegian flag, ragged at the edges, flapped from her mizzenmast, and there was a cowled four-inch gun on a platform raised above her poop. I was joining her as a passenger, but I didn't learn her name until I got close enough to read it on a small sign on the side of her bridge. This was because the Norwegian Trade Mission in London, through which I had booked my passage, believes in secrecy about ship movements. Since the German invasion of Norway, the Norwegian Government-in-exile has chartered most of the Norwegian ships in the world to the British Ministry of War Transport. The ships still fly Norway's flag, have predominantly Norwegian crews, and are, for the duration, in the custody of the Trade Mission.

An official at the Trade Mission, knowing I was ready to leave on short notice, had called me up at my hotel in London one Saturday morning and said that if I didn't mind sailing from London instead of a west-coast port, they had a ship for me. I said I didn't mind, although this would add several days to the voyage. Next morning I took a taxi to the Mission offices on Leadenhall Street and there handed over my passage money. The man who had telephoned me said that the ship was bound for New York in water ballast to take on cargo there. He gave me a sealed envelope addressed to one Captain W. Petersen and a slip of paper bearing written instructions for getting to the ship. I was to take a certain train at Fenchurch Street Station early Monday morning and travel to a small station near the Essex shore, a ride of an hour and a half. A taximan would meet me at the station and drive me to a pier, where I would find a boatman named Mace. Mace would put me aboard Captain Petersen's ship.

Shortly after eleven o'clock on Monday, December 1, I found myself in Mace's launch, moving through the water of the Thames Estuary toward the tanker, which lay about a mile offshore. The only other passenger in the launch was a Norwegian port engineer who was going out to examine the ship's motors. "Look at that paintwork!" the engineer said as we neared the *Regnbue*. "Tankers

166

make such quick turn-arounds the crews have no chance to paint. Discharge in twenty-four hours or less, take bunker and water, and out to sea again. Oil docks are always in some place like *this,* too—miles from the center of the city. The men don't get a chance to see the town. I know. I was in tankers in the last war." Before he had time to tell me more about them, we were under the rope ladder leading to the *Regnbue's* main deck. It was an extremely uninviting ladder, but the engineer went up it as if it were an escalator. A seaman dropped a line to Mace, who made a loop through the handles of my suitcase and portable typewriter, which then rose through the air like Little Eva going to heaven. I went up the ladder in my turn with neither grace nor relish. My style must have amused one of the several men who were leaning over the rail, because he looked down at me, then turned to the man next to him and said, "Commando."

This fellow, who was wearing a white jacket, was obviously a steward. He was of medium size but had long arms, so the jacket sleeves ended midway between elbow and wrist, baring the tattooing on his wide forearms. On the right arm he had a sailor and his lass above the legend, in English, "True Love." The design on the left arm was a full-rigged ship with the inscription "Hilse fra Yokohama," which means "Greetings from Yokohama." His head was large and bald except for two tufts of red hair at the temples, looking like a circus clown's wig. He had a bulging forehead and a flat face with small eyes, a turned-up nose, and a wide mouth. As soon as I got my breath, I said, "Passenger," and he took me in charge with a professional steward's manner, which, I afterward learned, he had acquired while working for a fleet of bauxite freighters that often carried tourists. The bauxite freighters had operated out of a port the steward called Noolians, and most of the tourists had been vacationing schoolteachers from the Middle West. Fearing emotional involvement with a schoolteacher, he had switched to tankers. "Tankers is safe," he said. "No schoolteachers." His name was Harry Larsen.

The steward led me along the rust-stained steel deck to the ship's forward deckhouse. The main deck of a tanker is simply the steel carapace over the tanks. In rough weather the seas break over this deck. The human activities of the ship are concentrated in two deckhouses, fore and aft. The forward one is like a four-story house rising from the main deck and contains the bridge and the captain's and deck officers' quarters. A long catwalk ten feet above the main deck serves as the highroad between the deckhouses, and even on the catwalk you are likely to get doused when there is a sea running. The engine room and the galley, the ship's one funnel, the cannon, the refrigerator, the crew's quarters, and the cat's sandbox are all jammed in and around the stern deckhouse. The steward showed me to my cabin, which was the one called the owner's, although the owner had never used it. It was next to the captain's office. His bedroom was on the other side of the office, and we were to share a bathroom. It was a fairly good cabin, with two portholes, a bed, a divan, and a desk. The steward said that the captain was still ashore but I should make myself at home.

I went out on deck to look around and was pleased to see one of the British Navy's barrage-balloon boats alongside. A balloon boat is a lighter with a half-dozen or so bright, silvery balloons floating above it, each attached to a slender wire. The *Regnbue* dropped a wire cable aboard the lighter, and a couple of naval ratings rove the end of a balloon cable to ours. They let go the cable and the balloon rose above our foremast, securely attached, as we thought, to the *Regnbue*. It wasn't, though. It blew away two nights later, but it was a pretty embellishment as long as we had it. While I was watching the transfer, a little man in a blue uniform came over and stood next to me. I asked him when he thought we would get under way. He said that he was the pilot and was going to take the ship a short distance farther down the river that afternoon. The captain was coming aboard after we got down river. The pilot was a black-haired, red-faced Londoner with a habit of laughing nervously after practically everything he said. "Good thing about a tanker in water ballast," he said. "She's just a box of air, what? Tanks half full of sea water, all the rest air—wants a long time to sink if she's torpedoed. Much as forty minutes, perhaps, eh?" He laughed. I said that I thought this was very nice, and he said that now you take a loaded tanker, it was just the opposite—the very worst sort of ship to be torpedoed aboard. "Flaming oil all about. Rather depressing, what?" he said. I agreed.

The steward came along and told us that dinner was on the table in the saloon, so the pilot and I followed him down a flight of stairs into a large, rectangular room with paneled walls and a dark green carpet. The most impressive feature of the saloon was a portrait, nearly life-size, of an old gentleman with a face the color of a Killarney rose and a bifurcated beard that looked like two blobs of whipped cream. The artist had used plenty of paint of the best quality. I could imagine a jury of boatswains giving the picture grand prize at a *salon*. "The founder of the line that owned this ship," the pilot said.

"Capitalist!" the steward said, simply and with distaste.

"Rum thing on Norwegian ships," the pilot said, "the captain doesn't eat with the other officers. As a passenger you'll mess down here in the saloon with the captain, and there'll be just the two of you at every meal. But in every other respect they're more democratic than our ships. Odd, what?"

The pilot had been at Dunkirk, he told me a bit later on. "I was in command of seven motorboats," he said, with his laugh, "transferring troops from the beach to destroyers. I lost the boats one by one. A motorboat doesn't take much smashing, does it? When the last one foundered, my two ratings and I swam to a destroyer's boat. What I shan't forget," he said, after a pause, "is the motorbike races on Dunkirk beach. Chaps waiting to be taken off, you know. Never saw better sport. There were soldiers making book on the races. Couldn't leave the beach until all bets were settled or they'd be known as welshers."

The dinner of pea soup, corned beef, and baked beans, ending with a double-size can of California peaches for the pilot and me, was big by London standards. The portions were on a scale I had almost forgotten, and there was a lot of butter. The steward said the food had been loaded at Corpus Christi, Texas, in October. "We don't take any food in England," he said. "I hope we get to New York for Christmas. I got nothing to make Christmas at sea— no newts, no frewts, no yin for drinking."

"We ought to make it," I said, with the confidence of inexperience.

"It depends what kind commodore we get," the steward said. "If we get slow commodore, old man retire from Navy fifty year and only come back for the war, we lucky to get New York for New Year's. I don't care much for New York anyhow," he added loftily. "Too much noise, too many Norweeyans in Brooklyn, argue,

argue, argue! I like better Camden, New Yersey, go with the Polish girls."

The ship moved slowly down the estuary during the afternoon. We dropped anchor again before dark at a point where the Thames had definitely ceased to seem like a river and where half a dozen other ships already rode at anchor. Our men looked at them curiously, as one surveys the other occupants of the lounge car at the beginning of a long railroad journey. There were a couple of British tankers with fancy Spanish names, a gray, medium-sized Dutch freighter, and a big, boxlike Elder Dempster boat that had once been in the West African service. I have seen the Dutch freighter's name in a newspaper since. She had shot down a German plane. There was also a stubby, soot-black Norwegian steamer of not more than three thousand tons, which had a single funnel so narrow and long that it reminded me of an American river boat. The third officer, a husky blond chap who wore an orange turtle-neck sweater, pointed to the stubby ship and said to me, "That is the slowest ship in the world. Once she made one trip from Cape Town in four convooeys. They started two weeks apart, and she kept on losing one convooey and getting into the next. She was going full speed the whole time." All the ships were, like ourselves, light and bound for America to get a cargo.

The pilot came down from the bridge and joined me when the ship was at anchor. I asked him when he thought we should get to New York, and he said that with luck we ought to make it in about twenty days. It depended a lot on what connections we made at the assembly ports, he said. The *Regnbue* was going all the way around Scotland to get to the west coast of Britain. We would spend the first few days of our voyage in a small convoy sailing up the east coast of England to our first assembly port. From there, we would go to the west coast in a larger convoy, but we might have to wait a couple of days while this larger convoy was being assembled. Then we would proceed to the second assembly port and go through the same business there. We might be just in time to leave with a transatlantic convoy or we might have to wait a week. There was no way of telling. "The most ticklish bit in the trip begins about twelve hours above here," the pilot added consolingly. "If we get off tomorrow morning, you'll be in it by night."

Captain Petersen came aboard shortly before nightfall. He was a small, stoop-shouldered man. His brown shoregoing suit was carefully pressed. He had a long, curved nose and lank, sandy hair, and he spoke English slowly but accurately, using American idioms. He had lived in Philadelphia, where he worked in an oil refinery, during part of the last war, he told me, and then had moved to Hoboken, where he had roomed in the house of an Irish policeman. After the war he had gone back to Norway to enter navigation school with the money he had earned in America. All the reminiscences of the United States that he politely introduced into our conversation dated from before 1919. He gave detailed accounts of several Chaplin comedies, like *The Count* and *The Cure,* which he had seen then. We went down to supper with the pilot, and Captain Petersen, pointing to the whiskered portrait, said to me, "That is a man who once owned eighty sailing ships. Even when he was ninety-two he combed his beard for one hour every morning. I remember seeing him in my home town when I was a boy. The company owns only a couple of ships now. It belongs to an old lady, who lives in my town also."

His town is a sleepy little city in southern Norway which in the nineteenth century was a great port for sailing ships. The *Regnbue,* the captain explained to me, is emphatically a ship from his town. Not only is she owned there—although, as he explained, owners captive in Norway had no control over their ships for the duration of the war—but skipper, chief officer, and second officer all came from there and had known each other as schoolboys. Both the captain and the chief officer, a man named Gjertsen, had even been married aboard the *Regnbue.* Their brides had joined them on the ship at Antwerp and Constanta, Rumania, respectively. Petersen had been second officer and Gjertsen third officer then, and they had honeymooned in turn in the captain's suite. The wives were at home now. "The second and third officers have wives in Norway, too," he said, "and so has the chief engineer. I was lucky enough to have a vacation in December 1939, so I saw my wife and boy only a little while before the Germans came."

Petersen told me that when the Germans invaded Norway the Norwegian Government had commandeered Norwegian ships all over the world, ordering those at sea to put into neutral or Allied ports. A radio message had been sufficient to accomplish this. Only a small part of the merchant marine had been caught at home. Now the exiled government's income from ship hire not only supported it but provided a surplus, which is to be used for the nation's reconstruction after the Germans are driven out. He didn't show any doubt that they would be driven out, nor did anyone I talked to on the *Regnbue*. The boatswain, a weathered gnome of a man, once said to me, "I couldn't sleep at night if I didn't believe on it." The owners of the ships were nearly all caught in the invasion. The Government had promised that after the war they would receive compensation for the use of their ships, provided they paid allotments to the sailors' families in the meanwhile. So the captive families had been receiving small amounts of money, but even with money there isn't much food.

There was a door at each side of the saloon. One led to the pantry and the steward's cabin, the other to the deck officers' quarters. The officers had their mess aft, in the other deckhouse. After supper on a normal evening aboard the *Regnbue*, I was to learn, the captain and the steward visited the deck officers. Then, at about eight o'clock, everybody visited the steward and drank coffee, made in a big electric percolator which the steward brought in from the pantry. I suppose a torpedo would have disrupted this routine, but nothing less could have. This evening marked my initiation into the ship's social life. Since we were still in port, it was a *soirée de gala;* none of the officers had to stand watch, and it was all right to use the short-wave radio in Gjertsen's cabin. Such sets are sealed at sea because they cause a radiation which can betray a ship's position. For news of the outside world you depend on what the wireless operator picks up on long-wave.

Around seven o'clock the captain, the pilot, the steward, and I marched into Gjertsen's cabin, where the other officers already were gathered. Gjertsen, a tall, dark man who looked something like Lincoln, was stretched out on his berth halfway between floor and ceiling. His wedding picture hung just above the berth. Gjertsen had not been home since 1937. Haraldsen, the second officer, who was small and jolly, turned the dials of the radio, with occasional professional counsel from Grung, the wireless operator, a serious young fellow whom the others considered something of a dandy. He came from Bergen, which is almost a big city. Bull, the third officer, the big fellow in the orange sweater, sat on the divan looking at a picture of the backsides of thirty-two bathing girls in *Life*. He didn't turn the page all evening. Nilsen, the gunner, sat on the floor and said nothing. He hardly ever said anything to anybody. The captain explained to me later that it was because Nilsen was a whaler. Whalers talk themselves out on their first voyage, the captain said. They exhaust all possible topics of conversation, then fall silent for life. "It isn't like a lighthouse-keeper," Petersen said. "He hasn't had a chance to talk in months, so he is bursting with it. But a whaling man is talked out." Gjertsen hated the radio, but he insisted on keeping the set in his cabin because he liked company. No matter what kind of music Haraldsen got, Gjertsen said it was rotten and Haraldsen should turn to something else. Whenever they got a news program he just fell asleep. He said there was enough trouble on the ocean without dialing for it. They were all low that evening because of a broadcast by the Norwegian radio of the news that the Germans were planning to cut off the money for their families. "I wonder how long people in the old country will be able to keep from starving," Haraldsen said helplessly. "Why don't the British start the invasion?" Grung demanded, looking sternly at the English pilot. "All the fellows who escape from Norway say there are only a few thousand Germans there."

"Full moon tomorrow night," the pilot said pleasantly, by way of changing the subject.

"Yes, fine moon for dive bombers," the radioman said resentfully. "We'll be right in the middle of E-boat Alley then."

"Maybe there'll be fog," the pilot suggested helpfully. "Fog is no good for bombers."

"Fog is fine for E-boats," Grung said. "Can't see them coming." Grung, I was to learn, liked to have something to complain about; actually, he worried little about enemy action. Danger at sea is like having a jumpy appendix: men can live with it for years, knowing in an academic way that it may cause trouble but forgetting about it most of the time. Haraldsen said that the *Regnbue* had always been a lucky ship—fourteen crossings since the war began and never a conning tower sighted. Everybody banged on wood. "The *Meddelfjord* always was a lucky ship, too, before the last time," Grung said, insisting on his right to grumble. "I lost a good pal on her, the second engineer. Burned to death in the sea. The oil was blazing on top of the water, and the fellows had to swim in it. That was a nice joke!"

"We didn't miss that by much ourselves," the captain said to me. "We were together with the *Meddelfjord* at Newcastle, both bound for London. We stayed to discharge some of our oil. The *Meddelfjord* and eight other ships went on. Three of them were sunk by planes and motor torpedo boats."

Bull put down his magazine and said in a matter-of-fact tone, "I like to catch a Yerman. Bile him in ile."

Unexpectedly, Nilsen, the silent, spoke up. "I have no respect for them," he said.

Before coming aboard I had calculated roughly that the chances are at least ninety to one against being torpedoed on any one crossing. Incidentally, the American marine-insurance companies then charged a premium of one per cent to insure tanker cargo, which indicated that they thought the odds are considerably longer than a hundred to one. It is not a great risk to take, once. The men in the *Regnbue* lived continually with this risk, which is quite a different thing. They seldom talked of danger except when they were angry about something else, like no shore leave or the British failure to invade the Continent.

Bull started turning the dials of the radio set again and got a program of jazz music from Stockholm. A woman was singing something that sounded like "Klop, klop, klop! Sving, sving, sving!" Bull and Haraldsen laughed so hard they could barely stand it. "I can't explain it to you," Haraldsen said to me, "but to a Norwegian the Swedish language sounds always very funny." We had three or four cups of strong coffee apiece in the pantry and then went to our cabins. Norwegians use coffee as a sedative.

Long before I got up next morning I could hear the anchor chain coming in, and when I got out on deck we were moving along in a column of eight ships. The strings of signal flags looked like holiday bunting, and each ship had its own bright new balloon. Half a dozen sloops and corvettes in pink-and-green camouflage milled around our column. The convoy was probably not moving better than eight knots, so the corvettes looked lightning fast. Machine guns were being tested on all the ships, and the intermittent bursts of gunfire added to the gaiety. The tracer bullets from the machine guns are fun to watch as they skitter over the water; they seem a superior kind of flying fish, with electric light and central heating. We had a pair of Hotchkisses mounted, one on each side of the bridge. If we were attacked they would be manned by the two sea-men on lookout. We also had two British machine gunners, who manned a small fort on the poop deck, where they had a couple of Lewis guns. There was not enough open space around for our gun crew to try out our four-inch gun, but an anti-aircraft battery on shore was practicing. Its guns went off at one-minute intervals, and the shells made a straight line of white smoke puffs across the sky, like pearls on a string. A couple of mine sweepers dragging magnetized floats went ahead of us, in case the Luftwaffe had planted any magnetics during the night.

We dropped the pilot at noon. Life on the ship picked up its sea rhythm. The crew consisted of the usual three watches, each of which was on duty four hours and then rested eight. Haraldsen, the second officer, was on the bridge from twelve to four, Gjertsen, the chief, from four to eight, and Bull, the third officer, from eight to twelve, when Haraldsen relieved him. I had a chance to get to know some of the sailors, because they came forward to stand their watches on the bridge. However, the engineer officers and the rest of the crew, down at the other end of the ship, remained relative strangers.

When the men came forward they wore life jackets. The officers, when they went up to the bridge, carried their life jackets with them and tied them to a stanchion. I had bought a kapok-lined reefer from Gieves, the naval outfitter in Piccadilly, a swank garment that purported to double as an overcoat and life jacket. It was supposed to close with a zipper, and each clash with the zipper presented a completely new tactical problem. The zipper changed its defensive arrangements to meet my attacks; I could never throw it twice with the same hold. Sometimes I could close it in a couple of minutes, but on other occasions it beat me. I was sure that if a torpedo ever struck us, I would go down in a death grapple with my zipper. I had an ordinary life jacket in my cabin, of course, but I had paid good money for the reefer. I was also given a huge, one-piece rub-ber suit, so stiff that it stood up in a corner of my cabin like a suit of armor. It was a Norwegian invention, Captain Petersen said, and everybody on the ship had one. The idea was to climb into its legs and tie yourself into the rest of it, so only your face showed. The air in the folds of the suit would both hold you up and insulate you from the cold of the water. This consoled me until Grung, the radioman, told me that a crew had once demonstrated the invention for the Norwegian Minister of Shipping and that while all of them had floated for hours, a couple of fellows who went in head first had floated upside down. Grung was a man of few enthusiasms. For example, we had a large escort for such a small convoy, and this made him unhappy. "There must be trouble expected or there wouldn't be so many," he said.

Late in the afternoon we reached the bad spot about which the pilot had told me. This is a lane along the East Anglian coast that London newspapers have named E-boat Alley. The commodore of the convoy was in the ship ahead of us, a British tanker. Commodores are usually commanders in His Majesty's Navy; they carry a pair of aides and a squad of signalmen with them and communicate their orders by flag signal or flash lamp. This commodore would go with us only as far as the first assembly port; he was an east-coast specialist.

I was in the saloon just before suppertime, reading Hakluyt's *Principall Navigations, Voiages and Discoveries of the English Nation,* when I heard a noise that sounded exactly like a very emphatic blast during the excavation of a building site. The ship quivered, as if she had taken a big sea. Larsen, the steward, was the only other man around; he was laying out a few plates of salami and ham and herring salad as table decorations. I took it for granted that the noise was a depth charge and said "My, my!" to show how calm I was. Larsen winked and said, "Mak raddy der bahding suit!" Both of us, I imagine, wanted to run out on deck and see what had happened, but since we had only recently met, we tried to impress each other. Captain Petersen came down to supper ten minutes later and said that a mine had gone off a hundred feet from the commodore's ship and almost knocked her out of the water. "Gjertsen was on the bridge and saw it," he said. "He says it threw a column of water higher than the ship's masts. She was hidden completely. Then, when the water settled, Gjertsen could see the ship was still there, but she had only a little way on. Then she hoisted two red lights to signal she was out of control. The blast must have damaged her rudder. So she has to go back to port."

"Good-by, Commodore," Larsen said unfeelingly.

"It must have been one of those acoustic mines," the captain said, "but it didn't work well. It went off too soon." There was a certain wonder in his tone, as if he felt that the Germans must be over-rated.

The explosion of the mine was the only evidence of enemy action we were to encounter during the whole trip.

Larsen, the steward, had it figured out that in order to get to New York by Christmas we would have to leave the west coast of England by December 7. "We get off with lucky seven and in seventeen days we come to New York," he said. "Get there Christmas Eve, the immigration officers ain't working, and we stay on the ship until December 26." This was a sample of what I got to know as Scandinavian optimism. We didn't reach even the first of our two assembly ports until December 5, so it looked certain that we would spend Christmas at sea. We were seventy-two hours going up the east coast from London, anchoring each night because of heavy fog. The second time we anchored, Larsen began getting out and repairing the green-and-red paper Christmas decorations that formed part of the tanker's stores. He went about his work during the day muttering a sad little refrain that I sometimes caught myself repeating: "No newts, no frewts, no yin for drinking."

The crew looked forward to spending its shore leave in Brooklyn, even if we got to New York after Christmas. To a Norwegian the finest part of the United States is Brooklyn. For the duration of the war it is the Norwegian fatherland. When a Norwegian seaman meets an American, he usually begins the conversation with, "I got a cousin in Brooklyn." Haraldsen, the second officer, had two brothers there. Larsen pretended to be supercilious about Brooklyn, but he fooled nobody on the *Regnbue*. The *Regnbue* had been in the Thames for only a couple of days, and few of her men had gone into London. The ship had been anchored at such an awkward distance from the city that it had hardly seemed worth the journey. Some men had got drunk at a hotel not far from the oil dock. Others had not even set foot on land. Corpus Christi, Texas, the ship's last American port of call, had not been exactly a Brooklyn, either.

Olsen the carpenter, Grung the radioman, and I were visiting the steward and drinking coffee on one of the foggy nights, and Olsen said, "The last time I was in Brooklyn I didn't take my shoes off for three weeks. My feet was so swollen I had to cut my shoes off." Olsen was a man who liked to startle people. "It must have been good liquor you were drinking," I said. This was just the kind of opening Olsen wanted. He put his head on one side and looked at me fixedly for a full half-minute, as if I were a dangerous lunatic. "Good liquor!" he finally said, contemptuously. "A man is a fool to drink good liquor. I never drink liquor that tastes good." He stared at me again, as if expecting me to leap at his throat, and then said, "Because why? I get drinking it too fast. Then I get drunk too quick. The best thing is whisky that tastes bad. Then you stop between drinks about ten minutes, until you need another one. Then you can keep on drinking for a month." The carpenter was a solid, rectangular fellow of fifty, with blue eyes set wide apart in a boiled-ham face. He could with equal competence make a davit out of iron pipe or reseat a rattan chair. He was the ship's delegate of the Norwegian Seamen's Union, to which all the men belonged.

The steward lay in his berth at the summit of a stack of drawers. There was no other place for him, because the rest of us occupied all the chairs. He said, "In Brooklyn I live in Hotel St. Yorge. Yentlemen! I don't go on Court Street in Eyetalian saloons. I yust buy good old bottle aquavit and go to my room and drink like yentleman. Go to Norweeyan church Sunday and put five dollars in collection. Brooklyn women too smart. Better leave 'em alone."

The radioman said that once he and some shipmates had been in a taxi-dance hall near Borough Hall and had asked a couple of hostesses to sit down and have a drink. The hostesses had charged them four dollars apiece for their time. "You got more for your money in Constanta," he said. Constanta, in Rumania, used to be a great port for Norwegian tankers before the war. "We had a man on one ship going down to Constanta," the carpenter said, "and he wouldn't believe all we told him about it. He said he had been in every other port in the world, and he wouldn't lose his head in Constanta. So he went ashore one night, and two days later we seen a man walking down on the dock with nothing on but his socks, and it was him. Always lots of fun in Constanta."

The steward found this so amusing that he reared up on the back of his neck and kicked the ceiling. He had been a leading light of the gymnastic society in a small town in southern Norway, and he liked to use the edge of his berth as a gymnastic bar. He spent a good deal of time composing to English and American girls on a portable typewriter he had in his cabin, and when he was at a loss for an English phrase he would get up, face his berth, and jump high in the air, twisting in time to land in a sitting position. Usually three or four jumps would bring him the phrase he wanted, and he would return to his typewriter. The steward called his cabin Larsen's Club, and the atmosphere was congenially ribald except when Captain Petersen was there. The skipper came in every night for his three cups of coffee. Captain Petersen was a friendly man who did not stand on formality, but he was a Methodist and a teetotaler. He didn't try to deter anybody else from drinking or talking randy, but Larsen seldom kicked the ceiling when the skipper was around. All the men were cut off from their home country and lonely, and the captain was the loneliest of all. Once he said to me, "It isn't so bad for a man who drinks and——" He stopped suddenly, as if just understanding what he had said, and went off to his cabin looking miserable.

At meals with Captain Petersen I had plenty of time for eating, because there was not much conversation. Once he said, as he began on his first plate of cabbage soup, "I have an uncle in New York who has been fifty-two years with the Methodist Book Concern." Twenty minutes later, having finished his second helping of farina pudding, he said, "He came over in a windyammer." On another occasion he said, "We had a Chinaman on the ship once. When we came to Shanghai he couldn't talk to the other Chinamen." After an interlude during which he ate three plates of lobscouse, a stew made of left-over meats and vegetables, he explained, "He came from another part of China." And once, taking a long look at the shipowner's portrait, he said, "I went to see an art gallery near Bordeaux." After eating a large quantity of dried codfish cooked with raisins, cabbage, and onions, he added, "Some of the frames were that wide," indicating with his hands how impressively wide they were. Once, in an effort to make talk, I asked him, "How would you say, 'Please pass me the butter, Mr. Petersen,' in Norwegian?" He said, "We don't use 'please' or 'mister.' It sounds too polite. And you never have to say 'pass me' something in a Norwegian house, because the people *force* food on you, so if you said 'pass' they would think they forgot something and their feelings would be hurt. The word for butter is *smor*."

It was morning when we reached our first assembly port, and the captain went ashore to see the naval authorities. He returned with word that we would sail next evening. In the afternoon a boat came out from shore and a naval officer climbed aboard to tell the captain that our destination had been changed from New York to Port Arthur, Texas. Luckily, the *Regnbue* had enough fuel for the longer journey or we would have lost more time taking bunker. The captain told me of the change and said he was sorry I would be carried so far from New York, but things like that happened all the time. The changes weren't made for strategic reasons, because no one could tell three weeks or a month in advance how the U-boats would be distributed off the American coast. It was just that there probably weren't enough "dirty" tankers to handle all the heavy oils from the Gulf of Mexico. A "clean" tanker handles only gasoline. A "dirty" tanker has tanks equipped with heating coils to keep heavy oils liquid. The *Regnbue,* the captain said with pride, was a first-class dirty tanker.

News of the change of destination quickly got about among the crew. There isn't much point in secrecy aboard a ship if none of the men are allowed to go ashore. Port Arthur is a dismal place compared to Brooklyn, and the seamen were disappointed. There are no Norwegians in Port Arthur, and no taxi-dance halls. Mik-kelsen, the electrician, said that you couldn't even buy whisky in a saloon in Port Arthur; you had to buy a bottle at a package store and take it into a soft-drink joint to get a setup. Perhaps the most disappointed men on the ship were the British machine gunners, Ramsay and Robinson. They had been out to India and Australia with other ships but never to America. "Where is Texas?" Robin-son asked me. "Will I be able to get up to New York for a week end?" Ramsay, who was a lance bombardier, laughed derisively. "You haven't got money enough to get that far," he said. "It's all of two hundred miles." Robinson earned three shillings and three-pence a day, of which the War Office sent one and three to his mother in Salford, slap up against Manchester. Ramsay drew nine-pence more for his single chevron, and he was always boasting to Robinson about his opulence.

The Britishers belonged to the Maritime Anti-Aircraft Regiment, generally called the Sea Soldiers at home. The Sea Soldiers ride on merchant ships in the manner of old-time American stagecoach guards. They have had more training with automatic arms than the seamen who man machine guns and are supposed to steady the seamen in a fight. Robinson and Ramsay had been partners on other ships and had been in a long running battle with some Axis submarines off the west coast of Africa just before they joined the *Regnbue*. Convoys were nearly always attacked off the African coast, they said. There was a belief among seamen that the Germans had a submarine base at Dakar, no matter what Pétain said. Robinson was a quiet lad who said, "A odn't been sottisfied i' infantry, so thought A'd try summat else, and this was fair champion—nowt to do." Ramsay was a Glaswegian, a hyperenergetic type who was always shadow-boxing on deck and shouting "Pooh!" or "Coo!" for no apparent reason. He used to brag about how many German planes he had shot down, although it is hard to apportion credit for bringing down a plane when a whole convoy is blazing away at it. One day he said that if we captured a German submarine—not a likely prospect—he would personally kill all the prisoners. Gjertsen, the chief officer, said to him seriously, "You can't kill anybody on this ship without the captain say so." This made Ramsay sulk. There were three other Britishers on the ship—a man in the engine room, a seaman, and a messboy. English seamen like to get on Norwegian ships when there is an opportunity, because the pay is better than the British scale. Nearly all seafaring Norwegians speak English, so there is no trouble about understanding orders. The only fellows on the *Regnbue* who knew no English were five youths who recently, and separately, had escaped from Norway by crossing the North Sea in small boats. They were all studying a textbook on Basic English. They had received word that after they had escaped their parents had been put in prison. News from Norway reaches England quite regularly by boat. There are even motorboats that smuggle mail between the two coasts.

Most of the men grew thoughtful when we cleared the first assembly port. We were within three hundred miles of Norway now, and they could not help thinking about it. Otherwise the tension, which had never been great, seemed to have completely vanished. There was no further danger from motor torpedo boats and not much from dive bombers. The big Focke-Wulf Kuriers and the submarine packs generally operated farther to the west, where the large convoys form, so we felt relatively safe. We had parted company with a couple of ships at the assembly port and picked up a couple of others. What bothered me was the weather. Captain

Petersen advised me to chew on dry crackers and drink no water. The steward said, "Don't use nothing yuicy. Yust dry stuff."

The prescription of "a brisk walk around the deck," classic on passenger liners, is not much good on a tanker, because deck space is so limited. You can take a few steps on the bridge or make a circuit of the forward deckhouse, picking your way among ropes, slings, boats, and the entrances to two companionways. If you go aft you have a slightly longer promenade around the after deckhouse, although you have to crawl under the gun platform once on each lap to complete the circuit. The main deck, between the two deckhouses and forward of the bridge, is low and lashed by spray. There is a catwalk, an elevated pathway between the two deckhouses, but men with work to do are constantly passing back and forth on it, so there is no room for a *flâneur*.

At the beginning of the voyage I had decided to let my beard grow until I got home again. The boatswain, who came from a port in the far north of Norway, counseled me to shave my beard, on the ground that it would bring fine weather and then the ship wouldn't rock. The boatswain was a small man who looked as dry and tough as jerked meat. He had ice-blue eyes and a long, drooping, ginger-colored mustache, and he repeated his joke about the beard every morning. Then, later in the day, he would manage to ask me the time and say, "I had two gold watches but they're on the bottom now." His last ship had been bombed and sunk at her dock in Liverpool, and he had lost all his gear on board. Fortunately, he had been spending the night on shore with a respectable lady friend—the widow of an old shipmate, he was always careful to explain when he told the story. He had a French wife in Caen, but he had not seen her in seven years, because big ships seldom went there. I once tried to talk French with him, but he said with a sigh, *"Ya goobliay toute."* The boatswain was aware that he said the same things every day, but he said them to be friendly. After all, nobody can think of something new to say when he sees the same shipmates daily for weeks on end. The quip about the beard contented the boatswain, and he laughed every time he said it. His laugh sounded like cakes of ice knocking together.

On December 7 we were in a gale. I turned in early and put my watch and fountain pen in the desk drawer, where they rattled like dice in a nervous crapshooter's hand. There is a difference of thirteen and a half hours between the time in Hawaii and Great Britain, and I was asleep before Grung, the radioman, picked up the first bulletin about the attack on Pearl Harbor. I heard the news when I went up on the bridge next morning. Bull, the third officer, pumped my hand and said, "We both allies now!" It felt more natural to be a belligerent on a belligerent ship than that anomalous creature, a neutral among belligerent friends. I tried to visualize New York. People at home must be frightfully angry, I imagined. I kept telling the Norwegians, "Americans aren't like the English. They get mad much quicker, and they stay mad." (I was to feel pretty silly about that after I got back to New York.) We all wondered why the fleet had been in Pearl Harbor and how the Japs had got there. The B.B.C. bulletins received by the radioman were skimpy. We were actually near the base of the British Home Fleet, but suddenly we felt far from the war. The ship had sailed with two neutrals aboard, and now it had none. The other neutral had been an ordinary seaman named Sandor, who was a Rumanian. Great Britain had declared war on Rumania a few days after we cleared, so Sandor had become an enemy alien. He took the news calmly. "Can't send me back now," he said. He had stowed away on the *Regnbue* at Constanta in the early summer of 1939 and had stayed with her ever since. He had learned Norwegian and English on the ship.

We were glad to get to our second assembly port, where we were permitted to turn on the short-wave radio in the chief officer's cabin. We sat around it for hours, listening to the B.B.C., the Norwegian broadcasts from London and Boston, and even Radio Paris, the Quisling station in Oslo, and Lord Hawhaw. We got some of our best laughs from an Italian English-language announcer who used to sink Allied shipping in astronomical quantities twice a day. It was a Norwegian broadcast from Boston, I remember, that told us Lindbergh had endorsed the war and a Free French announcer in London who said Senator Wheeler had done the same thing. The steward was amused. "Next thing, Quisling against Yermans!" he shouted.

As soon as we arrived at the second assembly port, the captain went ashore. When he came back he said that we were starting for America early the next morning. The port was at the head of a deep and narrow bay. The *Regnbue* and nine other ships were to start just before dawn and go to sea to meet vessels that would simultaneously leave other assembly ports. There would be from fifty to a hundred in the combined convoy, which was to be a very slow one. It would make only eight knots, because it included a lot of ships like the Norwegian steamer that Bull, the third officer, had pointed out to me some days before as the slowest ship in the world. We had lost her in the gale on December 7, but she had steamed into the second assembly port twelve hours behind us. She was called the *Blaskjell,* which means "mussel." An eight-knot convoy takes a long time to get across the ocean, Captain Petersen said, but going that way was better than hanging about waiting for a ten-knotter. Fast ships go alone, on the theory that they can run away from any submarine they sight, but the *Regnbue* was not nearly that fast.

It was about seven o'clock when we hove anchor next morning, but the moon was still high in the sky. The other ships that were going out showed one light apiece, and a corvette was talking to us in Morse code squawked out on a whistle that sounded like Donald Duck. A westerly wind was howling, and I remembered that we had received a gale warning the evening before. The moon slipped into a cloud abruptly, like a watch going into a fat man's vest pocket, and didn't come out again. When it is as dark as it was that morning it is hard for a landsman to tell if a ship is moving, because he can't see her position in relation to anything else. But after a while I was sure. When it began to get light I went up on the bridge and looked at the ships in front of us and astern. They were already plunging about. When you look at other ships in a heavy sea the extravagance of their contortions surprises you. Your own ship is going through the same motions, but you wouldn't believe they were so extreme unless you saw the other ships. The farther we got down the bay, the worse the weather grew. The commodore's ship, about a mile ahead of us, sent up a string of flags; the ships between us repeated the signal. Bull, who was on the bridge, said, "Commodore wants us slow down, says he can't hold his position." He threw the engine-room telegraph to "Half Speed." In heavy weather the *Regnbue* steered well only at full speed, and the men at the wheel had an unhappy time from then on. Now and then her bow came clear out of the water—from watching other tankers I could see exactly how it happened—and the sea gave her a ringing slap on the bottom. I felt that this was an impertinence, precisely the sort of thing a German would do if he were running the ocean.

By noon we were getting away from land. I went down to the saloon to have dinner with Captain Petersen and found him already ladling his third plate of milk soup out of the tureen. Milk soup is made of condensed milk and water, heavily sugared and full of rice, raisins, dried apricots, canned peaches, and anything else sweet the cook can find about the galley. It is served hot at the beginning of a meal, and only a Norwegian can see any sense in it. It appeared on the table regularly twice a week, and at each appearance the steward said, "Fawny soup today, Liebling." At the beginning of every meal, without exception, he would say to me, *"Vaer so god"* ("Be so good"), and bow. I would say the same thing to him and bow, and we would both laugh. It was like the boatswain's joke about the beard.

On the bridge that afternoon the captain was preoccupied. He said that unless we could go at full speed, he didn't see how we could get to the rendezvous before dark, but only about one other ship in our lot could keep up with us at full speed. Our entire escort was one 800-ton corvette, and if we left the convoy, we left the escort. Sometimes you have a big escort and sometimes you have a small one. It's like going into a shop in England: you get what they have in stock. Haraldsen, the second officer, who was also on the bridge, was as jolly as usual. "By and by Florida!" he would shout when water whipped across the front of the wheelhouse and splashed in our faces. That was *his* standard joke. The corvette seemed to stand on its head every time it went into a wave, and Haraldsen got a lot of fun watching it. "The little feller is doing good," he would say. "I hope they got a good belly." By three o'clock we had lost the *Blaskjell* and two of the others, and a half-hour later we could see the commodore's ship turning. The commodore was signaling us to return to port. He had judged that there was no chance of reaching the rendezvous before nightfall, and he didn't want us to be out on the ocean alone when morning came. "We made about thirty miles in nine hours," Captain Petersen said. We turned, and on the way back to the assembly port we picked up the *Blaskjell* and passed her. At nine o'clock we were again at anchor in our old berth.

The boatswain was not the only one who looked suspiciously at my beard after the return. "This has always been a lucky ship," the carpenter said. "I think we got a Rasmus on board now." A Rasmus is the Norwegian equivalent of a Jonah. The next day the weather was fine. The carpenter said that this was just what you might expect now that we had missed the convoy. Captain Petersen put on his brown suit and went ashore. He came back with word that we were stuck for at least a week. We had already been at sea for a fortnight. It was not entirely bad news to the boatswain and the steward. The boatswain could now put the men to work painting the ship. When a ship's paint gets streaky, a boatswain becomes melancholy and embarrassed, like a housewife who has not had time to wash the curtains. Griffin, the English seaman on board, once said to me, "If the bos'n ain't a bastard, the ship's no good." He added that the *Regnbue* was quite a good ship. The steward saw a chance to get the supplies he needed for Christmas. About all that the captain and I had been hearing lately at our meals was a monologue by Larsen about the horrors of Christmas at sea without newts or frewts or yin. Once a ship has left the port of origin, navy people permit only the captain and the radioman to go ashore—the radioman for a single conference before a convoy leaves—so Larsen gave the captain a list to take to a ship chandler. The captain found no nuts or fruits, but in a couple of days a lighter brought out a case of gin and two cases of whisky, which the steward put away in the pantry closet. Ordinarily, I was told, no liquor was served on the ship except to pilots and immigration officers, but Christmas was always an exception.

The days at anchor were tranquil. Every morning the captain went ashore and the rest of us painted and theorized about our false start for America. The officers worked alongside the men, and I daubed a bit for company. Some of the men argued that we should have started for our rendezvous at midnight instead of just before dawn, and others said that with a wind like that against us we shouldn't have started at all. Haraldsen said why complain, maybe the convoy we had missed would be attacked anyway. (A couple of days later we heard that all but fourteen ships out of seventy had had to turn back because of the weather.) Evenings, we listened to the radio and talked about the war. The men talked a lot about what they were going to do with Quislings in Norway after the war. They used Quisling as a generic term, just as we do. Some of the men wanted to put them on Bear Island, up north of Norway. Others just wanted to kill them. Even the messboys were angry at Knut Hamsun and Johan Bojer for having betrayed Norwegian culture. The ship had a library of four hundred volumes. None of the seamen would read Hamsun or Bojer now. Norwegians seem more interested in books than music, and the captain was the only one who mentioned Kirsten Flagstad to me. He said Wagner had gone to her head.

Often, when Captain Petersen sat down to a meal, he would look at the customary plates of cold meat on the table and say, "I wonder what they have to eat in the old country now," or "I wonder what my wife has to eat." When we had fish he would say, "My wife never liked fish. Her father was a butcher," or else "My father-in-law always said, 'Fish is fish, but meat is nourishment.' " Once he heard me humming that old barroom favorite, "M-O-T-H-E-R." He said, "I heard a fellow sing that in vaudeville in Philadelphia. He had his wife on the stage and their six children. When he sang it one kid held up a card with 'M' on it. The next kid held up 'O' and so on until the smallest one held up 'R.' It was the cleverest thing I ever saw on the stage." Often he showed me photographs of his wife and their little boy.

We put to sea again a few days before Christmas. Just before we left, a naval man came out to say that our destination was now Baton Rouge. Nobody even speculated about the reason for this second change. We took it for granted that there was some kind of a muddle. Despite my beard and the carpenter's forebodings, we had normal North Atlantic winter weather this time. Early in the afternoon we sighted a huge fleet of ships on the horizon. This was to be a ten-knot convoy, so we had left the *Blaskjell* and a couple of other tubs behind. "Now we'll have something to look at," Haraldsen, the second officer, said as the courses of the large group and our small one converged. Every ship in a convoy has a number. Number forty-four had been assigned to us at the assembly port, and as we joined the others we hoisted the four flag and the pennon that corresponds to a ditto mark. All we had to do was find the forty-three ship and fall in behind her.

The small convoys we had traveled in along the coasts had gone in either single file or a column of twos. This one was in a column of eights. We had ships to port and starboard as well as ahead but only an escorting corvette behind us, as we were a file-closer. This tickled Haraldsen, because we wouldn't have to repeat any of the commodore's signals. A signal is passed down a file of ships, each repeating it for the benefit of the one behind. All the file-closer has to do is run up the answering pennon to acknowledge the message. Grung, the radioman, came out of his shack to look at the escort. There were only four corvettes for fifty-six large ships. "It's a bad yoke," he said bitterly. "Those English lords are sitting with girls behind drawn curtains on large estates and we can go to hell." When we had had a large escort on the east coast, Grung had said that was a bad sign. Haraldsen said, "Oh boy, I wish I had one of them girls here! Some fun." He had worked as a carpenter in New York during the building boom from 1924 to 1929 and talked of this as the romantic period of his life. "I got fifteen dollars a day," he said. "Fellows would wait for you in front of your yob— Yews, you know—and say, 'Listen, come with me. I give you a dollar more.' I like Yews." He had been on sailing ships during the last war, but he did not recall them with the same affection as, for example, John Masefield or Lincoln Colcord. "A sailing ship is hell in cold weather," he once told me.

It takes a combination of keen eyes and accurate navigation to keep a ship in its proper position in a convoy during the night, and the fleet is usually rather jumbled in the morning. This situation helped to kill time aboard the *Regnbue*. In the morning everybody was eager to see how badly the convoy had broken ranks. Bull, the third officer, was always on watch at dawn, and every morning he would say, with a sort of pride, "Dis der vorst convooey I ever see. Every morning all over der Atlahntic." The *Regnbue* nearly always held its position in relation to the commodore; either we kept to our course accurately or there was a telepathy which made him and us commit the same errors. Some of the other ships, however, would be far off on the horizon. This would always amuse Bull and the lookouts. The forty-three ship, which was supposed to stay just ahead of us, was nearly always miles to starboard, and when she tried to get back into her place we would, for the fun of it, speed up so that she couldn't edge in. She was an old tanker and slower than the *Regnbue*. Her skipper must have been a rather fussy sort; she would break into an angry rash of signal flags, and her radioman would bring out his signal flash lamp and deliver a harangue in Morse. Finally we would let her ease into the column. It usually took an hour or so to get everybody aligned. The ships always reminded me of numbered liberty horses forming sequences in a circus.

After the convoy was re-formed we could kill another half-hour trying to count the ships. There were a few less every day. Ships drop out with engine trouble or get so far off the course during the night that they lose sight of the convoy. These run a bigger risk than the ones that keep pace, but most of them turn up in port eventually. Two ships carried catafighters; that is, Hurricane fighters that could be shot into the air from catapults if a Focke-Wulf appeared. In profile, the catapults looked like cocked pistols. We used to find comfort in looking at them, even though Grung said that the pilots were probably seasick and the planes would break away from their lashings in a storm just before we were attacked by an air fleet. Sometimes ships in convoy talk to each other out of boredom, like prisoners tapping on cell walls. One morning I found Bull, signal lamp in hand, carrying on a parley with a British tanker in the column to starboard. When at last he put the lamp down I asked what it was all about, and he said, "Oh, they invite us to come aboard for lunch."

"What did you tell them?" I asked.

"Oh," Bull replied, "I say, 'If you got a drop of yin, I wouldn't say no.'"

When you are in convoy it is sometimes impossible to remember whether a thing happened yesterday or the day before yesterday or the day before that. You watch the other ships and you read whatever there is to read and you play jokes on the ship's cat. You go to the pantry and slam the refrigerator door, and the cat runs in, thinking you are going to give him something to eat. Then you pretend to ignore him. Finally, when his whining becomes unbearable, you throw him a few bits of crabmeat. I had brought three books along with me on the *Regnbue*, but I had finished them in the three weeks we spent idling off the British coast. After that I read several ninepenny thrillers by Agatha Christie and Valentine Williams that happened to be aboard, and then a copy of *Pilgrim's Progress*, donated to the ship by the Glasgow Y.M.C.A. Eventually I was reduced to looking at September numbers of *Life*. Once I found an early 1939 issue of *Redbook*. I read every page of it grate-fully, though it contained six stories about husbands who strayed but found that they liked their wives best after all. There was a strict black-out every evening, but I didn't mind it as much as I had in London, because on the ship there was no place to go anyhow. One of the lifeboats had a fashion of working loose from its fastenings in heavy weather, and then the boatswain would summon a gang to heave on the ropes until he could make it fast again. I used to look forward to the chance of pulling on one of the ropes. Whenever the crew had to make the boat fast while I was napping in my cabin, I felt slighted.

Some of the men were always speculating about our destination, Baton Rouge. It didn't show on any of the maps on the ship. If it had, they figured, the size of the print might have given them an idea of how big the town was. My own guess was that it was a city of a hundred thousand. Actually, the population is thirty-four thou-sand. American cities weren't listed in *Hvem, Hvad, Hvor,* the Nor-wegian equivalent of the *World Almanac,* and the favorite reference work on board. *Hvem, Hvad, Hvor* means "Who, What, Where." The book contains street plans of every city in Norway, even places of as few as five thousand inhabitants. The men used to mark the locations of their houses and show them to each other and to me. Once, Gjertsen, the chief officer, showed me where he lived in his home town. The next day he came into my cabin looking for me, with *Hvem, Hvad, Hvor* in his hand. "I made a mistake," he said, pointing to the plan of the place. *"Here* is where I live," and he showed me a dot about a quarter of an inch from the one he had made before.

As Christmas drew near, Larsen, the steward, was often missing from his cabin during the evenings. He was aft in the galley with the cook, constructing great quantities of "fat things" and "poor men," the Norwegian terms for doughnuts and crullers, respec-tively. On his journeys aft he carried with him a thick, calf-bound Norwegian cookbook. Larsen had formerly been a cook; he some-times regretted his change-over from creative to executive catering. The cook was a tall, thin young man who looked as if he were built of candle wax. Together they elaborated on the plans for the Christ-mas Eve dinner. Rumors were spread by one of the British machine gunners, who had talked to the third engineer, who had it straight from a messboy, that there would be turkey. While the convoy moved along at its steady ten knots, nobody aboard the *Regnbue* talked of anything but the coming dinner.

On the great night the table was laid for a dozen persons in the saloon, where ordinarily the captain and I dined alone. We were lucky; the sea was reasonably calm. The steward and the boy who helped him in the saloon, which was forward, would have had a hard time in a gale, for the galley was in the after deckhouse and they had to carry all the food over the long catwalk between. Promptly at six o'clock the engineer officers came forward to dine with us. Larsen, the chief engineer, who was not related to Larsen the steward, was a girthy, middle-aged man who resembled Hendrik Willem van Loon. If I looked aft on a fair day I could generally see him standing by a door of the engine room with his hands in his pockets. He was a fixture in the seascape, like Nilsen, the gunner and ex-whaler, who silently paced the deck near the four-inch gun. Equally immutable was the British machine gunner on duty, wearing a pointed hood and sitting inside a little concrete breastwork on the poop deck, looking like a jack-in-the-box. Chief Engineer Larsen and his officers seldom came forward to visit us. To mark the occasion on this night, they were wearing collars and neckties. They looked scrubbed and solemn, and so did Captain Petersen and the three deck officers and the gunner and the radioman, all of whom were at the table.

Steward Larsen had set three glasses at each place—one, he told me, for port, one for whisky, and a third for gin. He had no aquavit for the Christmas dinner, and gin was supposed to replace it. To get the meal started, the steward brought in some porridge called *jul grot,* which is traditional and practically tasteless. Engineer Larsen said "Skoal" and emptied a glass of gin. We all said "Skoal" and did likewise. Then Steward Larsen served a thick soup with canned shrimp and crabmeat and chicken in it. We all drank again. The steward next served fish pudding, and there was more drinking of skoals. Then he brought in the turkey with the pride of a Soviet explorer presenting a hunk of frozen mammoth excavated from a glacier. The turkey had been in the ship's cold room since the September equinox, and ship chandler's turkeys are presumed to have been dead for quite a while before they come aboard. We had plenty of canned vegetables and, above all, plenty of gin. The teetotaler Methodist captain, who stuck to his principles and didn't drink, brought out a couple of songbooks that he had got from a Norwegian church and suggested we sing some Christmas hymns. His guests sang them, without much pleasure, it seemed to me, and we ate a lot of jello covered with vanilla sauce and drank some more gin. All the men's faces remained rigid and solemn. Engineer Larsen said, in English, "Merry Christmas to our American friend." The captain whispered to me, "You can tell he's from Oslo. He talks too much." The steward then brought in mounds of doughnuts and crullers, and some fancy drinks in tall glasses. He called the tall drinks Larsen's Spezials. They were triple portions of gin with lump sugar and canned cherries. Everyone said, "Thank you, Steward. Very good." The whisky was served straight, as a dessert liqueur. We all began drinking it out of jiggers and saying "Skoal" some more. The singing got fairly continuous and the choice of numbers gradually grew more secular. Most Norwegian songs, I noticed, have many verses, and the men who are not singing pay no attention to the one who is. They look as if they are trying to recall the innumerable verses they are going to sing in their turn. We all got together on one patriotic number, though. The last line, translated into English, was "If Norway goes under, I want to go too." We clasped hands on that one.

The captain asked me to sing "My Old Kentucky Home," which I couldn't remember many words of, but fortunately three other fellows started to sing three other songs at the same time. The steward, considering his official duties over, drew up a chair to the table and received congratulations. The cook, looking taller and more solemn than ever, came in and was hailed as a great man. The drinkers still made intermittent efforts to remain grave. They yielded slowly, as if they were trying to protect their pleasure. Now the dignitaries of the crew, who had finished a dinner with exactly the same menu in their own quarters, began to appear in the saloon and take seats at the table—first the argumentative carpenter, then the boatswain with the cackle, and finally the pumpman, a tall fellow who looked like a Hapsburg and spent his life shooting compressed air into clogged oil tanks. The carpenter arose to sing a song. He had the same argumentative, deliberate delivery that he had in conversation, and he paused so long between verses that the chief officer, who had come down off the bridge and entered the saloon just after the carpenter had finished a verse, thought the all-clear had sounded and began a song of his own. The usually timid cook, buoyed up by one of Larsen's Spezials, thundered, "Shut up, Chief Officer! Let the carpenter sing!" As the chief officer and the fourth engineer joined the party, the third officer and another of the engineers left to stand their watches. The machine gunner from Glasgow arrived to wish the captain a merry Christmas and snitch a bottle of whisky. Two seamen, lads of about eighteen, came in to convey the respects of the crew. They had, I imagine, thought of this mission themselves. One, a small, neat boy with a straw-blond mustache, sang a long song with the refrain *"Farvel, farvel"* ("Farewell, farewell"). It appeared to make him very unhappy. Nearly all the seamen on the *Regnbue* were youngsters, which would have been true on a Norwegian ship even before the war. After three and a half years at sea they are eligible to take a course at a mates' school if they can save or borrow the price. Boys who don't like the sea quit before then.

Presently Steward Larsen pulled me by the arm and took me off with him to visit the rest of the crew. Before leaving the saloon, he had handed out a bottle of whisky to each four men, and on the whole they were doing all right with it. "I am a Commoonist," he kept saying to me on our way aft, "so I want you to love these fellers." Everybody on the ship had received as a Christmas greeting from the Norwegian Government a facsimile letter signed "Haakon, Rex." The letters, which had been put aboard at London for the captain to hand out, told Norwegian seamen that they were their country's mainstay. The "Commoonist" read this letter over and over again and cried every time. The Government had also sent the crew a set of phonograph records of patriotic songs. The favorite was called *"Du Gamle Mor"* ("Thou Old Mother"), which means Norway. The boys aft were all wearing blue stocking caps, which had come in a Christmas-gift bundle with a card saying they had been knitted by a Miss Georgie Gunn, of 1035 Park Avenue, New York City.

By the time Larsen and I staggered back over the catwalk to the saloon, everybody but Captain Petersen was unashamedly happy. It was very close in the blacked-out saloon with all the ports shut, and I went up to the bridge for air. Bull, the third officer, was on watch up there. He had been moderately dizzy when he had gone on watch at eight o'clock after eating his dinner, he told me, but now he felt only a sense of sober well-being. "I see ships all around," he said, "so ve must be in de meddel de convooey." Sandor, the Rumanian seaman who had stowed away on the ship in 1939 and remained aboard ever since, was on lookout duty. He said, "This makes three Christmas on ship since I left home. No good. On ship you see thirty, thirty-five peoples. On shore you see hoondreds peoples. I like to get one Christmas ashore." Sandor's chances were not bright. The British immigration officers at our second assembly port had told him that, since he was now an enemy alien, he would not be allowed on shore in Britain for the remainder of the war. They had added that the Americans would probably also refuse to let him land, so he might have to remain afloat indefinitely. Griffin, the English seaman, was at the wheel. When Sandor spelled him, Griffin came out of the wheelhouse and we wished each other Merry Christmas. I had heard so much talk about home towns and traditions that night that I asked Griffin where he was from. "Blowed if I know," he said cheerfully. "Sandor don't know where 'e's going and I don't know where I come from."

When I went down to my cabin, a row that would have done credit to an early convention of the American Legion was going on in the saloon. I looked in, but everybody was shouting in Norwegian and no one looked sufficiently detached to translate for me, so I didn't hear what it was all about until the next day, when I was told that someone had been trying to get subscriptions to the Norwegian Air Force Spitfire Fund and that Grung, the radioman, had protested that the Norwegian Government, even in exile, was giving $300,000 a year to missionaries in China and Africa. "Let them spend the missionary money for Spitfires before they bother workingmen," he had said. The steward had called Grung a bad name and Grung had pushed him over a case of empty whisky bottles. Later, when I happened to see Grung coming out of the radio shack, I asked him what Larsen had called him. "He called me a Commoonist," Grung said.

The party gave us something to talk about for a couple of days afterward. The carpenter went around repeating a line he had memorized from the label of an Old Angus whisky bottle: "Yentle as a lamb." He would say it and roll his eyes and then exclaim, "Yeezis!" On Christmas morning an English ship signaled to us, "Merry

Christmas. Keep your chins and thumbs up." Grung and Bull had a consultation and then, not being able to think of anything witty, just ran up the answering flag meaning "Message noted."

One morning, when we were about halfway across the Atlantic, I found Bull in a particularly good humor. "Look around," he said, handing me a glass. "Vare is escort?" I had a good look around and there wasn't any. The corvettes had disappeared during the night. "Does that mean we've reached the safe part of the Atlantic?" I asked. "Safe yust so long ve see no submarine," Bull said. Captain Petersen, who came up a half-hour later to look around, said, "Maybe the escort from America was supposed to meet us here, and it didn't, and the British corvettes had a date to meet an eastbound convoy off Iceland. We don't count as much as eastbound ships, because they're loaded." We went on all day without an escort. Grung came out of his shack and stared at three hundred and fifty thousand tons of valuable shipping moving placidly on, unprotected and unattacked. "Admiral Raeder must be lousy," he said at last.

Next morning a force of Canadian destroyers met us. No harm had been done. It wasn't the only time the *Regnbue* had traveled in an unconvoyed convoy, Bull said. Once she had left Halifax in a convoy escorted by a battleship that was returning from an American dockyard. A couple of hundred miles out, the battleship had been summoned to help hunt the *Bismarck,* so she had moved off at thirty knots and left the merchantmen to push on by themselves to England. There were never enough vessels for convoy duty, Bull said, but luckily there never seemed to be enough submarines, either. The Battle of the Atlantic sounded imposing, but it was rather like a football game with five men on a side.

A few days after we met the Canadian, the ships bound for Gulf ports split off from the convoy. We were one of them. Each ship was to proceed as an individual, the theory at that time being that waters within a few hundred miles of the American coast were fairly safe. We had always cherished a notion that we were one of the fastest ships in our convoy. When dispersal day came, however, most of the others bound for the south quickly left us behind. Twenty-four hours after the split we were alone in the ocean, without another ship in sight. We steered southwest within a couple of hundred miles of the coast for nearly two weeks and saw only two vessels, neither of them a warship. Nor did we sight a single patrol plane. We hoped that no hostile aircraft carrier would ever have the same luck. The *Regnbue,* now that she was alone, zigzagged in a constant series of tangents to her course. This lost a mile an hour, which still further delayed my home-coming.

The weather stayed seasonably rough. We never ran into the kind of storm that sends smashed ships to port to make pictures for the newspaper photographers, but for days on end we couldn't see the sun long enough to get a position, and on New Year's Eve, when we were thirty-one days out of London, we had a sixty-mile gale, which made a second holiday party impossible. The day before we left the convoy I had been standing at the wheelhouse window watching the extraordinary antics of the tankers around us. A tanker in water ballast is a good sea boat but not a comfortable one. It rides the waves like a canoe, but it has a tendency to twist from side to side as it comes down. As I have already noted, this is even more disconcerting to watch than to endure. I was thinking about this when Mikkelsen, the electrician, a big, snaggle-toothed West Norwegian, came up and stood next to me. He looked at the ships for a while, then said quietly, "Fine weather." According to his lights it probably was.

After you leave your convoy you may have no other ships to watch and discuss, but you have a chance to fire your gun. That is an event to look forward to for days. Admiralty regulations require a ship to fire at least two shots on each trip. The captain gave Nilsen, the gunner, the order to prepare to fire these ritual shots. A day was set for the performance—not too soon, because, on account of scarcity of ammunition, we couldn't afford such pleasures more than once and we wanted to prolong the period of anticipation. The ordinarily silent Nilsen became the embodiment of the busy-executive type. The other members of the gun crew were the Hapsburg pumpman, two Diesel motormen, the fourth engineer, and the little sailor who had sung *"Farvel."* They assumed new dignity among their fellows during the days before the gun practice. Everybody on the *Regnbue* told jokes about the last time the gun had been fired. Some said that Larsen, the chief engineer, had been asleep in his cabin when the gun went off and had been knocked off his divan. Others told the same story about the cook, the steward, or the second officer. All of this was invention, because nobody on a merchant ship sleeps when the gun is to be fired. One might as well expect a small boy to sleep late on Christmas morning.

On the big day the raised gun platform served as an excellent stage for the gun crew and the protagonist, the gun. The boatswain had distributed pounds of cotton batting, and we had stuffed our ears with wads of the stuff. The little sailor, a romantic chap, had carefully smudged his forehead with black grease so that he would look like one of Admiral Tordenskjold's powder monkeys. An empty oil drum would serve as target. A couple of sailors threw it off the stern. Nilsen's crew loaded the gun. Then, after the ship had gone an estimated two thousand meters, they fired. There was a great spat of flame from the gun's muzzle, a satisfactory roar, and something splashed in the water a long distance away. I could not see the oil drum, but Haraldsen, the second officer, who had once been an ensign in the Norwegian Navy, said that the shell had not missed by much. We all shouted "Hurrah!" It was better than the Fourth of July. The gun was reloaded and fired again. After the second shot we all felt much safer, because we knew that the gun would not burst until the next trip.

The days continued alike as we went on, but they had a different feeling. After we had passed Hatteras even the carpenter and the radioman, the ship's leading grousers, began to admit it was probable we would make port. And all through the ship men made plans for whatever shore leave they might get. Larsen, the steward, who had once worked out of the port of "Noolians," proposed to the cook and a couple of others that they hire a taxi at Baton Rouge and drive straight to the French quarter in New Orleans. "I always say I'm going to save money," he told me, "but when I get near land I can't keep my temper." Captain Petersen looked forward to renewing acquaintance with the pastor of the Norwegian church in New Orleans, where he planned to go by train. A few of the men owned electric flatirons, and these were in heavy demand by shipmates who wanted to press their pants. Grung, the radioman, was in charge of the pay list. All of the men had fairly large sums coming to them, and each signified to Grung the amount he wanted to draw at Baton Rouge. Usually a man changed his mind several times, raising the ante each time. The cook and the steward held long conferences about stores, occasionally asking me how to spell "bitterscots pewding" or "tomates cetseps." The steward said that he would send the list ashore to a ship chandler in "Noolians" when we went through customs and have the stuff trucked up to Baton Rouge.

The ship had not taken stores for more than three months now, and the eggs caused a daily argument between the steward and me. For several mornings he had served them hard-boiled, a sign he had no real confidence in them. Each morning I would open my first egg and say, "*Darlig*," which is Norwegian for "Bad."

The steward would protest, "*Naj, naj.*"

"But this one has green spots inside the shell," I would say.

"Ex like dot sometimes," he would maintain.

The captain always ate his eggs without any remark; his silence accused me of finicking. At last, one morning toward the end of the voyage, he opened an egg and looked at the steward. "*Darlig,*" he said. The steward looked embarrassed. Then the captain ate the egg; a bad hard-boiled egg is probably as nourishing as a good one.

Next morning the steward brought me an amorphous yellow mass on a plate. It tasted mostly of sugar, but he offered me a jug of maple- and cane-sugar syrup to pour on it. I took a spoonful, fancying it some Norse confection, and said, "Not bad. What do you call it?" The steward said, "I call it ummelet. Same ex." Once the captain opened up a bit more than usual and talked about the Oxford Movement. The Movement had been strong in Norway, he said, and had frequently coincided with Quislingism. "A shipowner in my town," he once said to me, "got crazy about the Oxford Movement. He took his wife and children to a public meeting, and then he got up in the meeting and said that when he went to Antwerp on business he used to use bad women. His wife fainted. I don't call that a Christian." Several times the captain talked about his native town. "It has two fine hotels, and the harbor is full of beautiful little islands," he said once. "You can take your family in a boat fishing and then have a picnic on an island. In the winter we go skiing. My boy is three years old, and he has his second pair of skis. In the summer we used to have lobster parties, or dumpling-and-buttermilk parties. But it probably isn't like that now."

"By and by Florida" had been a gag line with Haraldsen, the second officer, throughout the voyage, but one day we really got

THE WORLD ON ONE KNEE

there. It was the first land we had sighted since leaving Britain, and it looked exactly like the newsreels, with fine, white hotels and palm trees and scores of spick-and-span motorboats in the blue water off-shore, fishing for whatever people fish for in Florida. The weather was clear but cold. When we got close to shore we were permitted to use the radio receiving set in the chief officer's cabin again, and one of the first things I heard was an announcer saying, "There is no frost in Florida. This morning's temperature was thirty-seven." I tried to get some war news and heard another announcer saying, "The slant-eyed specialists in treachery continue their advance toward Singapore." One, two, three, four, five seconds. "You could not employ them better than by making a lather of creamy Sweetheart soap." We sailed along the shore. There were plenty of airplanes overhead now. They swooped almost to our masthead and looked us over every five minutes. It made all the men happy just to see the coast. From the bridge we kept looking through our glasses for bathing girls, but the weather was too cold for them. We wondered what the people in the Palm Beach and Miami hotels thought of our rusty ship, with its wheelhouse fortified with concrete slabs and its ragged red flag with the blue cross. Fellows kept making attempts at jokes, like "There's the dog track; let's go" or "Grung, get out the flash lamp and signal women that want a date yust wait on the beach. I going to swim in."

That afternoon the steward came into my cabin and said that the captain and the officers were giving me a farewell supper that evening. As on Christmas Eve, it was formal dress—collars and neckties. The occasion itself was solemn; Norwegians are not effusive. My companions just sat there, talking Norwegian among themselves and ignoring me. Nobody made a speech, but at the end of the meal the cook carried in a cake about the size and shape of an Aztec calendar stone. It was encrusted with slightly damp sugar. He held it out to me, and I stood up and reached for it. It nearly pulled me forward on my face, and as I looked down on the top, I saw, written in icing, *"Farvel."*

A few nights later we were at the mouth of the Mississippi, waiting for a pilot. A northerly gale howled down at us straight from Lake Michigan. There were plenty of lights visible on the shore, more than I had seen at a comparable hour since leaving New York in the summer. Somehow I had expected our lights to go out when we entered the war. It seemed strange coming in our blacked-out ship to a country that was neither neutral *nor* dark. A boy in a rowboat brought out the pilot, a heavy-set, shivering man in a leatherette jacket who announced as soon as he came aboard that it was the coldest damn winter he had ever known in Louisiana. He brought aboard a copy of the New Orleans *Times-Picayune,* containing a lot of basketball scores and society notes and a few stories about a war that seemed to be on some remote sphere. A naval party came aboard and sealed the radio shack. The pilot took us seventeen miles up the river and then was relieved by a second pilot, who was going to take us the eighty remaining miles to New Orleans. I turned in.

We dropped anchor off quarantine in New Orleans at about ten o'clock on the morning of the forty-second day out of London. It was Sunday. We had to pass the immigration and public-health officers' inspections before the *Regnbue* could continue up the river. I had my suitcase packed before the government officers arrived, hoping that I would be able to go back to shore with them. It was the sort of day we had had off Florida, chilly but bright, and the city looked good in the sunlight. The *Regnbue's* men, lining the rails, talked about how fine it would be to be going ashore again. I had been at sea for only six weeks, but few of them had set foot ashore in four months. The immigration-and-health boat came out soon after ten with a party including a doctor and a rat inspector. The immigration men brought five armed guards to post about the ship to see that none of our allies would try to land too soon. Soon a customs officer came aboard and asked the captain if any man on the ship had more than three hundred cigarettes. Seamen buy their cigarettes in America, and our men had started to run short a fortnight before. Captain Petersen did not seem astonished by the question. He sent Grung to take a census of the cigarettes on board. Grung came back after a half-hour with word that only the second engineer had more than three hundred cigarettes. He had three hundred and twenty-five. The customs man asked if the twenty-five were loose, and Grung said that five of them were. The customs man said he thought he could let the second engineer keep the other twenty, although, he pointed out, he was making an exception. I pictured a large convoy missing a tide while the United States Customs counted cigarettes. Then the customs man asked about liquor, because he would have to seal up what we had on board. Grung went on a search for liquor and reported back that we had had two bottles of whisky and one of gin but that one of the public-health men had drunk about half of one of the bottles of whisky.

Next the immigration men came to the consideration of me. They said that since I had a good passport and had apparently been born in New York, I probably had a right to land in the United States, but not until my baggage had been passed by a customs appraiser. Unfortunately, they said, no appraisers had come along. "The last thing I expected to find on this ship was a passenger," the head immigration man said, giving me a rat inspector's look. He said that unless I wanted to stay on the ship for twenty-four hours longer I would have to pay two days' wages for the appraiser myself. Double pay for Sunday work. I said that would be all right, and they sent for an appraiser. It cost me $13.33. While waiting for the appraiser, I went out on deck. Captain Petersen came out too, and we stood looking at the shore. He was quiet, as usual, but he seemed to be struggling with an unusual emotion. At last he said, "Say, is it true the Hippodrome has been torn down?"

I said, "Yes, and the Sixth Avenue El, too."

Again he looked troubled, and I thought he was going to say he would miss me, but he said, *"The Big Show* were a wonderful play." That was an extravaganza that had played at the Hipp in 1917, when the captain had lived in Hoboken.

I said, "Yes, with Joe Jackson."

"A very funny man," Captain Petersen said.

A shabby motorboat came toward us from the left bank of the river. Captain Petersen said, "It must be a ship chandler after our business." There was a man on the forward deck with a megaphone, and as the boat came under our bow he called up inquiringly, "Captain, Captain?" Petersen pointed to his peaked cap, his emblem of office. The fellow shouted, "We got orders to send you on to Curaçao! You got enough bunker?" Curaçao is nine days from New Orleans for a ten-knot boat. Petersen showed no sign of surprise or disappointment. "We need bunker," he shouted back, "but we can get out in twenty-four hours!"

An hour later, when I was in a boat going ashore, I could see most of the *Regnbue* fellows on deck, leaning over the rail. There was the carpenter, with his square head and his obstinate shoulders,

201

and the tall pumpman, and the electrician, and the two British gunners in their khaki uniforms. I could make out the bearish form of Sandor, the Rumanian, who would not have to stay on board alone now, because the others would stay with him. And there was Larsen, the steward, in a belted, horizon-blue overcoat and a bright green hat, his shoregoing uniform. He wouldn't go ashore, after all.

BOOK III

THE WORLD GETS UP

CHAPTER I

Toward a Happy Ending

PEARL HARBOR had left slight trace on the public mind, it seemed to a man coming off a boat in mid-January of 1942, but it had closed the second phase of the war. The first had ended with the disaster of the Pétain armistice. The second had been a negative success because our side had avoided collapse. The third, however unpromisingly it might start, however long it might last, was bound to end in the defeat of the avowedly fascist powers, because the combination of peoples they had attacked was too big, too strong, and too game for them. Hitler's chance to own the world had depended on a successful bluff. If, with the aid of the French industrialists and their counterparts in Great Britain and the United States, he could have secured a dominance of the West without war, isolating Russia, he might have brought it off. He still had had a chance as long as he could keep Russia and the United States neutral. But with all the holders of high cards in the game he was in the position of a poker player who has tried to steal a pot with no pair. He could keep on raising until he ran out of chips in order to delay the showdown; that would be an insane card player's reaction. His situation made me, personally, extremely and perhaps unreasonably happy. Millions of men meriting better than I have lived and died in humiliating periods of history. Free men and free thinking always get a return match with the forces of sadism and anti-reason sometimes. But I had wanted to see a win, I had wanted my era to be one of those that read well in the books. Some people like to live in a good neighborhood; I like to live in a good age. I am a sucker for a happy ending—the villain kicked in the teeth, the stepchildren released from the dark basement, the hero in bed with the heroine. Maybe the curtain will go up on the same first act tomorrow night, but I won't be in the audience.

By 1942 I had my personal hurts as well. I had Suzette's letter, which had taken nearly a year to reach me, telling of her father's death, cold, undernourished and humiliated, in the Montmartre flat where we had so often broken bread. Jean, the son, had won a Croix de Guerre and had been demobilized, Suzette had written— I could imagine him dodging about France to avoid conscription for German factory labor. Sauvageon, living in the *zone interdite* between occupied and unoccupied France, had managed to get a letter out to me too, through Switzerland. He had written of the mass emigration of the Alsatians and Lorrainers who had chosen to retain their French nationality.

The third round would be the good one, I thought, and I didn't stay long at home waiting for it to begin. I made the return trip to England by another Norwegian ship, this time a fast one that traveled without escort. The chief excitement of this trip was a long series of after-dinner checker games between me and the chief engineer, Johansen, who referred to himself as "some of the oldest engineers afloat." I once beat him with a quadruple jump, in a game for three bottles of beer.

London had changed more than New York since our entry into the war. It was full of Americans now, and one more attracted about as much attention as an extra clam at a shore dinner. I felt like an until recently only child whose mother has just given birth to quintuplets. And I was more of a stranger to the American news sources with whom I now had to deal, the Army and Navy Public Relations offices, than correspondents who had been in London for only three months, because the organizations had been set up since the time I had left.

I had a high idea of what the American Army in the European theater of operations would eventually be, and my first clues to it did not disappoint me. There were few ground combat troops in Great Britain as yet and many less Air Corps people than I had expected to find, but the preparations of the Services of Supply indicated how great the fighting force would soon be. The S.O.S. was building, for example, a depot in the South of England for the repair of American Army motor vehicles, and from its size one could get a fair idea of how many vehicles would be in operation and how big an army they would serve. It was like estimating an elephant's size from the print of one foot. The dimensions of the A.E.F. would certainly be elephantine, which pleased me because it indicated that the Government had not been impressed by the Sunday-supplement strategists who talked about an exclusively air war.

I knew that the quality of American troops would be good, once they had paid their entry fee with a couple of bobbles, because Americans are the best competitors on earth. A basketball game between two high-school teams at home will call forth enough hardness of soul and flexibility of ethic to win a minor war; the will to win in Americans is so strong it is painful, and it is unfettered by any of the polite flummery that goes with cricket. This ruthlessness always in stock is one of our great national resources. It is better than the synthetic fascist kind, because the American kid wears it naturally, like his skin, and not self-consciously, like a Brown Shirt. Through long habit he has gained control over it, so that he turns it on for games, politics, and business and usually turns it off in intimacy. He doesn't have to be angry to compete well.

While I had been away from London, Manetta, the manager of the Savoy Grille, had taken over the restaurant in my old hotel in Half Moon Street, and it was now one of the busiest and noisiest pubs in London, with a British version of a swing band, no tables available on less than three days' notice, American colonels crowding the members of refugee governments away from the ringside, and Jack, the cockney bartender who during my first visit had drooped disconsolately in front of a fine assortment of whiskies, now overworked and understocked, like the wine waiter. The hotel portion of the establishment looked much as it always had, although because of the Americans it was harder to get a room. Some of the old county women, having booked weeks in advance, would arrive there and in time descend from their rooms, leading either a spaniel or a small grandniece wearing a blue hair ribbon. They would march stiffly toward the once tranquil dining room, hear the first blast of the swing band, enter the gabble of the cocktail lounge where the

207

new clientele waited for tables, and then turn and hobble desperately away, dragging dog or child after them.

London had the atmosphere of a town where people are gathering for a gold rush or an opera festival; everybody felt that something good was going to begin soon. Psychologically we had already passed to the attack. The correspondents, while they waited to be let in on the time and place, wrote stories about the growing American forces in Britain. After three years of going out to French, British, and Polish troops for stories, I enjoyed the novelty of being with Americans, although the uniform I now had to wear when I went out to troops made me feel that I was play-acting. I had passed through British railway stations so often and so unremarked in mufti that the salutes of British noncoms now took me by surprise and I was generally well past the saluter before I realized I had left him with a poor view of American military courtesy. It would have been hopeless to explain each time that a correspondent didn't rate a salute—I was bald enough and old enough to be a field officer and was wearing an officer's uniform.

The Air Corps, which was just beginning to take over a few British fields, reminded me of a football squad beginning its training for the season. It would win a lot of games if it was not rushed into heavy competition too soon. My favorite unit in the first weeks was a Flying Fortress bombardment group that resembled a football squad physically too. There is an official maximum size for fighter and medium bombardment pilots, but the really big boys in the Air Corps get into the big ships, where there is relatively a lot of head room. The commander of one squadron of the group had been All-Southern at Mississippi State; one of his pilots had played tackle for Alabama in the Rose Bowl, and another had understudied an All-American halfback at Duke; Tommy Lohr, a rugged little lightweight back from Brown, was another pilot in the group, and altogether they would have made a good squad for any coach in a normal season. But this time they had other business.

The original public-relations crew in London, being for the most part newspapermen who had recently acquired uniforms and lived in deadly fear of irritating real soldiers, were not of much help in getting out to see troops. According to them the C.O. of any unit a correspondent wanted to see was sure to be busy, and anyway there were no living accommodations for newspapermen at the fly-

ing field. I arranged all that with my Fortress fellows by always occupying the bed of a man who had gone on forty-eight-hour leave
to London. While the man was in London he would sleep in my
room at the hotel. When the regular occupant of the bed at the field
returned there was always somebody else going up to town and I
would move into his bed while he took mine in London. I never
really interviewed anybody, just lived around the place and learned
by osmosis, until I sometimes thought of myself as a redundant
member of the group, a goldbricker nobody had yet caught up with.
We were living in hutments and sleeping on cots; there were toilets
that flushed and showers; between meals and after dinner we would
sit in the lounge of the officers' club, where there were deep chairs
and a bar. In retrospect, after we all got to Africa, it seemed a most
luxurious period.

The Fortresses made their first flights over France while I was
living with this group. The accuracy of their bombing, even in their
first raids, astonished officers of British Bomber Command and the
Ministry of Economic Warfare, who had selected the targets. The
British thought at first that these were selected crews of veterans
and that the accuracy couldn't be retained in large-scale operations.
But I knew that they were boys who had had at most a year and a
half in the Air Corps, and that there were thousands more like them
at home. The factories would furnish the planes, the American system of public education would furnish the crews; it couldn't be
anything but a win. And the ground forces, I felt confident, would
be up to the air people in efficiency. The factories and the schools
would work for them, too. And the good American food that the
boys had eaten had given them the bone and lungs and recupera-
tive power that no Nazi state system of physical education could
superimpose on rickety frames.

The boys themselves, I thought, were the best proof they had
something to fight for. Four officers fly in each Fortress, and every
one of them at that time had to be a college man. You could look
around the lounge in the evening and see 250 officers, all giving a
common impression of fitness and good humor. There wasn't a
raddled, vicious face in the lot. They had come from state universities and technical schools and little denominational colleges all
through the country, where tuition fees were nominal or nonexist-
ent. This brazen public defiance of the profit system had resulted in

the creation of our greatest national asset. They hadn't had to spend their elementary-school days getting up competitive examinations which would admit them to secondary school, or their secondary-school days preparing competitive examinations for college. They had had time to play. Some of them were sons of rich men, a few were sons of mechanics, and most were in between, but there was no trace of class accent to distinguish one from another. There were regional accents, of course. And the standard of training in all those schools that to me had for years been just names in columns of football scores must have been pretty good, because the kids could all do their stuff as well as the few members of the group who had been to Ivy colleges.

I hadn't been with so many Americans so young in twenty years, and I thought they had an edge on my own college generation, although maybe I was less than fair in retrospect because I had been an insecure, intolerant undergraduate myself. All the boys had to do, I thought, was to look around at each other and they would understand that democracy was worth defending. The noncoms they flew with, six sergeants to a Fortress, were just as different from products of other regimes as the officers. They were all high-school men, even though in civil life they had clerked in grocery stores or driven laundry trucks. They had no idea that they were bound down in any social class, and they thought for themselves about everything they saw and did. They were good stuff.

The officers of the different ships wore no insignia to show which Fortress they belonged to, but it was easy to pick out crewmates in the lounge of the club. They were the men who usually occupied adjacent chairs, engaged in long sessions of insulting one another, and lent one another money in crap games. One of my favorites, a boy named Jones from Memphis, used to sit next to the phonograph, changing the records. The songs they liked were full of sobs: "I'll Be Around When He Is Gone," or "Someone's Rocking My Dream Boat," or "This Is the Story of a Starry Night." A psychiatrist has since told me that he considers such fare extremely depressing for men about to go out on bombing missions, but there were no suicides. I never hear those songs now without seeing the faces of the kids in the lounge, and sometimes I forget which of them are dead.

There was one Fortress pilot whom his colleagues called the

Baron, who once told me that his only ambition for after the war was to sit in the grandstand at the Yankee Stadium every afternoon and watch the ball game. He was known as the Baron because once when he had been doing some drinking in the club he had said, "When we get to Germany I will be a baron if I feel like it because my family has a castle on the Rhine and I can walk in and claim it any time." His father had been an officer in the German Army in the war previous to this one, but that did not prevent the Baron from being the kind of suburban boy who shoots a good game of pool, plays semipro baseball on Sunday while he is still in college and officially an amateur, and is perennially worried about a pending charge of driving while under the influence of alcohol. When the home-town papers began to arrive at the station after the first few Fortress raids the fellows from small cities had a lot of fun reading each other their clippings. One town had had a Joe Snodgrass Day in honor of a navigator from there who had been in a raid, and it had raised a fund of $62 to buy candy and chewing gum for him, but not cigarettes because some of the subscribers objected to smoking. The Baron said to me, "In the town I come from the people think I am a bum, and I guess they would be surprised I am here at all." He had played varsity baseball at three colleges, none of them tough academically, and you could deduce that he had not been exactly a studying type from the fact that he had been thrown out of two of them. He was a good pilot, and he flew in a careless, easy-looking way. "Flying is the hardest thing in the world to learn," he once said to me, "and the easiest thing to do after you've learned it." He had met a co-ed at the third college where he had played ball, and married her. He was always showing new acquaintances a picture of his wife, tall and dark, and she was very pretty. The Baron had a hard time emotionally in England. He didn't like anything he had heard about Hitler, but it used to make him angry when Englishmen referred to Germans as Huns. "My old man is all right," he used to say.

Quite a while afterward I met a bomber crew from that group in Africa, and they told me they thought the Baron had been killed over Lorient. "At least, when we last saw that ship it was blazing and only five hundred feet off the ground, and nobody had bailed out," the bombardier said. "It wasn't the Baron's regular crew. There was something the matter with a supercharger in his own

211

ship that morning, and the pilot of the ship he was lost in had a heavy cold and the co-pilot was green, so the Baron volunteered to fly them. That was a raid when we had to come down lower than usual to get through cloud over the target. We don't know whether flak or fighters got the Baron's ship, but just as it made the turn after bombing, smoke and flames began pouring out of it and it began losing altitude. They could have bailed out all right, but they were heading into a group of German fighters, so they kept the guns going and they blew two 109's to bits on the way down. They were too goddam busy to jump."

I used to sometimes try to get fliers talking about what they wanted after the war, but most of them had ambitions rather like the Baron's. One fellow wanted to stay on his honeymoon until all his bonus money ran out, another wanted to play golf all day and poker all night every night and drink whisky constantly, and a lot of them wanted to stay in the Air Corps or get jobs in commercial aviation. They didn't have very much to say about the future of the world, if they thought about it. They weren't vindictive, either. They liked to hear me talk about my Polish friends. "I guess those boys are really bloodthirsty," they would say with objective astonishment. "It's better for us not to get mad," one of them said to me. "The type of precision bombing we do you've got enough to do without being angry."

CHAPTER II

Birds of My Country

I SAILED FOR AFRICA from England on the night of November 9, twenty-four hours after the first African landings had been announced in London. For nearly two weeks before I left I had been subject to call at my hotel on twelve-hour notice. I had known there must be colleagues waiting for the same call, but I had never admitted that I was one of the elect, and none of the others had said anything to me. The secret of our destination had been well kept until November 8, but after the news of the first landings we who were still in London knew where we were going. We also knew that we had been only second-grade elect, having been left out of the first wave. Personally I felt all right about that, since I had never wanted to see a fight between Americans and Frenchmen. Our party, the second echelon of prose masters, left London late in the evening from a spur railroad station used only for troop movements, in an atmosphere thick with fog and mystery. It included Ernie Pyle, of Scripps-Howard, Bill Lang of *Time, Life,* etc., Red Mueller of *Newsweek,* Gault MacGowan of the New York *Sun,* Ollie Stewart of the Baltimore *Afro-American,* and Sergeant, now First Lieutenant, Bob Neville, whom I had known when he was on the *Herald Tribune* and *PM* and who was now going to Africa as a correspondent for the army magazine, *Yank.* I recognized a kindred spirit in Ollie the moment I saw him. "Where do you hope we land at?" he asked me. "Someplace where resistance has ceased," I told him. That established a perfect rapport.

I had had an attack of the gout in my right foot two days before pulling out, and I went limping off to the war instead of coming limping back from it. I had always previously felt a bit of pride in the recurrences of this fine eighteenth-century disease, a tribute to the high standard of living I had attained at a relatively early age, but this time I was peeved with it. I figured that someone might think it was psychogenic. It made me feel worse to find the Roosevelt Hospital unit from New York on the transport we boarded for the voyage; there were fifty-two nurses who got a first impression of decrepitude that I never consequently had a chance to overcome, because each was immediately appropriated by three Air Corps officers. Lieutenant Colonel Gurney Taylor, who was, I think, second in command of the unit, then turned traitor to his class by telling me about a ten-cent specific for the malady, a breach of confidence which will cost the civilian medical profession several hundred dollars a year for the rest of my life expectancy. I had to go to war to get a gout remedy. Except for the gout and the nurses the trip was without event; we docked at Mers-el-Kebir on November 21 without having seen any more enemy action than I had experienced in my two other sea passages.

There was a light air raid at Oran on the night of our arrival. The reaction to it of the local population seemed to me exaggerated; then I realized that there were still French-speaking people to whom an air raid was a novelty. I spent the next four weeks in and around Oran, making one excursion into eastern Morocco with the reconnaissance troop of the First Infantry Division when it seemed that the frontier of Spanish Morocco might become a war front. The fighting in Tunisia, as we heard about it from officers and correspondents who passed through Oran after visits to the front, was on a small scale, and few American troops were engaged. I used my time getting the feel of North Africa and gaining a gradual and unforced familiarity with the First Infantry Division, which had captured Oran, and remained in the Department. The First had many enlisted men from the sidewalks of the Bronx and Brooklyn, and a rich New York accent had new charms for me in Africa. There is an analogical sentiment in a chanson of Gace Brule, the thirteenth-century Champenois poet:

> *"The little birds of my country*
> *Have sung to me in Brittany,"*

where he was in exile, I think.

"Give da passwoy," I once heard a First Division sentinel challenge.

"Nobody told me nuttin,'" the challenged soldier replied.

"What outfitchas outuv?"

"Foy Signals."

"Whynchas get on da ball? Da passwoy is 'tatched roof.' "

"What is it mean?"

"How do I know? Whaddaya tink I yam, da Quiz Kids?"

It looked and acted and talked like a good division even then, making you know it could do the fine things it has since done. I got the same feeling from it that I had had the first time I had seen my Fortress group in England, before the Fortresses had been on a single operation.

CHAPTER III

What Do You Think That Bugle's Blowing For?

ORAN WAS THE FIRST PART of metropolitan France I had been in since June 1940. I thought I might be able to gauge from it the effects of all the events since then upon the French. I knew how strong the anti-British sentiment had been at the armistice time, how guilty the French must have felt because of the Armistice nonetheless, and how greatly a sensation of guilt increases bitterness. A corresponding sense of guilt toward France underlies the most extreme instances of British francophobia. So I did not expect to find undiluted enthusiasm for the Allied cause. But Oran disappointed even me, and I was astonished by the American policy of coddling the most obviously disaffected Oranais. These were the high civil and military officials and the large landowners.

The Prefect, a M. Boujard, had come in during the Popular Front government of Léon Blum in 1936 and had performed a star turn in political contortionism by remaining at the head of the Department ever since. He had carried out economic collaboration with the resident German and Italian commissions, enforcing the Nuremberg-patterned anti-Jewish laws and exalting the rest of the Vichy program. No one had held a pistol at his head to compel him to stay. The General of Division, one Boisseau, a furtive gray fox of a man, had insisted on the determined defense of Oran that had lasted sixty hours and cost several hundred American and perhaps a thousand French lives. This resistance had been inspired by his belief that the Allies would be chased out of Africa and he would then lose his promotion and pension rights if he had not fought against them. I had the pleasure of hearing him address some of his officers on the firing range at near-by Arzeu when American soldiers were demonstrating material that was to be turned over to the French. An American mortar put in a couple of bad shots. "I had no illusions about the American Army!" the general announced with loud satisfaction. Officers suspected of having fa-

215

vored the Americans even in thought, like a Zouave major I met (who had, by the way, fought like a lion against us), were practically ostracized. Liaison officers assigned to American units were scolded for "fraternizing" with the Americans—nearly two months after we had officially become allies. Most of the officers above the grade of battalion commander were a sad lot; those not definitely hostile, because they owed their promotions to Vichy, were apathetic because in their hearts they had never expected to fight again and hated the prospect.

"They are selfish!" my friend the Zouave major said, "they are in love with their pensions. Let it pass! But the blasphemy is that they do not want to fight!" He was a Basque who had escaped from Occupied France and then asked for service in Africa in the spring of 1941 when he had become convinced that Great Britain would not be conquered. "I have been suspect here," he told me, "so that it was more necessary for me than for the others to fight well against the Americans. Else the higher officers would have said, 'His sentiments were dictated by cowardice.' I could not have remained in the army."

The higher civil servants were in the same category as the higher officers. The minor functionaries, like postmen and cops, were in the main decent enough, but had had to conform.

The great landed proprietors of the Department, grandsons of immigrant French peasants, had piled up huge fortunes in paper francs during the armistice period by exporting to Germany their grain, their fruit, and the alcohol made from their brandy. They were the most implacable enemies we had. The poor Oranais noticed a slight improvement in nutrition soon after we landed, because dates and oranges could no longer be exported and were sold for home consumption. But this was of no benefit to the big farmers. They had never suffered personally and would have preferred to continue exporting their fruit. The money that they had been piling up would have been eventually worthless, for the Reichsbank, turning out unbacked francs by the trillion, would have inevitably forced a howling inflation. We, by pegging their franc at seventy-five to the dollar, had turned their paper into real money, and a good many of them into real millionaires. But they were angry because we had not given them a better rate. When, a couple of months later, we hiked the franc up to fifty to the dollar, we pushed a lot more money their way, still without gaining their gratitude. The leading stevedoring firm, to which the American port authorities threw the army business, was Italian-Fascist. The harbor was wide open for sabotage. A few of the ships that the American naval salvage crew had raised with great difficulty after they had been sunk by the French naval authorities were "accidentally" rammed and resunk by towboats. The French naval people retained their posts. In the first days after our arrival, I learned, some of the business had been given to a smaller competing stevedore firm. The Prefect had made representations to the American command that the owner of this smaller firm was suspected of being a British sympathizer! So the business went to the Italian.

The great landowners of the Department are of a distinct species, French only in the sense that the pre-Revolutionary Carolina rice planters were English. They are African-born; they visit France only to make a splurge in Paris or to treat their obesity at Vichy, and they are reactionary to an extent only possible in a country where a few white men live by the exploitation of a large native population. The miserable Arabized Berbers who work their great estates get almost nothing. The planters say that if you give a native anything above the lowest subsistence level he will quit work; he would not really like adequate food or clothes. They talk exactly like Mississippians. Naturally they are not in favor of manhood suffrage, labor unions, or any talk about the equality of races. They had not really collaborated with the Nazis: the Nazis had come along belatedly and collaborated with them. While they had been included in one of the ninety-odd departments of a democratic nation they had been restrained from complete self-expression. The apparent German victory had started them saying, "I told you so, democracy couldn't last." Our arrival desolated them.

These landowners, and the Prefect and the general, were the solid people who entertained Major General Lloyd R. Fredendall, the local ranking American general officer, at their homes. He let them think they were translating public opinion for him and apparently accepted what they said. He was a soldierly man who may have felt that his position had been eased by the decision of the Vichy people and the local big shots to retain all their old perquisites and keep on running the Department. He received masses of alarming reports every day from his own counterintelligence serv-

217

ice, the intelligence officer of the battalion of American infantry in the town, and the intelligence section of First Division, but these were filed away. One point the solid people were always careful to impress upon the general was the depth and fervor of anti-Semitic feeling in Oran. The solid people and their henchmen were administering Jewish real estate and cafés; their friends and relatives of the professional class were enjoying the practices Jewish doctors and lawyers had been forced to abandon. But they even got the American military administration to discharge French-English interpreters on the docks because the interpreters were Jewish (and of course pro-Ally). They said the Arab dockworkers would resent having Jews placed over them.

There was in truth a violent anti-Semitism in the city of Oran, but it was of the same kind as the anti-Semitism of Harlem, the result of deliberately inciting one exploited race against another. The Algerian-born French citizens of Spanish descent, colloquially called Néos, together with immigrants from Spain make up about a third of Oran's population. Another third is Moslem, and the two groups furnish practically all the manual labor of the city. About fifteen per cent of the population is composed of Algerian Jews. These Jews, Europeanized in varying degrees, had enjoyed French citizenship until Vichy adopted the German anti-racial laws. They had been neither great landlords nor important bankers, but shopkeepers, small moneylenders, renting agents or owners of a poor type of housing, craftsmen, chafferers, and professional people. The Oranais of French origin, a small minority, are mostly functionaries, skilled workmen or money people. A French physician, the official leader of the anti-Semitic movement in Oran, told me that there was a disproportionate number of Jewish doctors and lawyers, the classic complaint. The number of French physicians and lawyers in relation to the total Arab-Néo-Jew-French population was more disproportionate still, however. There were neither physicians, lawyers, nor men of property among the Arabs and Néos, the two most numerous groups of the population. But Arabs and Néos, as helpless against their major exploiters as a Harlem rioter against his, had been encouraged to hate the convenient Jew.

Oran is as odd as its ruling class. It has between 150,000 and 200,000 inhabitants and looks like a cross between Miami Beach and Washington Heights, although it is dirtier than either. The harbor lies in the shape of a crescent, with a continuous ridge of hills rising behind it, and the city is built on their slopes and crests.

Along the boulevards that offer good sea views there are *style-moderne* apartment houses with rounded corners, lots of glass, and balconies in the European manner of 1929. The older buildings are dingy but equally un-Oriental, and the climate is so cold in winter that the scattered palm trees look like a real-estate man's importation. A third of the population is *indigène*, which is the French term for the commingled Arabized Berbers and Berberized Arabs, but in weeks of walking about town I never saw a mosque. The only indigène who looked even faintly picturesque was an old fellow employed by a tintype photographer to pose with American soldiers in the Place du Maréchal Foch. The French say that Oran is the least French city in Africa, but it is at the same time the least African. Néos, Jews, native Oranais with French grandparents, and even the few indigènes who adopt European clothes and vocations seem to merge into the same vague Mediterranean type.

But since the Department of Oran, like the two other Algerian departments, was technically a part of metropolitan France, every action of the French and American authorities there might set a precedent for the reconquest, and I was shocked by the mess things were in. It was as if continental United States had extended statehood to Puerto Rico and Hawaii and had then itself been occupied by an enemy power, leaving the untypical new states to carry on pro tem as the United States of America, and the sugar companies had then been left free to run Puerto Rico and Hawaii.

Members of uniformed fascist organizations had left the city or at least hidden their *sturm* duds when the Americans marched in. They had sniped at our people all through the battle and might legitimately have expected to be backed against a wall and shot. But within a couple of weeks they reappeared in the cafés wearing their capes, monocles, and high boots and talking loudly about the day of revenge, not against the Germans, but us. The Légion des Anciens Combattants, the opposite number of the Sturm-Abteilung, paraded, the Service d'Ordre de la Légion, which corresponded to the Schutzstaffel, strutted; the Compagnons de France, facsimile of the Hitlerjugend, made early morning hideous with their marching song, *"Maréchal, Nous Voilà."* The civil servant who had been the local head of the Légion Tricolore, the battalion being recruited to fight against our Russian ally on the eastern front, was mobilized as a major in the French Army to fight by our side against the Germans. I had a faint suspicion he would not fight too hard. The Darlan government refused to mobilize Jews with their regiments. The Falange operated openly among the Néos, its leaders telling them that the Germans would soon appear in Oran and hand it over to Franco. Spain had held the city for two hundred and fifty years, until the Barbary Pirates had driven the Spanish garrison out in 1790. The French had moved in about forty years later.

The greed and violence of the ruling clique in Oran had provoked a more articulate reaction there than in any other African city. Long before 1939 Oran had been known as a city where political passions were strong. The Left Republicans, who drew their main strength from among the skilled workers and small functionaries born in France, had somehow managed to keep up a daily newspaper, *l'Oran Républicain,* even during the Pétain regime. It had had occasional issues suppressed and had appeared many times with large blank spaces created by the censor; its plant had been searched dozens of times for weapons or communist propaganda, but it had survived. Perhaps the Prefect, that pluperfect trimmer, had not wanted to neglect any possible hedge. The editors of *l'Oran Républicain* were by the time of my advent among the angriest and most disappointed people in North Africa. We had even left the old Vichy censorship undisturbed, so that when the *Républicain's* leader writer prepared a pro-American editorial, the censors bluepenciled it. All through the Department Jews and Frenchmen who had publicly expressed satisfaction at our landing were now serving jail sentences for their bad taste. Post-office clerks and railway conductors who had been discharged for suspected pro-Ally sympathies were still out of jobs, and those who belonged to the uniformed fascist groups were being given more responsible jobs than ever. I asked a profound-appearing major in the British Political Warfare office at Oran about this, and he said, "People should not expect to profit from their patriotism." The slogan of the occupation was, "Keep the rascals in."

General Fredendall obviously did not formulate our policy for the North African theater. He got his directives from Algiers, where General Eisenhower and Robert Murphy of the State Department were running the show, and it was of course impossible to know whether they themselves were making policy or receiving it from Washington. But Fredendall's complacency in matters of detail jarred me. I spent part of one Sunday afternoon talking to him about the Service d'Ordre de la Légion, commonly spoken of as the S.O.L., the members of which had formed an elite guard of uniformed fascism, like the German SS after which they were patterned. The next time he saw me, in the lobby of the town's principal hotel, which had been requisitioned by the Army, he graciously approached me and said, "You don't have to worry about those S.O.L.'s anymore. Their secret intelligence section is working with us now." Within a few days they had probably turned in the name of every De Gaullist in Oran as a candidate for a concentration camp. There was a general understanding that the policy of leaving the Vichy people in power was in accord with the famous agreement with Admiral Darlan signed by Eisenhower or Murphy or both, but Fredendall said he had never seen a copy of the agreement. I would have liked to know its exact terms.

State Department special agents had done the undercover work of preparation for the Oran landing and had studied the local political situation for two years while they had the German and Italian commissions living in the same hotel with them. These agents were as surprised and nearly as angry as the Allied sympathizers in Oran at the turn political affairs had taken. Their attempt to organize a militant fifth column to aid the landing had not come off, but they had furnished the landing force with excellent intelligence, and the people who had risked their lives to secure this intelligence were now being openly threatened by the S.O.L. A very beautiful Scandinavian woman, married to a Frenchman, who had been one of our most effective agents, told me that she had received repeated menaces through the mail and that Fascists regularly scrawled insults on her door.

Toward the middle of December I began to think I had used up the material that interested me in Oran, but it was not until the day before Christmas that I actually got started toward Algiers. I went down to the airfield, about fifteen miles from the city, to get on a transport plane, but was stranded by a combination of low priority and bad weather. The field was deep in a quality of mud worse than Mississippi gumbo, or so Southern soldiers informed me. One plane got out loaded with lieutenant colonels and high-priority freight, which I subsequently discovered at Algiers was toilet tissue and laundry soap, both rated ahead of correspondents. Then the base operations officer announced that the weather had closed down and there would be nothing more that day. I was in the operations shack, madder than hell, when Lieutenant Colonel Joe Crawford, commander of the second battalion of the Sixteenth Infantry, wandered in and invited me home with him for a quiet infantry Christmas. His battalion was stationed about three miles from the airport, and he said he could bring me in again next day if the weather improved and get me on a plane. I liked the battalion, and I was so tired of Oran that I didn't want to go back to it even for one night, so I thanked Crawford and came along.

Headquarters company was billeted in the buildings and courtyard of a wealthy colonist's farm; the other companies were in tents on the slopes of a couple of hills. I had just pulled off one gumboot and broken a thumbnail doing it when the bugle began to blow assembly in the farmyard. The first note had hardly sounded, it seemed, when the top sergeant began to yell. The top sergeant of headquarters company was a New Yorker with a frozen movie-gangster smile and a hard mind, and he yelled, "C'mon, get goin'! Whaddaya tink dat bugle's blowin' for?" I looked out of a window and he was handing out bandoliers of rifle ammunition, spieling all the while like a peddler pitching popcorn at Coney Island, "C'mon, get your ammunition. Da mora dis we use da shorter it'll be!" He turned his head toward me and added, "We hope!" I didn't know what the bugle was blowing for, until Don Kellett, the battalion intelligence officer, came in and said that the radio had announced a state of alert ordered for American forces all over North Africa. The battalion was to get ready to move and fight on five minutes' notice, but the reason for the alert had not been stated. He surmised that the Spaniards had let the Germans through Spanish Morocco. Crawford thought there might be an outbreak of sabotage organized by the Fascists throughout North Africa, and Chuck Horner, the executive officer, bet on a plague of parachutists. Night was falling, and our Christmas carol was "What do you think that bugle's blowing for?"

It was a good battalion of a good regiment. In an unbelievably short time the company officers reported that their outfits were ready to go. No further orders came to the battalion, and the soldiers waited under arms, packs on backs. Then a rocket appeared over the airfield. It was a green one followed by half a dozen whites and some reds and blues. Kellett said he didn't know what the signal meant, but it looked like trouble. "Maybe parachutists have landed and those mugs are too excited to get off regular signals!" he said. The wind was toward us, and we could hear machine-gun fire. We tried to raise the airfield on the telephone and couldn't. "Get a couple of patrols over there," Crawford ordered.

The tough top sergeant went out himself with one patrol. They walked out into the dark, and Crawford and Horner and Kellett and I awaited their return in the command post, the nerve center of the area. Every couple of minutes Kellett would walk to the door and come back, saying, "More rockets. Blue and green now," or "More shooting." Horner said, "It's a tough one to sweat." The sergeant returned after three quarters of an hour.

"We had to work our way onto the field to find out what all the shooting was for, sir," he said, "and their patrols fired at us. It was lucky it was the Air Corps that was shooting, because they can't hit nothing. When we got over on the field we found it was just a lot of drunks shooting off rockets and machine guns because it was Christmas Eve. They never heard of no alert." Crawford was pretty mad. He said, "That Air Corps mentality again!" He finally got the executive officer at the field on the telephone and said, "I have a lot of men with itchy trigger fingers here and your people are pretty lucky they didn't get brassed off." Crawford was so conscientious that he had even kept me sober, and we were all angrier about the Air Corps having such a good time than about anything else. The battalion slept in its clothes and on its weapons that night.

The first thing I heard in the morning was Kellett coming into the big sleeping room and saying to Crawford, "We got a flash that Darlan's been assassinated."

Crawford said, "Merry Christmas!"

CHAPTER IV

The Hat of M. Murphy

ALGIERS ON CHRISTMAS DAY, when a C-47 transport plane got me
there from Oran, was calmer than any city had a right to be after
having witnessed within the space of eight weeks a partially successful *coup d'état,* the landing of an army from another hemi-
sphere and the assassination of an equivocal admiral. It was hard
to determine whether the calm was due to apathy or to the Algerois'
fear of expressing any anti-Axis sentiment when we might be looking for another Darlan to take the defunct cheat's place. Certainly
the average European or Moslem inhabitant of the city seemed
more preoccupied with alimentation than with war.

The driver of the army car that brought me into town from the
airfield told me that good billets were scarce, but that I might as
well try my luck at the best hotel in the city first. Allied Headquarters had set aside six double rooms for correspondents, he said,
and since there were departures and arrivals every day I might find
a bed. I recognized the hotel from the motion picture *Pepe le Moko.*
It was the one where Pepe's mistress stayed with her rich protector
while Pepe pined in the Casbah.

My luck was in. As I started into the revolving door I met a
fellow named Dave Brown whom I had known in New York for
years. He said he had a room with one vacant bed in it. Dave, an
American, had worked in the financial department of the New
York bureau of Reuters, Ltd., the British news agency, for twelve
years without ever being sent out of the office to cover a story. At
last Reuters had sent him with the American force that landed in
Morocco, as a trial assignment, I suppose, and he was doing a fine
job of it. In New York Dave had long lived above an Armenian
restaurant near Radio City and played the horses in partnership with
the proprietor. I had always suspected the Armenian of giving Dave
good tips when the rent was due and bad ones when it looked as
if Dave were getting prosperous enough to move. Living with a
spot-news man during a busy news period is a great luxury for a

magazine correspondent, because the spot-news fellow has to keep up with the hour-to-hour situation and file frequent news bulletins. The magazine writer keeps posted without any exertion. For a week after the Darlan assassination Dave would be summoned from his bed two or three times a night to go up to General Eisenhower's headquarters for handouts, sometimes during air raids. I could lie snug beneath my Berber blanket and snore.

I found it difficult to distinguish at first, on walking through the climbing streets of the city, whether I was in a friendly place or an occupied enemy town. One could walk interminably without seeing a single caricature of Hitler in a shop window or an Allied newsreel advertised by a theater. The windows of the bookstores near the University of Algiers were crammed with Germanophile apologetics —testimony, perhaps, to Anglo-Saxon belief in freedom of the press. There were no signs of patriotic street demonstrations, such as one occasionally saw even in the Paris of 1939–40. I gathered from café conversations that there had been a few immediately after the debarkation of the Allies, but that the local officials had discouraged them as examples of Jewish bad taste. The place had a restful, neutral surface quality like Dublin.

Perhaps the mysterious agreement with Darlan had included a clause barring pro-Ally propaganda; I could think of no other reason why up-to-date films presenting the best aspects of American life had not been rushed in almost with the first assault wave. As it was, the leading American film attraction in the city was a 1935 film featuring Victor Moore as a henpecked husband, a role peculiarly difficult for Moslems to sympathize with. Even Darlan's death had not cleared the air of the heavy smudge of ambiguity that had hung over Africa since the deal with him. On one of my first walks I went into a crowded restaurant for a change from army food. There was less nourishment but more flavor in civilian cooking, and you could afford the change once in a while if you had the solid army rations to fall back on when you got hungry. The only vacant chair was at a table, with a small blond man who soon told me that he was a Syrian-born Jew, owned the best jewelry shop in town, had been educated at the American University at Beirut, and knew Arabic so well he composed poems in it. He said that he didn't know what to make of the Allies' "desertion" of their pre-landing "friends," exactly the same turn of words I had heard many times in Oran. Here, however, the desertion seemed even more weird, because the friends had come out with arms in their hands and risked their lives for us on the night of our landing. The jeweler offered to introduce me to some of the men who had led the *coup* which had paralyzed the defense forces for several hours, and I accepted. We took a rendezvous for five o'clock that afternoon, at the apartment of Dr. Henri Aboulker, of the faculty of medicine of the university. It had been an uncommonly good lunch for a within-the-law restaurant in Algiers: some indistinguishable kind of stew meat cooked with a reddish sauce and olives.

You can hope for lucky encounters only if you walk around a lot. A distinguished blackface comic once told George Lyon, a former city editor of mine, that there are only three kinds of people in the world worth talking to, whores, newspapermen, and actors, and they all need sturdy legs in their business. After a roundabout stroll I got back to Dr. Aboulker's apartment on the Rue Michelet in time for my appointment.

Dr. Aboulker was seventy-eight years old. He was permitted to continue his practice and remain on the faculty of medicine, although a Jew, because citizens who had been wounded or received military decorations in the last World War were as yet exempt from the provisions of the racial laws. The stage in which they too would be barred would undoubtedly have been reached later, but even Vichy had hesitated to do it. It would have looked awkward for that professional war veteran, the Marshal.

The Pétainist African regime which had remained in under Darlan and had now apparently survived him had taken measures to avoid any future repetition of this awkward situation by excluding Jews from the new mobilization, however. No Jew would be able to say twenty-five years after *this* war that he had deserved well of his country, the Darlanois were determined. They had left one loophole, at the insistence of General Giraud, who was as stubborn in military affairs as he was politically indifferent Jews, Moslems, foreigners held in concentration camps, former soldiers of the Foreign Legion, and anybody not formally enrolled with a regular class of the Army Reserve could volunteer in a new catch-all organization called the Corps Franc d'Afrique, which was promised immediate service in the front line. "If they want to fight, let them fight," Giraud said. "Nobody stops them." He was constitutionally impervious to the argument that segregation impaired their rights as Frenchmen. He meant it when he said that the only right that counted was the right to kill Germans. But the Pétainist civil officials considered the Corps Franc a beautiful invention for silencing obstreperous fellows of all creeds. "If you are such a patriot, join the Corps Franc," they said. Meanwhile they remained in their grandiose offices five hundred miles from the firing line, scheming to requisition all the most comfortable villas in Algiers and move into them before British or American bigwigs did. The competition for palaces was keen and absorbed a deal of the war energy of all three allies.

Dr. Aboulker had both wounds and decorations in profusion. His right leg had been shattered by machine-gun bullets and then ingeniously patched together again, but he could walk only with the aid of a cane, a detail the humorous significance of which will become apparent shortly to the reader. His apartment, a collection of large high-ceilinged rooms on the second or third floor of a fine *immeuble* dating from about 1900, reminded me irresistibly of that of Dr. Perrot, the anti-Semitic physician I had visited in Oran. A man's taste is formed more by his culture, his profession, and the period in which he is young than by his race or politics. The two apartments contained the same mixture of pretentious nineteenth-century furniture, which looked archaic, and of painting which had been revolutionary in the two physicians' youth and still seemed fresh, from the late impressionists through *les fauves*. The doctor was a somber old man who kept his hat on in the house for fear of drafts. One of his sons, a straight, slender lad in his early twenties, was in the group that received me. The others, all, I think, Jews, included my jeweler friend, a philosopher, a couturier, and several others whose callings I do not remember, a paradoxical group of putschists. Two of the younger men there, they told me, had been at the by-now famous conference between General Mark Clark, Murphy, and the two French officers who had prepared the plan for our Algiers landing, when Clark had been brought by submarine to a beach villa owned by one of the group. One of the young men had waded into surf up to his chest to steady the kayak in which the general had made his way back to the submarine. They said that Murphy had used the Aboulker apartment as his headquarters during the months of preparation for the putsch and even on the night when the landing was expected. According to the original plans for that night, they said, the Americans were supposed to land in the harbor of the city at one o'clock. At eleven the putschists, 540 young men of whom 450 were Jews, went out with arms which the United States Government had furnished to them and seized the telegraph office, the municipal power plant, the Préfecture of Police, and other nerve centers, and arrested the ranking army officers who were not in on the plot and Admiral Darlan himself. Some of them said they were sorry they had not killed Darlan then. He had temporized, saying he would join them, and they had only held him prisoner. "It would have been easy to finish him if killing had been part of our plan," one man said, "but we lacked the habit of ruthlessness." The Americans had not appeared on schedule, some of the officials whom the putschists had missed at their first swoop had alerted the troops stationed in the suburbs, and by two o'clock in the morning the putschists themselves had been besieged in the various buildings they had taken. The troops outnumbered them and had artillery. After a resistance during which several of their number had been killed, the pro-Allied civilians had surrendered. They had held Darlan for four hours, and it is easy to understand how much their attack had served to distract attention from our landing. By eight o'clock the next morning the Americans were in possession of the city. During the course of the day they freed the men who, if our attack had been a failure, would certainly have been tried and executed by Darlan's gang. "It is now almost impossible for one of us to see Mr. Murphy," the old doctor said. "He shuns us like a case of an extremely contagious disease."

"The army brass hats and the people of the Préfecture whom we arrested hate us," one of the younger men said. "They hate us because we know what cowards they are. You should have seen how miserably they acted when they saw the tommy guns, the brave Jew-baiters. The chief of the secret police, who has been of course restored to his position, kneeled on the floor and wept, begging one of my friends to spare his life. Imagine his feeling toward the man who spared him! Another friend, a doctor, is to be mobilized—in a labor camp, of course—under the military jurisdiction of a general whom *he* arrested." After a good deal more talk and the consumption of a couple of glasses of white wine—too sweet, exactly like that the anti-Semite had offered me—a couple of the younger men drove me home to my hotel in an automobile. I was too late to eat at the officers' mess, so I had dinner at a black-market restaurant that had been recommended to me. I had mushroom soup, *rouget de la Méditerranée meunière,* a couple of grilled thrushes, chicken en casserole, rum cake with cream, oranges, coffee, and a bottle of Veuve Clicquot of a year I hadn't heard of but which did well enough to wash down campaign fare. I was happy in the possession of a great deal of information which could do me no professional good because I couldn't have got it through the censor. But useless possessions are always the ones we revel in. I was also happy that night because I thought I knew that the pessimism of the Aboulker circle was exaggerated. "Be patient," I had told them, "the heart of the State Department is in the right place. It has only been temporarily mislaid—perhaps under a lettuce seed."

The telephone in our room summoned Dave Brown fairly early next morning to the downtown office building where the Allied Forces had set up their public-relations headquarters. I fancied it had something to do with politics but didn't worry much about it. At about eleven I had my breakfast of black imitation coffee, a dry piece of bread, and watery *confiture* and my cold bath. I could have had a good breakfast at the mess up until eight-fifteen, and there was hot water at the hotel until nine, but I never got up that early. I dressed and walked down to public relations myself to see if I had received any money. When I entered the correspondents' room there Dave told me that the French government of North Africa had announced the arrests of fifteen persons for plotting to assassinate General Giraud. Their names had not been announced, but anti-collaborationists had already supplied half a dozen correspondents with tentative lists. "You hadn't been out of Dr. Aboulker's apartment half an hour," Dave said, "when they arrested everybody there. They picked up the fellows who drove you home, too." It occurred to me immediately that the secret police whom our sympathizers had arrested on the landing night now were back in power, and that opportunities for a frame-up were excellent. The boy who had killed Darlan had been executed without any public hearing; the men of the Préfecture could attribute any statement they wished to him. Infallibly they would say he had implicated every prominent De Gaullist in town in a double murder plot, of which he had carried out the first half. That is what they did say.

A few days later—this incident is out of precise sequence, but it seems to belong here—a small, dapper young man called on me at the hotel and told me that the married daughter of Dr. Aboulker wanted to see me to relate the circumstances of his arrest, and that she and her husband would meet me in her father's apartment that afternoon. I went up there with Dave, whose superiors in London were continually bombarding him with requests for information on the political story that he couldn't send out. The daughter, whose married name I forget, was an extraordinarily pretty and spirited brunette. The political police, armed with tommy guns, had arrived soon after my departure, she said, when she was alone in the apartment with her father and her two children, aged three and eight. Her father was in an electric cabinet, treating the leg that had been shattered in the World War and that still bothered him. She had answered the door and a plain-clothes man had pushed a tommy gun into her stomach while another had pointed his sub-machine gun at her eight-year-old boy and ordered him to put his hands up. The brave Fascists were taking no chances. Then a dozen detectives had searched the apartment for weapons. "There weren't any, luckily," she said, "because we had got rid of those M. Murphy had furnished to us." They had dragged her father from his cabinet, not allowed him to dress, and hauled him off to jail without his trousers. "They would not let him take his cane," she said, "and without it he cannot stand upright, which amused them. They dragged him down the stairs. I haven't been allowed to see him in prison. By the way," she said, "I have something here that will amuse *you*."

She walked off into another room and came back carrying a black Homburg hat. She handed it to me. It was quite a good hat, made by Christy's of London, the kind that anybody who wanted to be mistaken for a Foreign Office man might be glad to wear.

"The hat of M. Murphy!" she said. "He left it here that evening of the landing. He said, 'I will be right back' and went out. He hasn't been here since!"

CHAPTER V

Giraud Is Just a General

THE WEEK THAT FOLLOWED the arrest of our former agents in Algiers restored all the esteem I had had for newspapermen when I was twenty years old. After enough years newspapermen begin to pall on other newspapermen; they begin to take their good qualities for granted and wince at their shortcomings, of which the most common are a vanity that sometimes borders on the thespian and a sort of perpetual mental adolescence that I think stems from starting work on a fresh story every day or every week or month and never having time to get to the bottom of anything. They forget that newspapermen as a class have a yearning for truth as involuntary as a hophead's addiction to junk. The question of whether the junkie really loves hop is academic; he can't get along without it. A newspaperman may write a lie to hold his job, but he won't believe it, and the necessity outrages him so that he craves truth all the more thereafter. A few newspapermen lie to get on in the world, but it outrages them, too, and I have never known a dishonest journalist who wasn't patently an unhappy bastard.

There were about thirty journalists in Algiers at the time, including radio reporters, and not one of them accepted the official French version of the arrests—that the motive had really been the safety of General Giraud—or the far more disturbing official American efforts to play down the whole affair. The journalists, like my cockney in Poplar, weren't 'aving any. It made me all the happier that not only the professing liberals, but the representatives of conservative papers, and the plain routine second- and third-string representatives of press associations all got the idea. I think it even impressed the Army and State Department people running the North African show. They could stop us from sending our stuff out, and they did, but they saw in us an articulate, tangible cross section of the opinion they would have to face at home. There was no division on national lines; British and American correspondents were in complete accord.

Largely, I think, because of the row we raised, General Bergeret, who had come to Africa as Darlan's personal assistant and had remained with Giraud, virtually running the civil side of the administration, and Rigault, a character in charge of public relations, became aware that people of the Allied powers would not accept so crude a return to Gestapo government. The Anglo-American press of Algiers was therefore summoned to an interview with General Henri Honoré Giraud himself. The general thought our protest an unwarranted intrusion into a routine administrative affair. He had not checked on the affair personally because he was too busy with his army. Giraud believed, as a military principle, in standing by one's subordinates. All his principles are military. He was therefore going to put us in our places.

The office where he received us was in a secondary school for boys, and we were herded into his presence much as if we were going before the headmaster. After we had stumbled forward one by one to have our hands crushed in his psychologically steely grip, we stood back and waited, in our habitual civilian postures. The general's eye wandered over us moodily, and I imagined that he had expected us to hold *"Fixe!"* until he had said *"Repos!"* Brigadier General Robert McClure of the United States Army, who was in charge of Allied public relations and censorship in the theater of war, was to attend the mass interview, but his automobile had been delayed in the blackout. I could see Giraud getting angrier by the second at having to wait for a general four stars down to him. Giraud wears five. A few wispy hairs which stood apart from the main body of his moustache and got in the path of his breath quivered like shreds of paper in front of a powerful electric fan. He sat down at his desk, and his aide ordered us all out of the room until McClure arrived. We went into one of the classrooms and sat on some benches, hoping we would not be expelled from school.

Giraud is as straight and nearly as tall as De Gaulle, but he is better-proportioned, more in drawing. Also he has been a general for so much longer that he has settled into the role more comfortably. De Gaulle's expression is occasionally irascible, as if he anticipated that somebody might challenge his authority. The thought has not occurred to Giraud for years. The painter he suggests is not El Greco, but Meissonier. He is, as I had known ever since the Battle of France, a good general.

When General McClure arrived at the schoolhouse, we all filed into the Giraud presence again. McClure is happily ignorant of French; Giraud could not say anything to him except through the intermediary of an officer far junior to a brigadier general. One cannot say to a captain, "Ask the brigadier general, in English, where the hell he has been." According to military protocol the situation was impossible. All Giraud's actions are limited by military conceptions. He therefore said nothing to McClure.

He began his discourse to us by saying that he was happy to be making war by the side of an ally so rich in the most modern material. When his army had marched through Belgium and into Holland to engage the Germans in 1940 he had had only seven airplanes for a quarter of a million men. Now he had 50,000 men fighting in Tunisia, and fighting well, and he had hoped to have modern equipment for them. He had been promised modern equipment, but it was not here. He looked accusingly at us, as if some correspondent might be wearing a 2½-ton truck in a shoulder holster. He could not for the life of him, he said, see why there was so much fuss about a dozen civilians, who might or might not be guilty, when hundreds of his people were being killed every week because they were fighting with only rifle ammunition and little of that. A British captain named Hyphensmith translated for the benefit of those who could not understand French.

"I am not interested in politics," the general said, "I make war."

One of the correspondents said that since this was a war for democracy, a word which brought no change in the general's expression, it was important that the people of occupied countries should not get the idea that if they helped us we would after our arrival permit them to be put in jail. I said that many of the current North African officials who remained in power had been put in by Vichy as selected watchdogs who could be depended upon. The general said he did not know of one such official. Since he had been a prisoner of war through most of the Armistice and had arrived in Africa only after our landing, he may not have known much, but he had certainly heard a lot.

Frank Kluckhohn of the New York *Times,* through the intermediary of Captain Hyphensmith, passed up a list of the reported prisoners to the general and asked him to verify it. There were about a dozen names on the list, including those of a couple of men high in the political police who had known about the plot to aid the Allied landing and helped conceal it. There were Dr. Aboulker and two of his sons, a man named Brunel who was the son of a former mayor of Algiers, and some others. Giraud said, triumphantly, "See how accurate your information is!" and crossed off a couple of names, including that of Aboulker, who we all knew quite well was in jail. Giraud's manner recalled Napoleon calling a grenadier by name, after having just received the information from the grenadier's corporal. I was sure he had been misinformed by his Gestapo, even to the identity of the men arrested. When he came to the extremely Corsican names of the two police officials—one of whom he later appointed Prefect of Algiers—he said, "These men withheld information from their superiors. A good policeman does not withhold information from his superior!" He himself had been in a submarine on his way to Africa when the policemen had "withheld," and if these men had informed their superiors the landing would have been opposed and Giraud perhaps captured. But it was hard for him to pardon a breach of discipline, even in the enemy's camp. He said that no trials of the accused men were contemplated. He seemed genuinely puzzled by our exaggerated interest in the affair.

Giraud, although entitled to dozens of decorations, wore none. His un-ribboned, khaki chest would have been conspicuous even on a French captain. As we were about to leave, one of the British correspondents asked him why he wore no decorations.

"Because I have taken an oath not to wear any until I enter Metz at the head of a victorious army," Giraud said. I thought that his choice of an objective made the man clear. A politician would have said Paris, a sentimentalist would have named his own native province. But Metz is a garrison town, the most important strategically on the Franco-German frontier. The soldier wanted to get back to his barracks.

Giraud, I felt, would react to any attack on Bergeret and Rigault as De Gaulle had to reflections on his precious Colonel P———— in London a year or so earlier, by suspecting the detractors of his subordinates. But more than anything else he wanted to fight and beat the Germans, and he was as susceptible to a gift of matériel as a little child to candy. I had known civilian intellectuals incapable of visualizing the reality of war; Giraud was the reverse of the

medal. He had no civilian imagination. Freudians would be astonished by a human 100 per cent masculine or 100 per cent feminine.
Giraud is even more astonishing in his way. He is 100 per cent a
general.

The dressing down of the correspondent corps by General Giraud
having produced no carminative results, we were invited to the
villa of M. Murphy for cocktails and a conference on New Year's
Eve. This was a parallel to the hard and soft method employed by
New York detectives in reducing a prisoner to reason. M. Murphy
lived in a fine villa high on the fashionable hill. The cocktails were
good, there was a fire on the great hearth, a dog wandered among
the guests to soften their hearts toward its master, after the English
manner. Everything was *très gentleman*. M. Murphy deprecated
the importance of the arrests, regretted that the strict censorship of
political despatches would have to stay on, implied that Darlan had
not been such a bad fellow after all, and in general tried to pour
gin on the troubled waters. He got so many arguments from correspondents that one of the headquarters colonels who was there
for the free drinks became quite petulant about us. Military petu-
lance is usually in proportion to the distance from the firing line and
in inverse ratio to the probability of the officer who is being petulant ever getting there. "We have war to get on with!" this colonel
said, fiercely biting the olive out of a martini. M. Murphy introduced the name of Marcel Peyrouton and asked us what we thought
of him. Everybody who had been in France thought he was terrible,
so Murphy decided to bring him on anyway. Personally, I think
now that it was a good idea. Peyrouton had decided that we were
going to win the war, and he made an excellent ferret for us, bringing numerous collaborationist rats out of the administrative sewers
they were hiding in.

Within the next few months the political situation in Algeria got
much better. The suspected "assassins" were released. Peyrouton
replaced Chatel, the left-over governor general, and then got rid
of the prefects of Algiers and Oran, who were replaced by anti-Axis
men; Brunel, the former mayor, a De Gaullist, got an important
place in the Government; the curious Rigault disappeared from
the office of information and was replaced by General René
Chambe, an aviator and man of letters who had recently escaped
from France and a really topnotch sort; Bergeret lost his importance

235

and was posted to an unimportant command in West Africa. The S.O.L. and the Légion were dissolved, although the Compagnons de France were not, De Gaullist publications from London were allowed into North Africa, the racial laws were abolished and General Giraud went on record in favor of a republican form of government for a redeemed France. I imagine that he did so after the same kind of an educational course that had preceded De Gaulle's *"Liberté, Egalité, Fraternité"* speech from London, but he said it. Critics of the regime complained of the slowness with which reforms were put into effect, but with the diminishing flagrancy of the things they objected to they began to seem merely querulous.

Along with this improvement in political matters, State Department officials in Africa tried to sell the idea that they had intended things thus all the time, and that the stand of the press at home and of the correspondents on the spot had had nothing to do with the change. If so they had certainly concealed their sentiments as expertly as their intentions. I do not think that anything would have changed if we had not got up on our hind legs and yelled. The thesis that the department goes serenely on its way, indifferent to the press, does not always accord with developments.

The trouble was that—

African political affairs had been in a frightful mess while Darlan lived and for about a month thereafter—what would have happened had he survived will always be a subject for unpleasant speculation. A bungling censorship had prevented the British and American publics from getting any exact information, and afterward the public would not believe reports of improvement even when they were true. Ken Crawford, of *PM* and the Chicago *Sun,* arrived in Algiers in February or March and found little to get indignant about. When he told his employers so they decided he had gone over to the enemy. But he hadn't been there in the bad time. Remembering the Darlan days, the liberal press refused to accept *anything* that Washington said about North Africa thereafter. I strongly suspect that the Free French publicity organization here—it sounds a bit absurd to call people on Fifth Avenue Fighting French, to distinguish them from Giraud's troops in Tunisia—took advantage of this opening in their smear-Giraud campaign last spring. They even invented a "Giraudist" movement which they said had been set up by the State Department against De Gaulle. The term

Giraudiste simply doesn't exist in Africa, any more than "Eisen-howeriste" or "Pattoniste," or "Montgomeryiste." Giraud, by his own fervent wish, is just a general.

The time between January 1 and January 23, 1942, was from a military point of view the most ticklish of the whole North African campaign. In November and December the British force with American attached fragments in Tunisia had been small and the Americans along the Algerian coast few and extremely preoccupied with the possibilities in Spanish Morocco. But the German army at Tunis had been even more limited. It had been brought in by troop carrier, glider, and an occasional furtive steamer from Sicily, and it lacked heavy equipment, although it had a short line of supply to the land forces from numerous African ports. Rommel was too far to the east to help the Tunis force, and the supplies pouring into Tripoli went to him. When in January he fell back clear to Tripoli, however, he was in a position where he could shift troops up to Tunisia at will. A force that would not be important in the Libyan theater, where the armies were relatively large, might be strong enough to upset the whole balance of strength in Tunisia, where battalions were still considered important units. Then too there was always the chance that Rommel might pull all his troops out of Tripoli and race for Constantine and Algiers with his whole army.

The problem was eased when the British secured the port of Tripoli on January 23 before Rommel had acquired too much of a head start in the race north. With the short supply line they now had they could keep on his heels all the way, which they did, while the British First Army and the Americans were steadily adding strength in the west. After that he was cooked. Action, if it came at all during January, was bound to begin in southern and central Tunisia, where the Rommel territory overlapped that of Von Arnim, the northern commander. Northern Tunisia was bogged down in mud. Early in January I decided that I had stalled Ross long enough without contributing a story on the shooting war, so I started for the advanced area. I was fed up with the political atmosphere in Algiers anyway.

The easiest way to get into the war was to ride a transport plane out to an advanced airfield, where we had a fighter group, and then if there was not enough to write about there arrange to go by truck or jeep up to one of the two or three detachments of American ground troops in the area. It turned out that the transports were booked full for the morning I had chosen for my departure. An Air Corps major whom I had known in England and re-encountered at Algiers said he could fix that by reserving a place for me on the French courier plane which made a circuit of British and American airports east of Algiers every day, carrying mail and local passengers.

This plane, which was of a type that the French had been allowed to use for courier service even after the Armistice, because it used so little gasoline, did not look as if it could fly into a strong wind. When I first saw it I was conscious of a lack that I could not define. At last it came to me. It was like an illustration from a 1922 magazine and there should have been a Coles Phillips girl in the foreground. A little man in a long overcoat and a soft gray hat came up to me while I stood gazing and asked me where I was going. I told him, thinking he was some kind of a ticket collector, and he opened the door of the plane, climbed in, and said, "Come along, you're the only passenger." He was the pilot. Before he sat down at the controls he pulled a Guide Michelin out of his pocket, looked at it, put it back and said, "*Ça va.*" Then he took off.

We made our first landing at Telergma, south of Constantine, where we picked up a technical sergeant and a box of dates addressed to a lieutenant in a fighter squadron. The man in the long overcoat said to me, "Up to here it's all right, but I've never been to your field, and it's said to be difficult to find, in between some mountains." We carried the tech sergeant to Canrobert and got two British aircraftsmen who said they were on pass and were going back to Algiers with the little man, clean around the circuit via Biskra.

When I had first asked my friend the major about means of flying into the advanced field he had said, "First you get a transport, and then you get about a dozen Spits to act as escort, and then you go in." The man in the long overcoat dropped into the field very nicely, begged me to be so good as to speed the box of dates on its way, tipped his soft hat and flew away, leaving me in the middle of the war.

CHAPTER VI

The Foamy Fields

IF THERE IS ANY WAY you can get colder than you do when you sleep in a bedding roll on the ground in a tent in North Africa two hours before dawn, I don't know about it. The particular tent I remember was at an airfield in a valley. The surface of the terrain was mostly limestone. If you put all the blankets on top of you and just slept on the canvas cover of the roll, you ached all over, and if you divided the blankets and put some of them under you, you froze on top. The tent was a large, circular one with a French stencil on the outside saying it had been rented from a firm in Marseilles and not to fold it wet, but it belonged to the United States Army now. It had been set up over a pit four feet deep, so men sleeping in it were safe from flying bomb fragments. The tall tent pole, even if severed, would probably straddle the pit and not hit anybody. It was too wide a hole to be good during a strafing, but then strafings come in the daytime and in the daytime nobody lived in it. I had thrown my roll into the tent because I thought it was vacant and it seemed as good a spot as any other when I arrived at the field. I later discovered that I was sharing it with two enlisted men.

I never saw my tentmates clearly, because they were always in the tent by the time I turned in at night, when we were not allowed to have lights on, and they got up a few minutes before I did in the morning, when it was still dark. I used to hear them moving around, however, and sometimes talk to them. One was from Mississippi and the other from North Carolina, and both were airplane mechanics. The first night I stumbled through the darkness into the tent, they heard me and one of them said, "I hope you don't mind, but the tent we were sleeping in got all tore to pieces with shrapnel last night, so we just moved our stuff in here." I had been hearing about the events of the previous evening from everybody I met on the field. "You can thank God you wasn't here last night," the other man said earnestly. The field was so skillfully hidden in

239

the mountains that it was hard to find by night, and usually the Germans just wandered around overhead, dropping their stuff on the wrong hillsides, but for once they had found the right place and some of the light anti-aircraft on the field had started shooting tracers. "It was these guns that gave away where we was," the first soldier said. "Only for that they would have gone away and never knowed the first bomb had hit the field. But after that they knowed they was on the beam and they come back and the next bomb set some gasoline on fire and then they really did go to town. Ruined a P-38 that tore herself up in a belly landing a week ago, and I had just got her about fixed up again, and now she's got shrapnel holes just about everywhere and she's hopeless. All that work wasted. Killed three fellows that was sleeping in a B-26 on the field and woke up and thought that was no safe place, so they started to run across the field to a slit trench and a bomb got them. Never got the B-26 at all. If they'd stayed there, they'd been alive today, but who the hell would have stayed there?"

"That thrapnel has a lot of force behind it," the other voice in the tent said. "There was a three-quarter-ton truck down on the field, and a jaggedy piece of thrapnel went right through one of the tires and spang through the chassix. You could see the holes both sides where she went in and come out. We was in our tent when the shooting started, but not for long. We run up into the hills so far in fifteen minutes it took us four hours to walk back next morning. When we got back we found we didn't have no tent." There was a pause, and then the first soldier said, "Good night, sir," and I fell asleep.

When the cold woke me up, I put my flashlight under the blankets so I could look at my watch. It was five o'clock. Some Arab dogs, or perhaps jackals, were barking in the hills, and I lay uncomfortably dozing until I heard one of the soldiers blowing his nose. He blew a few times and said, "It's funny that as cold as it gets up here nobody seems to get a real cold. My nose runs like a spring branch, but it don't never develop."

When the night turned gray in the entrance to the tent, I woke again, looked at my watch, and saw that it was seven. I got up and found that the soldiers had already gone. Like everyone else at the field, I had been sleeping in my clothes. The only water obtainable was so cold that I did not bother to wash my face. I got

240

my mess kit and walked toward the place, next to the kitchen, where they were starting fires under two great caldrons to heat dish water. One contained soapy water and the other rinsing water. The fires shot up from a deep hole underneath them, and a group of soldiers had gathered around and were holding the palms of their hands toward the flames, trying to get warm. The men belonged to a maintenance detachment of mechanics picked from a number of service squadrons that had been sent to new advanced airdromes, where planes have to be repaired practically without equipment for the job. That morning most of the men seemed pretty cheerful because nothing had happened during the night, but one fellow with a lot of beard on his face was critical. "This location was all right as long as we had all the planes on one side of us, so we was sort of off the runway," he said, "but now that they moved in those planes on the other side of us, we're just like a piece of meat between two slices of bread. A fine ham sandwich for Jerry. If he misses either side, he hits us. I guess that is how you get to be an officer, thinking up a location for a camp like this. I never washed out of Yale so I could be an officer, but I got more sense than that."

"Cheer up, pal," another soldier said. "All you got to do is dig. I got my dugout down so deep already it reminds me of the Borough Hall station. Some night I'll give myself a shave and climb on board a Woodlawn express." Most of the men in camp, I had already noticed, were taking up excavation as a hobby, and some of them had worked up elaborate private trench systems. "You couldn't get any guy in camp to dig three days ago," the Brooklyn soldier said, "and now you can't lay down a shovel for a minute without somebody sucks it up."

Another soldier, who wore a white silk scarf loosely knotted around his extremely dirty neck, a style generally affected by fliers, said, "What kills me is my girl's brother is in the horse cavalry, probably deep in the heart of Texas, and he used to razz me because I wasn't a combat soldier."

The Brooklyn man said to him, "Ah, here's Mac with a parachute tied around his neck just like a dashing pilot. Mac, you look like a page out of *Esquire*."

When my hands began to feel warm, I joined the line which had formed in front of the mess tent. As we passed through, we got bacon, rice, apple butter, margarine, and hard biscuits in our mess tins and tea in our canteen cups. The outfit was on partly British rations, but it was a fairly good breakfast anyway, except for the tea, which came to the cooks with sugar and powdered milk already mixed in it. "I guess that's why they're rationing coffee at home, so we can have tea all the time," the soldier ahead of me said. I recognized the bacon as the fat kind the English get from America. By some miracle of lend-lease they had now succeeded in delivering it back to us; the background of bookkeeping staggered the imagination. After we had got our food, we collected a pile of empty gasoline cans to use for chairs and tables. The five-gallon can, known as a flimsy, is one of the two most protean articles in the Army. You can build houses out of it, use it as furniture, or, with slight structural alterations, make a stove or a locker out of it. Its only rival for versatility is the metal shell of the army helmet, which can be used as an entrenching tool, a shaving bowl, a washbasin, or a cooking utensil, at the discretion of the owner. The flimsy may also serve on occasion as a bathtub. The bather fills it with water, removes one article of clothing at a time, rubs the water hastily over the surface thus exposed, and replaces the garment before taking off another one. This is called taking a whore's bath.

There was no officers' mess. I had noticed Major George Lehmann, the commanding officer of the base, and First Lieutenant McCreedy, the chaplain, in the line not far behind me. Major Lehmann, a tall, fair, stolid man had told me that he lived in Pittsfield, Massachusetts, where he had a job with the General Electric Company. When I had reported, on my arrival at the field, at his dugout the day before, he had hospitably suggested that I stow my blanket roll wherever I could find a hole in the ground, eat at the general mess shack, and stay as long as I pleased. "There are fighter squadrons and some bombers and some engineers and anti-aircraft here, and you can wander around and talk to anybody that interests you," he had said.

Father McCreedy is a short, chubby priest who came from Bethlehem, Pennsylvania, and had been assigned to a parish in Philadelphia. He always referred to the pastor of this parish, a Father McGinley, as "my boss," and asked me several times if I knew George Jean Nathan, who he said was a friend of Father McGinley. Father McCreedy had been officiating at the interment of the fellows killed in the raid the evening before, and that was all he would talk about during breakfast. He had induced a mechanic to engrave the men's names on metal plates with an electric needle. These plates would serve as enduring grave markers. It is part of a chaplain's duty to see that the dead are buried and to dispose of their effects. Father McCreedy was also special-services officer of the camp, in charge of recreation and the issue of athletic equipment. "So what with one thing and another, they keep me busy here," he said. He told me he did not like New York. "Outside of Madison Square Garden and the Yankee Stadium, you can have it." He wore an outsize tin hat all the time. "I know a chaplain is not supposed to be a combatant," he said, "but if parachute troops came to my tent by night, they'd shoot at me because they wouldn't know I was a chaplain, and I want something solid on my head." He had had a deep hole dug in front of his tent and sometimes, toward dusk, when German planes were expected, he would stand in it waiting and smoking a cigar, with the glowing end of it just clearing the hole.

When I had finished breakfast and scrubbed up my mess kit, I strolled around the post to see what it was like. As the sun rose higher, the air grew warm and the great, reddish mountains looked friendly. Some of them had table tops, and the landscape reminded me of Western movies in Technicolor. I got talking to a soldier named Bill Phelps, who came from the town of Twenty-nine Palms, California. He was working on a bomber that had something the matter with its insides. He confirmed my notion that the country looked like the American West. "This is exactly the way it is around home," he said, "only we got no Ayrabs." A French writer had described the valley bottoms in southeastern Algeria and Tunisia as foamy seas of white sand and green alfa grass. They are good, natural airfields, wide and level and fast-drying, but there is always plenty of dust in the air. I walked to a part of the field where there were a lot of P-38's, those double-bodied planes that look so very futuristic, and started to talk to a couple of sergeants who were working on one. "This is Lieutenant Hoelle's plane," one of them said, "and we just finished putting a new wing on it. That counts as just a little repair job out here. Holy God, at home, if a plane was hurt like that, they would send it back to the factory or take it apart for salvage. All we do here is drive a two-and-a-half-ton truck up under the damaged wing and lift it off, and then we put the new wing on the truck and run it alongside the plane again and fix up that eighty-thousand-dollar airplane like we was sticking together a radio set. We think nothing of it. It's a great ship, the 38. Rugged. You know how this one got hurt? Lieutenant Hoelle was strafing some trucks, and he come in to attack so low he hit his right wing against a telephone pole. Any other plane, that wing would have come off right there. Hitting the pole that way flipped him over on his back, and he was flying upside down ten feet off the ground. He gripped that stick so hard the inside of his hand was black and blue for a week afterward, and she come right side up and he flew her home. Any one-engine plane would have slipped and crashed into the ground, but those two counter-rotating props eliminate torque." I tried to look as though I understood. "Lieutenant Hoelle is a real man," the sergeant said.

I asked him where Hoelle and the other P-38 pilots were, and he directed me to the P-38 squadron's operations room, a rectangular structure mostly below ground, with walls made out of the sides of gasoline cans and a canvas roof camouflaged with earth. A length of stovepipe stuck out through the roof, making it definitely the most ambitious structure on the field.

Hoelle was the nearest man to the door when I stepped down into the operations shack. He was a big, square-shouldered youngster with heavy eyebrows and a slightly aquiline nose. I explained who I was and asked him who was in charge, and he said, "I am. I'm the squadron C.O. My name's Hoelle." He pronounced it "Holly." There was a fire in a stove, and the shack was warm. Two tiny black puppies lay on a pilot's red scarf in a helmet in the middle of the dirt floor, and they seemed to be the center of attention. Six or eight lieutenants, in flying togs that ranged from overalls to British Army battle dress, were sitting on gasoline cans or sprawled on a couple of cots. They were all looking at the puppies and talking either to them or their mother, a small Irish setter over in one corner, whom they addressed as Red. "One of the boys brought Red along with him from England," Hoelle said. "We think that the dog that got her in trouble is a big, long-legged black one at the airport we were quartered at there."

"These are going to be real beautiful dogs, just like Irish setters, only with black hair," one of the pilots said in a defensive tone. He was obviously Red's master.

"This is a correspondent," Hoelle said to the group, and one of the boys on a cot moved over and made room for me. I sat down, and the fellow who had moved over said his name was Larry Adler but he wasn't the harmonica player and when he was home he lived on Ocean Parkway in Brooklyn. "I wouldn't mind being there right now," he added.

There was not much in the shack except the cots, the tin cans, a packing case, the stove, a phonograph, a portable typewriter, a telephone, and a sort of bulletin board that showed which pilots were on mission, which were due to go on patrol, and which were on alert call, but it was a cheerful place. It reminded me of one of those secret-society shacks that small boys are always building out of pickup materials in vacant lots. Adler got up and said he would have to go on patrol. "It's pretty monotonous," he said, "like driving a fast car thirty miles an hour along a big, smooth road where there's no traffic. We just stooge around near the field, and at this time of day nothing ever happens."

Another lieutenant came over and said he was the intelligence officer of the squadron. Intelligence and armament officers, who do not fly, take a more aggressive pride in their squadron's accomplishments than the pilots, who don't like to be suspected of bragging. "We've been out here for a month," the intelligence officer said, "and we have been doing everything—escorting bombers over places like Sfax and Sousse, shooting up vehicles and puncturing tanks, going on fighter sweeps to scare up a fight, and flying high, looking for a target and then plunging straight down on it and shooting hell out of it. We've got twenty-nine German planes, including bombers and transports with troops in them and fighters, and the boys have flown an average of forty combat missions apiece. That's more than one a day. Maybe you'd like to see some of the boys' own reports on what they have been doing."

I said that this sounded fine, and he handed me a sheaf of the simple statements pilots write out when they put in a claim for shooting down a German plane. I copied part of a report by a pilot named Earnhart, who I thought showed a sense of literary style. He had had, according to the intelligence officer, about the same kind of experience as everybody else in the squadron. Earn-hart had shot down a Junkers 52, which is a troop carrier, in the episode he was describing, and then he had been attacked by several enemy fighters. "As I was climbing away from them," he wrote, "a 20-millimeter explosive shell hit the windshield and deflected through the top of the canopy and down on the instrument panel. Three pieces of shell hit me, in the left chest, left arm, and left knee. I dropped my belly tank and, having the ship under control, headed for my home base. On the way I applied a tourniquet to my leg, administered a hypodermic, and took sulfanilamide tablets. I landed the ship at my own base one hour after I had been hit by the shell. The plane was repaired. Claim, one Ju 52 destroyed." The intelli-gence officer introduced Earnhart to me. He was a calm, slender, dark-haired boy, and he persisted in addressing me as sir. He said he came from Lebanon, Ohio, and had gone to Ohio State.

Still another lieutenant I met was named Gustke. He came from Detroit. Gustke had been shot down behind the German lines and had made his way back to the field. He was a tall, gangling type, with a long nose and a prominent Adam's apple. "I crash-landed the plane and stepped out of it wearing my parachute," he told me, "and the first thing I met was some Arabs who looked hostile to me, and as luck would have it I had forgotten to bring along my .45, so I tripped my parachute and threw it to them, and you know how crazy Arabs are about cloth or anything like that. They all got fighting among themselves for the parachute, and while they were doing that I ran like the dickens and got away from them. I got to a place where there were some Frenchmen, and they hid me overnight and the next day put me on a horse and gave me a guide, who brought me back over some mountains to inside the French lines. I had a pretty sore tail from riding the horse."

A pilot from Texas named Ribb, who stood near by as Gustke and I talked, broke in to tell me that they had a fine bunch of fel-lows and that when they were in the air they took care of each other and did not leave anybody alone at the end of the formation to be picked off by the enemy. "In this gang we have no ass-end Char-lies," he said feelingly.

I asked Lieutenant Hoelle what was in the cards for the after-noon, and he said that eight of the boys, including himself, were going out to strafe some German tanks that had been reported working up into French territory. "We carry a cannon, which the P-40's don't, so we can really puncture a tank the size they use around here," he said. "We expect to meet some P-40's over the target, and they will stay up high and give us cover against any German fighters while we do a job on the tanks. Maybe I had better call the boys together and talk it over."

A couple of pilots had begun a game of blackjack on the top of the packing case, and he told them to quit, so he could spread a map on it. At that moment an enlisted man came in with a lot of mail and some Christmas packages that had been deposited by a courier plane. It was long after Christmas, but that made the things even more welcome, and all the pilots made a rush for their packages and started tearing them open. Earnhart, one of the men who were going on the strafe job, got some National Biscuit crackers and some butterscotch candy and a couple of tubes of shaving cream that he said he couldn't use because he had an electric razor, and the operations officer, a lieutenant named Lusk, got some very rich homemade cookies that an aunt and uncle had sent him from Denver. We were all gobbling butterscotch and cookies as we gathered round the map Hoelle had spread. It was about as formal an affair as looking at a road map to find your way to Washington, Connecticut, from New Milford. "We used to make more fuss over briefings in England," the intelligence officer said, "but when you're flying two or three times a day, what the hell?" He pointed out the place on the map where the tanks were supposed to be, and all the fellows said they knew where it was, having been there before. Hoelle said they would take off at noon. After a while he and the seven other boys went out onto the field to get ready, and I went with them. On the way there was more talk about P-38's and how some Italian prisoners had told their captors that the Italian Army could win the war easy if it wasn't for those fork-tailed airplanes coming over and shooting them up, a notion that seemed particularly to amuse the pilots. Then I went to the P-38 squadron mess with Adler, who had just returned from patrol duty and wasn't going out on the strafe job, and Gustke, who was also remaining behind. This mess was relatively luxurious. They had tables with plates and knives and forks on them, so they had no mess tins to wash after every meal. "We live well here," Adler said. "Everything high-class."

"The place the planes are going is not very far away," Gustke said, "so they ought to be back around half past two."

When we had finished lunch, I took another stroll around the post. I was walking toward the P-38 squadron's operations shack when I saw the planes begin to return from the mission. The first one that came in had only the nose wheel of its landing gear down. There was evidently something the matter with the two other wheels. The plane slid in on its belly and stopped in a cloud of dust. Another plane was hovering over the field. I noticed, just after I spotted this one, that a little ambulance was tearing out onto the field. Only one of the two propellers of this plane was turning, but it landed all right, and then I counted one, two, three others, which landed in good shape. Five out of eight. I broke into a jog toward the operations shack. Gustke was standing before the door, looking across the field with binoculars. I asked him if he knew whose plane had belly-landed, and he said it was a Lieutenant Moffat's and that a big, rough Texas pilot whom the other fellows called Wolf had been in the plane that had come in with one engine out. "I see Earnhart and Keith and Carlton, too," he said, "but Hoelle and the other two are missing."

A jeep was coming from the field toward the operations shack, and when it got nearer we could see Wolf in it. He looked excited. He was holding his right forearm with his left hand, and when the jeep got up to the shack he jumped out, still holding his arm.

"Is it a bullet hole?" Gustke asked.

"You're a sonofabitch it's a bullet hole!" Wolf shouted. "The sonofabitching P-40's sonofabitching around! As we came in, we saw four fighters coming in the opposite direction, and Moffat and I went up to look at them and they were P-40's, coming away. The other fellows was on the deck, and we started to get down nearer them, to about five thousand, and these sonofabitching 190's came out of the sun and hit Moffat and me the first burst and then went down after the others. There was ground fire coming up at us, too, and the sonofabitches said we was going to be over friendly territory. I'm goddam lucky not to be killed."

"Did we get any of them?" Gustke asked.

"I know I didn't get any," Wolf said, "but I saw at least four planes burning on the ground. I don't know who the hell they were."

By that time another jeep had arrived with Earnhart, looking utterly calm, and one of the mechanics from the field. "My plane is all right," Earnhart told Gustke. "All gassed up and ready to go. They can use that for patrol."

The telephone inside the shack rang. It was the post first-aid station calling to say that Moffat was badly cut up by glass from his windshield but would be all right. The mechanic said that the cockpit of Moffat's plane was knee-deep in hydraulic fluid and oil and gas. "No wonder the hydraulic system wouldn't work when he tried to get the wheels down," the mechanic said. The phone rang again. This time it was group operations, calling for Earnhart, Keith, and Carlton, all three of them unwounded, to go over there and tell them what had happened. The three pilots went away, and a couple of the men got Wolf back into a jeep and took him off to the first-aid station. Hoelle and the two other pilots were still missing. That left only Gustke and me, and he said in a sad young voice, like a boy whose chum has moved to another city, "Now we have lost our buddies."

A couple of days later I learned that Hoelle had bailed out in disputed territory and made his way back to our lines, but the two other boys are either dead or prisoners.

A couple of days later I was standing in a chow line with my mess tins at another airfield, over the line in southern Tunisia, waiting to get into a dugout where some mess attendants were ladling out a breakfast of stew and coffee. The field is enormous, a naturally flat airdrome of white sand and alfa grass that doesn't hold rainwater long enough to spoil the runways. All around the field there are bulky, reddish mountains. The sun was just coming up over one of them, and the air was very cold. The mess shack was covered on top and three sides by a mound of earth. It served officers and men of a squadron of P-40 fighters, and on that particular Monday morning I stood between a corporal named Jake Goldstein, who in civilian life had been a Broadway song writer, and a private named John Smith, of New Hope, Pennsylvania, who used to help his father, a contractor, build houses. Goldstein told me about a lyric he had just written for a song to be called "Bombs." "The music that I think of when it goes through my head now," he said, "is kind of a little like the old tune called 'Smiles,' but maybe I can change it around later. The lyric goes:

> *There are bombs that sound so snappy,*
> *There are bombs that leave folks sad,*
> *There are bombs that fell on dear old Dover,*
> *But those bombs are not so bad.*

The idea is that the real bad bomb is when this girl quit me and blew up my heart."

"It sounds great," I told the corporal.

"It will be even bigger than a number I wrote called 'What Do You Hear from Your Heart?'" Goldstein said. "Probably you remember it. Bing Crosby sang it once on the Kraft Cheese Hour. If you happen to give me a little write-up, remember that my name in the song-writing business is Jack Gould." Private Smith started to tell me that he had once installed some plumbing for a friend of mine, Sam Spewack, the writer, in New Hope. "His wife, Bella, couldn't make up her mind where she wanted one of the bathroom fixtures," Smith said, "so I said——"

I never heard any more about Bella Spewack's plumbing, because Major Robert Christman, the commanding officer of the squadron, came up to me and said, "Well, it's a nice, quiet morning." He had his back to the east. I didn't get a chance to answer him, because I started to run like hell to get to the west side of the mound. A number of soldiers who had been scattered about eating their breakfasts off the tops of empty gasoline cans had already started running and dropping their mess things. They always faced eastward while they ate in the morning so that they could see the Messerschmitts come over the mountains in the sunrise. This morning there were nine Messerschmitts. By the time I hit the ground on the lee side of the mound, slender airplanes were twisting above us in a sky crisscrossed by tracer bullets—a whole planetarium of angry worlds and meteors. Behind our shelter we watched and sweated it out. It is nearly impossible to tell Messerschmitts from P-40's when they are maneuvering in a fight, except when one plane breaks off action and leaves its opponent hopelessly behind. Then you know that the one which is distanced is a P-40. You can't help yelling encouragement as you watch a fight, even though no one

250

can hear you and you cannot tell the combatants apart. The Messerschmitts, which were there to strafe us, flew right over the mess shack and began giving the runways and the planes on the field a going over.

We had sent up four planes on patrol that morning, and they tried to engage the strafing planes, but other Germans, flying high to protect the strafers, engaged the patrol. Some "alert" planes that we had in readiness on the perimeter of the field took off in the middle of the scrap, and that was a pretty thing to watch. I saw one of our patrol planes come in and belly-land on the field, smoking. Then I saw another plane twisting out of the sky in a spin that had the soldiers yelling. We all felt that the spinning plane was a Messerschmitt, and it looked like a sure thing to crash into one of the mountains north of us. When the plane pulled out and disappeared over the summit, the yell died like the howl at Ebbets Field when the ball looks as if it's going into the bleachers and then is snagged by a visiting outfielder. It was a Messerschmitt, all right. A couple of minutes later every one of the German planes had disappeared, with our ships after them like a squad of heavy-footed comedy cops chasing small boys.

The fellows who had ducked for cover hoisted themselves off the ground and looked around for the mess things they had dropped. They were excited and sheepish, as they always are after a strafe party. It is humiliating to have someone run you away, so you make a joke about it. One soldier yelled to another, "When you said 'Flop!' I was there already!" Another, who spoke with a Brooklyn accent, shouted, "Jeez, those tracers looked just like Luna Park!"

We formed the chow line again, and one fellow yelled to a friend, "What would you recommend as a good, safe place to eat?"

"Lindy's, at Fifty-first Street," the other soldier answered.

"The way the guys ran, it was like a Christmas rush at Macy's," somebody else said.

Everybody tried hard to be casual. Our appetites were even better than they had been before, the excitement having joggled up our internal secretions. There were arguments about whether the plane that had escaped over the mountain would crash before reaching the German lines. I was scraping the last bits of stew from my mess tin with a sliver of hard biscuit when a soldier came up and told me that Major Rudenburg, whom I had never met, had been killed on the field, that five men had been wounded, and that one A-20 bomber had been ruined on the ground.

After I had washed up my tins, I walked over to the P-40 squadron operations shack, because I wanted to talk to a pilot familiarly known as Horse about the fight he had been in two days before, when I had seen eight P-38's go out from another field to attack some German tanks and only five come back, two of them badly damaged. A lot of Focke-Wulf 190's had attacked the P-38's over the target, and Horse and three other P-40 pilots, who were protecting the 38's, had been up above the 190's. Horse was a big fellow with a square, tan face and a blond beard. He came from a town called Quanah, in Texas, and he was always showing his friends a tinted picture of his girl, who was in the Waves. Horse was twenty-five, which made him practically a patriarch in that squadron, and everybody knew that he was being groomed to command a squadron of his own when he got his captaincy. He was something of a wit. Once I heard one of the other boys say that now that the field had been in operation for six weeks, he thought it was time the men should build a sit-down toilet. "The next thing we know," Horse said, "you'll be wanting to send home for your wife."

I found Horse and asked him about the fight. He said he was sorry that the 38's had had such a bad knock. "I guess maybe it was partly our fault," he said. "Four of our ships had been sent out to be high cover for the 38's. They didn't see any 38's or Jerries either, so when their gas was beginning to run low they started for home. Myself and three other fellows had started out to relieve them, and we passed them as they came back. The 38's must have arrived over the tanks just then, and the 190's must have been hiding at the base of a cloud bank above the 38's but far below us. When we got directly over the area, we could see tracers flying 'way down on the deck. The 190's had dived from the cloud and bounced the 38's, who never had a chance, and the 38's were streaking for home. We started down toward the 190's, but it takes a P-40 a long time to get anywhere, and we couldn't help. Then four more 190's dived from 'way up top and bounced us. I looped up behind one of them as he dived. My two wing men were right with me. I put a good burst into the sonofabitch and he started to burn, and I followed him down. I must have fired a hundred and twenty-five rounds from each gun. It was more fun than a county fair. Gray, my fourth man, put a lot of lead into another 190, and I doubt if it ever got home. The other two Jerries just kept on going."

The P-40 operations shack was set deep in the ground and had a double tier of bunks along three of its walls. Sand and grass were heaped over the top of the shack, and the pilots said that even when they flew right over it, it was hard to see, which cheered them considerably. The pilots were flying at least two missions a day and spent most of the rest of the time lying in the bunks in their flying clothes, under as many coats and blankets as they could find. The atmosphere in the shack was a thick porridge of dust diluted by thin trickles of cold air. Major Christman, the squadron leader, once said in a pleased tone, "This joint always reminds me of a scene in *Journey's End*." The pilots, most of whom were in their earliest twenties, took a certain perverse satisfaction in their surroundings. "Here we know we're at war," one of them said to me. "Not that I wouldn't change for a room and bath at a good hotel."

During most of my stay at the field I lived not in the *Journey's End* shack but in one known as the Hotel Léon because technically it belonged to a French lieutenant named Léon, a liaison officer between the French forces and our fliers. It was the newest and finest dugout on the field, with wooden walls and a wooden floor and a partition dividing it down the middle, and the floor was sunk about five feet below ground level. When I arrived at the field, there were plans to cover the part of the shack that projected above ground with sand, in which Léon intended to plant alfa. I had joined up with an Associated Press correspondent named Norgaard, whom I had met at the first field, and soon after our arrival Léon, a slender man with a thin, intelligent face and round, brown eyes, welcomed us to his palace. We put our stuff into the shack and emerged to find Léon throwing a modest shovelful of sand against one of the walls. Norgaard offered to help him. "There is only one shovel," Léon said with relief, pressing it into Norgaard's hands. "It is highly interesting for our comfort and safety that the house be covered entirely with sand. I am very occupied." Then he walked rapidly away, and Norgaard and I took turns piling sand around the Hotel Léon for endless hours afterward. Léon always referred to a telephone switchboard as a switching board, oil paper as oily paper, a pup tent as a puppy tent, and a bedding roll as a rolling bed.

After my talk with Horse, I walked over to the Hotel Léon and found it crowded, as it usually was. Only Léon and Norgaard and I, together with Major Philip Cochran and Captain Robert Wylie, lived in the hotel, but during the day Cochran and Léon used it as an office, and that was why it was crowded. When I had first come to the field, it had been operating for six weeks practically as an outpost, for there was just a unit of American infantry, fifty miles to the southeast, between it and the region occupied by Rommel's army. Cochran, though only a major, had run the field for almost the entire period, but by the time I arrived he had reverted to the status of operations officer. The shack had telephone lines to detachments of French troops scattered thinly through the hills to our east, and they called up at all hours to tell Léon where German tanks were moving or to ask our people to do some air reconnaissance or drop bags of food to a platoon somewhere on a mountain. The French had no trucks to transport food. Sometimes Cochran flew with American transport planes to tell them where to drop parachute troops, and sometimes he flew with bombers to tell them where to drop bombs. Because of Cochran's and Léon's range of activities, they always had a lot of visitors.

Attached to the partition in the shack were two field telephones, one of which answered you in French and the other in English. Two soldier clerks, who were usually pounding typewriters, sat on a bench in front of a shelf along one wall. One of them was Corporal Goldstein, the song writer. The other was a private first class named Otto, who wore metal-rimmed spectacles with round lenses and belonged to the Pentecostal brethren, an evangelical sect which is against fighting and profanity. Otto owned some barber tools, and he cut officers' hair during office hours and enlisted men's at night. That morning he was cutting the hair of Kostia Rozanoff, the commandant of the Lafayette Escadrille, a French P-40 outfit that was stationed at the field. Rozanoff was a blond, round-headed Parisian whose great-grandfather had been Russian. Otto, perhaps taking a cue from the shape of Rozanoff's skull, had clipped him until he looked like Erich von Stroheim, but there was no mirror, so Rozanoff was happy anyway. Cochran, dressed in a dirty old leather flying jacket, had just come back from a mission in the course of which he thought he had destroyed a 190, and was trying to tell about that while nearly everybody else in the shack was trying to tell him about the morning's strafing. Also in the shack was Colonel Edson D. Raff, the well-known parachutist, who had once unexpectedly found himself in command of all the American ground forces in southern Tunisia and for weeks had successfully bluffed enemy forces many times larger. He had flown in from his post in Gafsa in a small plane which he used as his personal transport. He was crowded in behind Otto's barbering elbow and was trying to talk to Cochran over Rozanoff's head. Raff is short and always wore a short carbine slung over his left shoulder, even indoors. He invariably flies very low in his plane to minimize the risk of being potted by a Messerschmitt. "I have one foot trailing on the ground," he says.

Lieutenant Colonel William Momyer, the commanding officer of the field, was sitting between Rozanoff and Corporal Goldstein, telling about a mission he had been on himself that morning, escorting a lot of A-20's over Kebili, a town where the Italians had begun to repair a dynamited causeway across the Chott Djerid. "I bet the wops will never get any workmen to go back to that place," Momyer said. "We scared hell out of them." Momyer had shot down a Junkers 88 and a Messerschmitt within a week. He was hot.

Among the others in the shack that morning were Norgaard, the Associated Press man, and a tall P-40 pilot named Harris, who kept asking Léon whether any French unit had telephoned to report finding the Messerschmitt he had been shooting at during the strafing episode, because he was sure it must have crashed. It was the Messerschmitt we had seen pull out of the spin over the mountain. The English-speaking telephone rang, and Captain Wylie answered it. He has the kind of telephone voice that goes with a large, expensive office, which he probably had in civilian life. It was somebody up the line asking for Major Rudenburg, the officer who had just been machine-gunned in the strafing. "Major Rudenburg has been killed," Wylie said. "Is there anything I can do for you?"

There was a variety of stuff on the field when I was there. In addition to Christman's P-40 squadron and the Lafayette Escadrille, there was a second American P-40 squadron, commanded by a Major Hubbard, which had a full set of pilots but only five ships. This was because the powers that be had taken away the other ships and given them to the Lafayettes in the interest of international good will. Hubbard's pilots were not sore at the Lafayettes, but they didn't think much of the powers that be. There was also a bomber squadron. The people on our field were not by any means sitting targets. They constantly annoyed the Germans, and that is why the Germans were so keen on "neutralizing" the field. But they didn't come back that day, and neither lunch nor dinner was disturbed.

The guests of the Hotel Léon often didn't go to the mess shack for dinner, because Léon would prepare dinner for them on the premises. He was a talented cook, who needed the stimulation of a public, which was, that Monday evening, us. He also needed Wylie to keep the fire in the stove going, Cochran to wash dishes, and me and Norgaard to perform assorted chores. He got eggs from the Arabs and wine from a near-by French engineer unit, and he had gathered a choice assortment of canned goods from the quartermaster's stores. He also bought sheep and pigs from farmers. Léon's idea of a campaign supper was a *soufflé de poisson,* a *gigot,* and an *omelette brûlée à Parmagnac.* He made the soufflé out of canned salmon. The only trouble with dining at Léon's was that dinner was seldom ready before half past eight and it took until nearly midnight to clean up afterward.

During that Monday dinner we speculated on what the enemy would do next day. Norgaard said it was hell to have to get up early to catch the Germans' morning performance, but Cochran, the airfield's official prophet, said, "They'll want to make this one a big one tomorrow, so you can sleep late. They won't be over until two-thirty in the afternoon." Momyer, who was having dinner at the "hotel" that night, agreed that there would be something doing, but he didn't predict the time of day. Léon said, "I think also that there is something cooking in." Momyer decided to maintain a patrol of eight planes over the field all day. "Of course, maybe that's just what they want us to do, use our planes defensively, so we will fly less missions," he said, "but I think this time we ought to do it."

I had such faith in Cochran that it never occurred to me that the Germans would attack us before the hour he had named, and they didn't. The only enemy over the field the following morning was Photo Freddie, a German reconnaissance pilot who had become a local character. He came every morning at about forty thousand feet, flying a special Junkers 86 job so lightened that it could outclimb any fighter. The anti-aircraft guns would fire, putting a row of neat, white smoke puffs a couple of miles below the seat of Freddie's pants, the patrol planes would lift languidly in his direction, like the hand of a fat man waving away a fly, and Photo Freddie would scoot off toward Sicily, or wherever he came from, to develop his pictures, thus discovering where all the planes on the field were placed. The planes were always moved around after he left, and we used to wonder what the general of the Luftwaffe said to poor Freddie when the bombers failed to find the planes where he had photographed them. Now and then some pilot tried to catch Photo Freddie by getting an early start, climbing high above the field, and then stooging around until he appeared. Freddie, however, varied the hour of his matutinal visits, and since a P-40 cannot fly indefinitely, the pilot would get disgusted and come down. I do not think anybody really wanted to hurt Freddie anyway. He was part of the local fauna, like the pet hens that wandered about the field and popped into slit trenches when bombs began to fall.

At about twenty minutes past two that afternoon Norgaard and I returned to the Hotel Léon to do some writing. An Alsatian corporal in the French Army was working in front of the shack, making a door for the entrance. The corporal had been assigned by the French command to build Léon's house, and he was a hard worker. He always kept his rifle by him while he was working. He had a long brown beard, which he said he was going to let grow until the Germans were driven out of Tunisia, so I wouldn't recognize him if I saw him now. Only Goldstein and Otto were inside the hut this time. I said to Goldstein, "Why don't you write a new number called 'One-Ninety, I Love You'?" Otto, who had been reading the *Pentecostal Herald,* said, "I do not think that would be a good title. It would not be popular." At that precise moment all of us heard the deep *woomp* of heavy ack-ack. It came from one of the British batteries in the mountains around the field. We grabbed our tin hats and started for the doorway. By the time we got there, the usual anti-aircraft show was on. In the din we could easily distinguish the sound of our Bofors guns, which were making their peculiar seasick noises—not so much a succession of reports as one continuous retch. The floor of the shack, as I have said, was five feet below ground level, and the Alsatian had not yet got around to building steps down to the entrance, so we had a nice rectangular hole just outside from which to watch developments. The Germans were bombing now, and every time a bomb exploded, some of the sand heaped against the wooden walls was driven into the shack through the knotholes. The only trouble was that whenever a bomb went off we pulled in our heads and stopped observing. Then we looked out again until the next thump. After several of these thumps there was a straight row of columns of black smoke a couple of hundred yards to our right. I poked my head above ground level and discovered the Alsatian corporal kneeling and firing his rifle, presumably at an airplane which I could not see. The smoke began to clear, and we hoisted ourselves out of the hole to try to find out what had happened. "I do not think I touched," the Alsatian said. A number of dogfights were still going on over the mountains. Scattered about the field, men, dragging themselves out of slit trenches, were pointing to the side of a mountain to the north, where there was smoke above a downed plane.

Léon had a little old Citroën car, which he said had become, through constant association with the United States Army, "one naturalized small jeeps." He had left it parked behind the shack, and as Norgaard and I stood gawping about, Léon came running and shouted that he was going out to the fallen plane. We climbed into the "naturalized jeeps" and started across the field toward the mountainside. At one of the runways we met a group of P-40 pilots, including Horse, and I yelled to them, "Was it theirs or ours?" "Ours, I think," Horse said. We kept on going. When we reached the other side of the field, we cut across country, and Léon could not make much speed. A couple of soldiers with rifles thumbed a ride and jumped on the running boards. As we went out across plowed fields and up the mountain toward the plane, we passed dozens of soldiers hurrying in the same direction.

When we arrived where the plane had fallen, we found three trucks and at least fifty men already there. The plane had been a Messerschmitt 109 belonging to the bombers' fighter escort. Flames were roaring above the portion deepest in the earth, which I judged was the engine. Screws, bolts, rings, and unidentifiable bits of metal were scattered over an area at least seventy-five yards square. Intermingled with all this were widely scattered red threads, like the bits left in a butcher's grinder when he has finished preparing an order of chopped steak. "He never even tried to pull out," a soldier said. "He must have been shot through the brain. I seen the whole thing. The plane fell five thousand feet like a hunk of lead." There was a sour smell over everything—not intolerable, just sour. "Where is the pilot?" Norgaard asked. The soldier waved his hand with a gesture that included the whole area. Norgaard, apparently for the first time, noticed the red threads. Most of the soldiers were rummaging amid the wreckage, searching for souvenirs. Somebody said that the pilot's automatic pistol, always the keepsake most eagerly sought, had already been found and appropriated. Another soldier had picked up some French and Italian money. While the soldiers walked about, turning over bits of the plane with their feet, looking for some object which could serve as a memento, an American plane came over, and everybody began to run before someone recognized it for what it was. Just as we came back, a soldier started kicking at something on the ground and screaming. He was one of the fellows who had ridden out on our running boards. He yelled, "There's the sonofabitch's goddam guts! He wanted my guts! He nearly had my guts, God damn him!" Another soldier went up to him and bellowed, "Shut up! It ain't nice to talk that way!" A lot of other men began to gather around. For a minute or so the soldier who had screamed stood there silently, his shoulders pumping up and down, and then he began to blubber.

Léon picked up a large swatch of the Messerschmitt's tail fabric as a trophy, and as the soldiers walked away from the wreck most of them carried either similar fragments or pieces of metal. After a while Norgaard and I climbed into Léon's car, and the three of us started back toward the field. When we arrived we learned that a lieutenant named Walter Scholl, who had never been in a fight before, had shot down the Messerschmitt. He was the fellow who, in the Cornell-Dartmouth football game of 1940, threw the famous fifth-down touchdown pass for Cornell, the one that was completed for what was considered a Cornell victory until movies of the game showed that it shouldn't have been Cornell's ball at all and the decision had to be reversed. Two other pilots had shot down two

Junkers 88 bombers. One of our planes on the ground had been destroyed, and a slit trench had caved in on two fellows, nearly frightening them to death before they could be dug out.

Norgaard often said that southern Tunisia reminded him of New Mexico, and with plenty of reason. Both are desert countries of mountains and mesas, and in both there are sunsets that owe their beauty to the dust in the air. The white, rectangular Arab houses, with their blue doors, are like the houses certain Indians build in New Mexico, and the Arabs' saddle blankets and pottery and even the women's silver bracelets are like Navajo things. The horses, which look like famished mustangs, have the same lope and are similarly bridlewise; burros are all over the place, and so is cactus. These resemblances are something less than a coincidence, because the Moors carried their ways of house-building and their handicraft patterns and even their breed of horses and method of breaking them to Spain, and the Spaniards carried them to New Mexico eight hundred years later. All these things go to make up a culture that belongs to a high plateau country where there are sheep to furnish wool for blankets and where people have too little cash to buy dishes in a store, where the soil is so poor that people have no use for heavy plow horses but want a breed that they can ride for long distances and that will live on nearly nothing.

"This horse is young," an Arab once said to Norgaard and me as he showed us a runty bay colt tied in front of a combined general store and barbershop in a village about a mile from the airfield. "If I had had a little barley to feed him, he would be bigger, but what barley we had we have ourselves eaten. It is a poor country."

We used to go down to this village to get eggs when we were too lazy to make the chow line for breakfast or when we felt hungry at any time of day. We'd take them back to the shack a bunch of us were living in and cook them. Solitary Arabs squat along the roadsides all over North Africa, waiting for military vehicles. When one comes into sight, the Arab pulls an egg out from under his rags and holds it up between thumb and forefinger like a magician at a night club. The price of eggs—always high, of course—varies in inverse ratio to the distance from a military post. Near big towns that are a long way from any post the Arabs get only five francs (ten cents at the new rate of exchange) for an egg, but in villages close to garrisons eggs are sometimes hard to find at any price. Norgaard and I followed a standard protocol to get them. First we went into the general store and barbershop, which was just a couple of almost empty rooms that were part of a mud house, and shook hands with all the male members of the establishment. Naturally, we never saw any of the females. Then we presented a box of matches to the head of the house, an ex-soldier who spoke French, and he invited us to drink coffee. The Arabs have better coffee and more sugar than the Europeans in North Africa. While we drank the coffee, we sat with the patriarch of the family on a white iron bed of European manufacture. The patriarch had a white beard and was always knitting socks; he stopped only to scratch himself. Once, as we were drinking coffee, we watched our French-speaking friend shave a customer's head. He started each stroke at the top of the cranium and scraped downward. He used no lather; the customer moistened his own poll with spittle after each stroke of the razor. Once, when the customer made a particularly awful face, all the other Arabs sitting around the room laughed. During the coffee-drinking stage of the negotiations we presented the Arabs with a can of fifty English cigarettes. After that they presented us with ten to fifteen eggs. Soldiers who were not such good friends of theirs usually got twenty eggs for fifty cigarettes, but it always costs something to maintain one's social life. One day I asked the barber why the old man scratched himself, and he said, laughing, "Because of the black spots. We all have them, and they itch." With much hilarity the Arabs showed us the hard, black spots, apparently under their skins, from which they were suffering. I judged the trouble to be a degenerate form of the Black Death, tamed during the centuries by the rugged constitutions of our hosts. Norgaard thought that the spots were just chiggers.

The Germans had come over our airfield on a Monday morning and strafed it, and they had come back on Tuesday afternoon and bombed the place. They were going to start an offensive in southern Tunisia, we later learned, so they wanted to knock out this, the most advanced American field. On Wednesday morning the Germans made no attack. That afternoon Norgaard and I decided that we needed some eggs, so we walked down to the Arab village. I carried the eggs home in my field hat, a visored cap which has long flaps to cover your neck and ears when it is cold and which makes a good egg bag. We got back to the Hotel Léon between five and six o'clock. Cochran was out flying, and Léon was out foraging. Jake and Otto, the two soldier clerks who worked there during the day, had gone to chow. There was less than an hour of daylight left.

Cochran, who had a fine instinct for divining what the Germans were likely to do, had been sure that they would come over for the third day in succession, and Lieutenant Colonel William Momyer, the commanding officer of the field, had maintained a patrol of P-40's over the field all day. Cochran was among those taking their turns on patrol duty now. In forty minutes more all the planes would have to come down, because the field had no landing lights. And nothing had happened yet.

The walk had made Norgaard and me hungry, and we decided to have our eggs immediately. We threw some kindling wood in the stove to stir the fire up, and I put some olive oil in the mess tin in which I was going to scramble the eggs. The olive oil belonged to Léon. I took the lid off the hole in the top of the stove, put the mess tin over the hole, and broke all the eggs into the oil. I think there were eleven of them. They floated around, half submerged, and although I stirred them with a fork, they didn't scramble. We decided that I had used too much oil, so we added some cheese to act as a cement. Before the cheese had had time to take effect, we heard a loud explosion outside—plainly a bomb—and felt the shack rock. Norgaard grabbed his tin hat and ran out the door to look, and I was just going to follow him when I reflected that if I left this horrible brew on the stove hole a spark might ignite the oil and thus set fire to the shack. I carefully put the mess on a bench and replaced the lid on the stove. I put on my helmet and followed Norgaard out into a kind of foxhole outside our door. More bombs exploded, and then all we could hear was the racket of the Bofors cannon and .50-caliber machine guns defending the field. I went back inside, removed the stove lid, and put the eggs on again. Just as some warmth began to return to the chilled mess, another stick of bombs went off. In the course of the next minute or so, I repeated my entire routine. Before I finished cooking dinner, I had to repeat it three times more. Finally the eggs and the cheese stuck together after a fashion and I drained the oil off. Then, since no bombs had dropped for a couple of minutes, I poured half the concoction into

Norgaard's canteen cup, I put what was left in my mess tin, and we ate.

After we had eaten, we left the shack and started toward the large, round pit, some fifty yards away, which served as a control room for the field. Night had closed in. There had been no firing now for ten minutes, but as we approached the pit, our anti-aircraft opened up again, firing from all around the field simultaneously. The Bofors tracer shells, which look like roseate Roman candles, reminded me of the fireworks on the lagoon at the World's Fair in Flushing. The burst ended as abruptly as it had begun, except that one battery of .50's kept on for an extra second or two and then stopped in an embarrassed manner.

We saw a lot of our pilots clustered around the pit. A corporal named Dick usually stood in the pit talking to our planes in the air by radio telephone, but Major Robert Christman was in Dick's place this time. I recognized Christman's voice as he spoke into the telephone, asking, "Did you see the gunfire? Did you see the gunfire?" You wouldn't ask a Jerry that if you were shooting at him, so I knew they were firing the anti-aircraft guns to light one or more of our planes home. Christman asked again, "Did you see the gunfire? Did you see the gunfire?" Then he said to somebody else in the pit, probably Dick, "Hold this a minute." He stuck his head up over the side of the pit and shouted in the direction of a near-by dugout, "They say they saw the fire! Cochran's going to lead in and land to show the other ship the way! Lord, how that Cochran swears when he's excited! Tell the ack-ack to hold everything!" The switchboard through which the control room communicated with all the ack-ack batteries was in the dugout. Nothing was convenient on that field. It sometimes seemed that one of the pilots had scratched the whole thing out of the ground with a broken propeller blade after a forced landing.

We could see a plane showing red and green lights slowly circling over the field, descending gradually in long, deliberate spirals, as if the pilot wanted somebody to follow him. Then there was a blast of machine-gun fire, and a fountain of tracers sprayed up from a distant edge of the field. "God damn them!" Christman yelled. "Tell them to hold that fire! What do they want to do—shoot Phil down?" The plane coasted slowly, imperturbably lower. It was Cochran's firm belief, I knew, that the ack-ack on the field had never hit anything, so he probably wasn't worried. The plane skimmed over the surface of the field. There was one pitiful red light on the field for it to land by, like the lantern a peddler would hang on the tail of a hobbled donkey to keep him from being hit by a motorcar. "He'll never make it that way," a pilot near me said. "What the hell is he doing? He'll overshoot. No, there he goes up again."

In a minute Christman, back at the phone once more, said, "Cochran went up because the other fellow couldn't see him. The other ship says he saw the gunfire, though. Now he wants a burst on the southern edge of the field only." Somebody in the switchboard dugout yelled, "Come on now! Battery C only, Battery C only! Everybody else *hold* it!" All the guns on the field immediately fired together. I could hear Momyer's voice yelling in the dugout, "God damn it, I'll have them all court-martialed!" Christman shouted, "He says he saw it and now he can see Cochran! He's coming in!" Cochran was again circling in the blackness above the field. The pilot next to me said, "This is sure sweating it out." I recognized him, partly by his voice and partly by the height of his shoulders, as Horse.

"Did we get any of theirs?" I asked Horse.

"Yes, sir," Horse said. "Bent got one for sure. He's in already. And a French post has telephoned that another one is down near there in flames and that pilot out there with Cochran had one smoking. He must have chased it so far he couldn't get back before dark. Must have forgot himself. I don't rightly know who he is."

The ack-ack batteries fired again. They apparently did what was wanted this time, because nobody cursed. Christman called up from the pit, "They want one more burst, all together, and then they're coming in!" The message was relayed, and the ack-ack fired another salvo. Now there were two planes, both showing lights, moving in the sky above the field, one high and one low. "Cochran's coming in," Horse said. "Look at him. Just like it was day and he could see everything." The lower pair of lights drifted downward, straightened out and ran forward along the field, and stopped. The other lights slowly followed them down, seemed to hesitate a moment, then slanted toward the ground and coasted into a horizontal. "Good landing," Horse said. "We sure sweated that one." The second pilot to land turned out to be a lieutenant named Thomas, who had become too absorbed in the pursuit of a Junkers

88 to turn back until he had shot it down. That made three Junkers for us, each carrying a crew of four men. I learned that the German bombs had spoiled, to use the airmen's term, two of our planes on the field. A couple of minutes later a jeep that had gone out to meet Cochran's plane brought him to where the rest of us were standing. He is a short, box-chested man, and the two or three flying jackets he was wearing made him look shorter and stockier than he really is. He was feeling good. "I'm sorry I cursed you out, Bob! I was excited!" he yelled down into the control pit to Christman. Momyer, who had come out of the dugout, made as if to grab Cochran and hug him, but stopped in astonishment when he heard Cochran being so polite. It seemed to remind him of something. Looking rather thoughtful, he went back into the dugout and called up the lieutenant colonel in command of the ack-ack, which he had been abusing. "Thank you very much, Colonel," I heard him say. "Your boys certainly saved the day."

That evening was a happy one. Léon's shack was crowded with pilots talking about the successful fight and scrambling eggs and eating them out of mess tins. Cochran felt so good that he decided to have his first haircut since he had left New York, three months before, so he sent over to the enlisted men's quarters for Otto to do the job. Otto is a young man with reddish hair and white eyebrows and a long nose, and he had a habit of getting interested in a conversation between two senior officers and breaking into it. Once, hearing Colonel Edson D. Raff, the parachute-troop commander, telling Lieutenant Colonel Momyer that he could take Tunis with no more than four hundred and fifty men, Otto blurted out, "How can you be so sure?" Aside from this failing he is a good soldier, and when he gives a haircut he really cuts off hair, so nobody can say he is looking for a return engagement in the near future. "I never cut human hair back home on the farm, but I used to clip all our horses," Otto once said.

It was well after dark when Léon came in from his foraging, which had been a success too. "I have bought three small peegs," he announced triumphantly, "and when they are theek enough we shall eat them." He had left them in the care of a *hôtelier* in a town a few miles away. They were subsequently taken, and presumably eaten, by the Germans. At the time, however, Léon thought it a safe *logement* for the pigs. "I have also talked with the aide of

General Koeltz," Léon said to Cochran and Momyer, "and he says that in the case any pilot sees any trucks moving on the road of which we have spoken yesterday, he is allowed to shoot without permission." While Otto cut Cochran's hair, we added up the box score of the three-day German attack on the field. The home team felt that it had done pretty well. During the Monday strafing the Germans had spoiled one of our planes on the field and another in the air and had killed one officer, a major, with machine-gun bullets. We had merely damaged one of their fighters. On Tuesday, while they had spoiled two more of our planes on the ground with bombs, we had shot down a Messerschmitt 109 and two Junkers 88's. That meant that we had lost a total of three planes but only one life while they had lost three planes and nine lives. One of our missions had also destroyed a Focke-Wulf 190 on Monday morning and a Messerschmitt had been badly damaged in the dogfight that had accompanied the strafing of our field. Wednesday evening we had destroyed three more planes and twelve men, and the Germans had succeeded only in damaging two planes on the ground, which gave us an imposing lead. "They won't be over tomorrow morning," Cochran said. "Maybe not all day. They'll want to think things over and try something big to make up for their losses and get the lead back. They'll be like a guy doubling his bet in a crap game."

That field had been fought over many times before in the course of history, and a corner of it had been the site of a Carthaginian city. Bent, a pilot who talked with a British accent and had once done some digging among old ruins in England, said that every time he flew over that corner he could plainly see the gridiron pattern of the ancient streets on the ground. Horse was irreverent about Bent's archaeological claims. "Maybe a couple of thousand years from now," he said, "people will dig around this same field and find a lot of C-ration cans that we've left and attribute them to archaeology. They'll say, 'Those Americans must surely have been a pygmy race to wear such small helmets. It scarcely seems possible they had much brains. No wonder they rode around in such funny airplanes as the P-40.' "

Another officer who turned up in Léon's shack that evening was Major (afterward Lieutenant Colonel) Vincent Sheean, who always points out these days that he was once a correspondent himself. He said he had been driving in a jeep on a road near the field when the bombing started, so he had stopped and jumped into a ditch. Sheean had come down from the second highest headquarters of the African Air Forces to see that the French pilots of the Lafayette Escadrille, which had recently arrived at our field, received understanding and kind treatment from their American comrades. A couple of the Lafayette pilots happened to be in the shack when he arrived; they had imbibed so much kind treatment that they could hardly remember the words of *"Auprès de Ma Blonde,"* which they were trying to teach to Momyer on a purely phonetic basis.

The next day, Thursday, was as quiet as Cochran had said it would be. The Germans left us completely alone. In the morning the Lafayette Escadrille fellows went on their first mission, covering a French local offensive in a mountain pass, and returned without meeting any enemy aircraft.

The exposed position of our mess shack had begun to worry Major Christman's men after the strafing we had received the Monday before, and he had ordered the chow line transferred to a place called the Ravine, a deep, winding gulch on the other side of the high road along one end of the field. Most of the men lived in the Ravine and felt safe there. They had scooped out caves in its sides and used their shelter halves to make doors. One stretch of the gully was marked by a sign that said "Park Avenue." Sheean and I stood in the chow line for lunch and then took an afternoon stroll along Park Avenue. Afterward I went back to Léon's shack to write a letter and found it crowded, as usual. An engineer officer who had been at the field a couple of days was asking Cochran how he could be expected to get on with the construction job he had been sent there to do if new bomb holes appeared on the field every day and his detachment had to fill them up. "We've been filling up bomb holes ever since we been here, and it looks like we won't get a chance to do anything else," the engineer said. "My colonel sent me down here to build revetments for airplanes, and he's going to expect me back soon." Another visitor, a captain in the Royal Engineers, asked him if there were any unexploded bombs on the runways. Men on the field always referred to this British captain as the booby-trap man, the planting of fiendish traps for the enemy being his specialty, and added with respect, "Even the parachute troops say he's crazy." He had made several jumps with Colonel Raff's parachutists to install his humorous devices in places where he thought German soldiers would later get involved with them. The American officer told him that there were several unexploded bombs on the runways and that he had marked off their positions with empty oil drums.

"But haven't you removed the fuses?" the booby-trap man asked with obvious astonishment.

"To hell with that!" his American colleague said with feeling. "They won't do any harm if they do go off. It's a big field."

"Oh, but they'll make quite a lot of noise," the booby-trap man said, still vaguely unhappy.

The American officer looked at the booby-trap man and Cochran as if they were both lunatics and went out of the hut without saying anything more. "How *extraordinary!*" the booby-trap man said. "He didn't even seem interested." He sounded hurt, like a young mother who has just learned that a visitor does not care for babies.

The booby-trap man looked like a conventional sort of Englishman, with a fair, boyish face and a shy smile. He spoke with the careful accent of the north countryman who has been to a university and he did not himself use the term "booby trap." He preferred to call his darlings, variously, trip mechanisms, push mechanisms, pull mechanisms, and anti-personnel switches. Trip mechanisms, for instance, are the ones soldiers inadvertently set off by stumbling over a concealed wire, and pull mechanisms are those they explode by picking up some innocent-seeming object like a corned-beef tin. The captain was an amateur botanist and seldom went out without a couple of pocketfuls of small devices to set about the countryside in likely spots as he ambled along, collecting specimens of Tunisian grasses. I asked him that afternoon how he had started on what was to become his military career, and he said with his shy smile, "I expect it was at public school, when I used to put hedgehogs in the other boys' beds. After a while the hedgehogs began to pall, and I invented a system for detuning the school piano, so that when the music master sat down to play 'God Save the King' it sounded god-awful."

"I sometimes try to imagine what your married life will be like, Captain," Cochran said. "Someday the baby will be in the crib and your wife will go to pick it up and the whole house will blow up because you've wired the baby to a booby trap."

"I trust I shall be able to restrain my professional instincts to fit the circumstances of domestic life," the booby-trap man said rather stiffly. He was a man who really took his branch of warfare seriously.

About a month later he blew himself up with a very special mine he was laying to protect our retreat from Kasserine. He simply disintegrated.

Sleep in the Hotel Léon was usually interrupted in the gray hour before dawn by the jangle of a field telephone that spoke French. Then Léon, whom the rest of us residents called *Monsieur le patron*, would sit up and pull the telephone from the holster in which it hung at the foot of his bed. He slept wearing all the clothes he possessed, which included several sweaters, a long military overcoat, and a muffler. When he grabbed the phone, he would say, *"Allo! Oui?"* (The rest of us sometimes would sing "Sweet Allo, Oui" to the tune of "Sweet Eloise.") The French voice at the other end of the phone was almost always audible, and, so that the half-awake American officers in the shack would get the idea of what was going on, Léon would reply in a hybrid jargon. He would say, for example, "One *ennemi appareil* flying sousewest over point 106? *Merci, mon capitaine.*" Then he would hang up and fall back into bed, muttering, *"Imbécile,* why he don't fly west? He will be losted."

A partition divided Léon's shack into a bedroom, in which four of us slept side by side, and an office, in which only two slept. In the bedroom were Léon, Major Philip Cochran, Norgaard, and myself. Captain Robert Wylie and Major Vincent Sheean slept in the office. We would ignore Léon's first morning call, but before long there would be another; Cochran would be asking what was going on, and we would hear the roar of motors warming up for the dawn patrol and the morning missions. Then we would hear Wylie clattering around our stove in his G.I. shoes, and there would be a glow in the shack when he put the match to the paper with which he started the fire. Wylie, who wasn't a flying officer, always tried to have the shack warm by the time Cochran got up, and he wanted the major to stay in bed until the last minute. He was as

solicitous as a trainer with a favorite colt, and the rest of us benefited from the care he took of Cochran, because we didn't get up
early, either. Wylie is a wiry man with a high forehead and a
pepper-and-salt mustache. He wears glasses and looks like an advertising artist's conception of an executive who is in good humor
because he has had an excellent night's sleep owing to Sanka. He is
a highly adaptable man. After Wylie had puttered around for a
while, we would sit up one by one and stretch and complain about
being disturbed or about the cold and then go outside to wash.
Mornings on which the anti-aircraft opened up against early visitors, the tempo was accelerated. Cochran undressed at night by
loosening the knot in his tie and drew it tight again in the morning
as a sign that he was dressed. These were symbolic gestures he never
omitted.

On the morning of the fifth and last day of the small private war
during which the Germans had been trying hard to knock out our
field, it was the anti-aircraft that brought us out of bed. We scrambled for the door, lugging our tin hats, our toothbrushes, and our
canteens. The Germans were already almost over our field, but
they were quite high, since our patrol planes had engaged them on
the way in and they could not break off the fight to strafe us. The
German planes were single-engined fighters, which sometimes carry
wing or belly bombs, but this time they were not bombing. Some of
the defending planes were marked with the tricolor *cocarde* of the
French Army. It was, I suppose, a historic combat, because the
pilots of the Lafayette Escadrille were making the first French air
fight against the Germans since the armistice of 1940. The Escadrille, which had been equipped with a number of our Curtiss
P-40's in Morocco, had been with us only a few days.

As we watched, a plane fell, apparently far on the other side of a
ridge of mountains near the field, and we yelled happily, thinking it
was a Messerschmitt. After the fight we were to learn that it had
been a P-40 with a French sergeant pilot. Cochran kept up an expert running commentary on what all the pilots were trying to do,
but he frequently didn't know which were French and which Germans. During the battle we simultaneously watched and brushed
our teeth. A couple of the French planes landed on the field while
the others were still fighting, so we knew that they must have been
shot up. Finally, one group of planes above the field started away

and the others chased them, but the first planes simply outclimbed their pursuers and left them behind; then there was no longer any doubt about which were Messerschmitts and which were Curtisses. One German plane remained over the field, at perhaps thirty thousand feet, even after the rest of the invaders had disappeared. "That's what kills me," Cochran said, pointing to the lone plane. "There's that sucker stooging around and casing the joint for a strafe job, and he's so high nobody can bother him." Finally the stooge, evidently having found out all he wanted to know, took his leisurely departure.

A group of P-40's from one of the two American P-40 squadrons at the field rose to relieve the Lafayettes, and the French planes came buzzing in like bees settling on a sugared stick. In a few minutes Kostia Rozanoff, commandant of the Escadrille, and his pilots had gathered in Léon's shack to discuss the fight. All of them had had combat experience in 1939 and 1940, but the engagement this morning had been the *rentrée,* and they were as excited as if they had never seen a Messerschmitt before. Despite the fact that they were old hands, Cochran said, they had fought recklessly, climbing up to meet the Messerschmitts instead of waiting until the Germans dived. "If they don't dive," Cochran had frequently warned his own pilots, "you just don't fight." The French pilots' ardor had got them a beating, for besides the pilot whom we had seen fall and who, Rozanoff said, had not bailed out and was quite certainly killed, the two planes that had landed during the combat were riddled and would be of no use except for salvage, and one of their pilots had been wounded. The Germans apparently had suffered no damage at all. Rozanoff is thirty-seven and has a deep voice like Chaliapin's. He said that the pilot who had been killed was his wing man, and he could not understand how he had failed to see the Messerschmitt that had attacked him from the rear. "I cry him turn," Rozanoff kept saying. "I turn. He turns not. Poor little one."

It was extremely sad that the first Escadrille combat had not been a victory; it would have been such a fine story to bolster French morale all over the world. I remembered the sergeant pilot, who had been a likable fellow. An officer of the district gendarmerie brought the sergeant's wedding ring back to the field later in the morning.

My friend Norgaard and I had chosen that Friday for our departure from the field. We were going in to the big city, where the censors and the cable officers were, to write some stuff and get it off. There was air transportation between our field and the more settled places to the west, where staff officers and diplomats lived, but the service did not run on a formal schedule. Big Douglas transports skimmed in over the mountains once and sometimes twice a day, carrying mail and supplies, and they usually had room for passengers going back. They came at a different hour each day to make it as hard as possible for the Germans to waylay them. When they came, they stayed merely as long as was necessary, and the only way to be sure of a ride was to have your bedding roll made up and to stay near the landing field, waiting for the transports to appear. When they did, an officer would drive you and your luggage out to them in a jeep and you would get your stuff aboard. Norgaard and I hung around in front of our shack that morning, waiting. As the day wore on, a strong wind came up and blew great clouds of sand. At about eleven o'clock two transports arrived, escorted by some Spitfires. Cochran had planned to drive us down to the transports, but he was called to the telephone, and Major Robert Christman said that he would drive us instead.

When we arrived where the transports were standing on the runway, the transport captain, whose name, I noted from the leather strip on the breast of his flying jacket, was Lively, came over to the jeep and asked where his Spits could get gas. The name painted on his ship was Scarlett O'Hara. He and Christman started discussing what was the quickest way to get the gas. Christman and Norgaard and I stayed in the jeep. Dust was blowing over the field a mile a minute. Suddenly Christman looked over his shoulder, called on God, and vanished. Simultaneously Lively was also gone. I turned around to speak to Norgaard and discovered that he too had evaporated. I hate to sit in an empty jeep when I don't know why the other passengers have jumped. I do not remember actually getting out myself, but I know that I was already running when I heard somebody yell, "Hit the dirt!" Under the circumstances, this sounded so sensible that I bellyflopped to the ground, and I landed so hard that I skinned my knees and elbows. No surface in the world offers less cover than a runway. I regretted that my body, which is thick, was not thinner. I could guess what had happened:

German strafers had ridden in on the dust storm, and nobody had seen them until they opened fire. I knew that the very nasty noises above me were being made by airplane cannon and that the even nastier ones close to me came from the detonation of the small explosive shells they fire. The strafers, I figured, were heading for the transports—large, expensive, unarmored jobs that you could punch holes in with a beer-can opener. I was therefore in line with the target and was very sorry to be where I was. I thought, illogically, "I am sorry to leave Liebling before I know how his life turns out."

As soon as there was a lull in the noises overhead, I got up and ran toward the edge of the runway to get away from the transports, but more noises came before I made it, so I flopped again. After they had passed, I got up and ran off the runway. I saw a soldier in a fine, large hole nearly six feet deep. He shouted, "Come right in, sir!" You can have Oscar of the Waldorf any time; I will always remember that soldier as my favorite host. I jumped in and squeezed up against him. Almost immediately the noises came a third time, and two transport pilots jumped down on my back. I was astonished that I had been able to outrun such relatively young men.

By this time all of our machine guns along the edges of the field were firing away, and there was a fourth pass, as the fliers say, and a loud crash, as if one of the Germans had dropped a bomb. A minute or two later the noise began to die down. Looking up from the bottom of the hole, we could see a man descending in a parachute. The big, white chute was swaying this way and that in the wind. The man had an awful time landing. We could see that even from a distance. The chute dragged him and bounced hell out of him after he landed. Afterward, word got around the field that he was an American. I didn't find out until a couple of days later, though, that the man with the chute had been Horse, the big, square-bearded, twenty-five-year-old Texan pilot I had come to know well. In landing, he hit his head against the ground and suffered a concussion of the brain. They put him in an ambulance and started for the nearest hospital, which was forty miles by road, but he had bad luck. The Germans had been strafing that road, too, that morning, and when the ambulance got within five miles of the hospital, it was blocked by two burning ammunition trucks. The shells on the trucks were exploding. The squadron surgeon and the ambulance driver

273

put Horse on a stretcher and carried him around the trucks to a safe point on the other side, and an ambulance from the hospital came out to pick him up, but by the time it got there he was dead.

When the shooting at the field was over, the pilots and the soldier and I got out of the hole and walked back toward the transports, which were still there. Norgaard climbed out of another hole not far away. He said that when he had jumped out of the jeep he had crawled under it, and there he had found a transport lieutenant who had had the same idea. They had given up the jeep after the first pass and run for it, just as I had already done. We stared at the parallel furrows the Messerschmitt cannon had plowed down the runway, as if they had been the teeth of a rake and ourselves the field mice between them. The transport boys borrowed our jeep to get gas for the Spits, which had been immobilized during the raid because their tanks were empty. When the boys came back, we climbed into one of the transports. The big planes took off almost immediately. "Leave them laughing," Norgaard said to me when he recovered sufficient breath to say anything.

We learned later that the strafing had been done by eight Messerschmitts flying in four loose pairs, and that was why there had been four passes. Another Messerschmitt, making a run by itself, had dropped one bomb, ineffectually. There had also been a high cover of Messerschmitts; one of them had accounted for Horse. We were told that Cochran had said, with a hint of admiration in his voice, "It is getting so that the Germans patrol our field for us." A lot of Air Forces generals who were on a tour of inspection visited the field shortly after we left, said that the situation was very grave, and left, too. This point in the war over the field may be compared to the one in a Western movie at which the villain has kicked hell out of the heroine and just about wrestled her to the brink of ruin in a locked room.

At about two-thirty that same afternoon the Lafayette Escadrille was patrolling the field, in the company of two pilots from the American P-40 squadron that was commanded by Major Hubbard. This squadron had its full complement of pilots but only five planes. The pilots took turns flying the five ships, so they were not getting a great deal of practice. Nevertheless, Hubbard's squadron had already scored two victories that week. The two American pilots in the air were Hubbard and a man named Beggs. Two of their mates,

Boone and Smith, were on the ground on alert call, sitting in their planes ready to reinforce the patrol if they were called.

This field didn't have one of those elaborate radio airplane-detectors that warn swank airdromes of the approach of enemy aircraft. It had to rely on its patrol system and on tips that watchers telephoned in. The tipsters were not infallible, as Norgaard and I had noticed that morning, and in the afternoon they slipped up again. Ten Junkers 88 bombers unexpectedly appeared, flying toward the field at three thousand feet. There was an escort of four fighters, unusually small for so many bombers, flying high above them and, as someone described it to me, acting oddly uninterested. The Frenchmen on patrol, also flying high, made one swipe at the escort and it disappeared, not to be seen again. Nine of the bombers were flying in three loose V's, and one ship was trailing the third V. Hubbard took the bomber on the right of the first V and shot it down. Beggs got the middle one, and a Frenchman knocked down the one on the left. The other Junkers had begun to drop their bombs. Boone and Smith came up off the field through the falling bombs to join the battle. Hubbard shot down another plane, and Boone, who had never fired a shot at a man or a plane before, came up behind one Junkers and blasted it out of the sky; it caromed against another Junkers on the way down, which gave Boone two planes with one burst of fire. He went on to destroy two more. Smith, opening fire at extreme range for fear that he would be shut out, blew the rudder off another Junkers, which also crashed. The tenth Junkers headed for home, but it never got there; the French picked off that one. It was the jack pot, ten out of ten. It was also the end of the five-day war over our airfield. No producer of Westerns ever wound up a film more satisfactorily. The Germans stayed away, in fact, for nineteen days and then came back only once, for a quick sneak raid.

Of the ten German bomber crews, only four men came out of the fight alive, and two of these died in the hospital. The two others said that the ten bombers had been escorted by four Italian Macchi C. 202 fighters, which had deserted them. Why the Luftwaffe should have entrusted four Macchis with the protection of ten Junkers 88's is harder to explain than the result. The Germans, fortunately for our side, sometimes vary their extreme guile with extreme stupidity.

I didn't have a chance to return to the airfield for about ten days, and then I stopped in on my way down to Gafsa, where the Americans were supposed to be launching a ground offensive. Captain Wylie, who told me about the big day at the field, said that Boone had come into the operations shack looking rather incredulous himself. "Probably I'm crazy," he had said to Wylie, "but I think I just shot down four planes." The Frenchmen said it was a victory for three nations: "The Americans shot down seven planes, we shot down two, and the Italians shot down the tenth so the crew couldn't tell on them."

The Americans left the field undefeated, for the two P-40 squadrons were relieved not long afterward by other outfits and sent back from the fighting zone to rest. Christman's squadron had been fighting there steadily for two months. I met the fellows from Christman's bunch again while I was trying to get a ride into civilization from another airfield, a bit west of the one where they had been stationed. A lot of trucks drove up and deposited the officers and men of the squadron on the field, with their weapons, their barracks bags, and their bedding rolls. Christman was there, and Private Otto, the squadron barber, and Corporal Jake Goldstein, the reformed song writer. I renewed my acquaintance with a pilot named Fackler, whom I remembered especially because he had once, finding himself in flying formation with two Messerschmitts who thought he was another Messerschmitt, shot one of them down, and I again met Thomas, the Oklahoma boy who had been lost in the air and had been lighted home by the fire of the field's antiaircraft guns, and a non-flying lieutenant named Lamb, who used to practice law in New York, and a dozen others. I felt as if I had known them all for a long time.

Eleven transports came in to take the squadron west, and I arranged to travel in one of them. I was in the lead ship of the flight, and the transport major who commanded it told me that his orders were to drop the squadron at a field only about an hour's flight away. Then the transports would go on to their base, taking me along with them. It was pleasant to see the faces of the P-40 boys aboard my transport when it took off. They didn't know anything about the field they were going to, but they knew that they were going for a rest, so they expected that there would at least be huts and showers there. They looked somewhat astonished when the transports settled down in a vast field of stubble without a sign of a building anywhere around it. There were a few B-25 bombers on the field, and in the distance some tents. A transport sergeant came out of the pilot's compartment forward in our plane and worked his way toward the tail of our ship, climbing over the barracks bags heaped in the space between the seats. "I guess this is where you get out," he told the P-40 fellows.

A couple of soldiers jumped out, and the rest began passing out bags and rifles to them. Pretty soon all the stuff was piled outside the plane and the soldiers were standing on the field, turning their backs to a sharp wind and audibly wondering where the hell the barracks were. A jeep with an officer in it drove out from among the tents and made its way among the transports until it arrived at our ship. The transport major talked to the officer in the jeep, and then they both drove over to the transport Christman was traveling in and picked him up, and the three of them drove back to the tents. Some soldiers who had been near the jeep had heard the field's officer say that nobody there had been notified that they were coming. The transport major had replied that all he knew was that he had orders to leave them there. The soldiers who had heard the conversation communicated the news to the others by army telegraphy. "Situation normal!" one soldier called out, and everybody laughed. Soldiers are fatalistic about such situations.

Some time before, a report had circulated among the men that the squadron was to go back to the United States. Now I heard one soldier say, "This don't look like no United States to me."

Another one said, "When we get back there, Freddie Bartholomew will be running for President." He didn't seem sore.

Somebody said, "I hear they're going to start us here and let us hack our way through to South Africa."

Somebody else began a descant on a favorite army fantasy: what civilian life will be like after the war. "I bet if my wife gives me a piece of steak," he said, "I'll say to her, 'What the hell is this? Give me stew.' "

Another one said, "I bet she'll be surprised when you jump into bed with all your clothes on."

The delicacy of their speculations diminished from there on.

After a while the jeep came back. The transport major got out and said, "There seems to be some mistake. You'd better put your stuff back in the ship." We all got back into the planes, and the major told me that this obviously wasn't the place to leave the men but that he would have to wait until base operations could get head-quarters on the telephone and find out their destination. We sat in the planes for an hour; then another officer came out in a jeep and said that nobody at headquarters knew anything about the squad-ron, so the major had better not take it any place else. The major told his sergeant to instruct the men to take their luggage off the planes. "We enjoy doing this. It's no trouble at all," one of the sol-diers in my plane said. The transports took off and left them stand-ing there. I learned later that they eventually got straightened out. After two or three days someone remembered them; the pilots were sent to western Morocco, and the ground echelon was moved to another field.

All this happened what seems now to be long ago, in the pioneer days of the American Army in Tunisia. The old field, from which I had watched the five-day war, was never knocked out from the air, but it was taken by German ground troops with tanks, and then the Americans took it back and went on. The Hotel Léon, if the Ger-mans hadn't burned it, was certainly full of booby traps for the Americans when they got there. I shouldn't have liked to sleep in it. Léon went back to Algiers, but he didn't like it and got back to the front for the last big push in April as liaison officer with a British tank outfit. Cochran has been promoted, and decorated several times and posted to a training command in the United States. He always said that he liked hatcheck chicks, but when he got back to New York, he says, he found that most of his favorites had become welders. I met the Alsatian corporal again in early May, on the Rue Bab-al-Zoun in Algiers. He was a sergeant by then and limp-ing, because he had walked into an anti-personnel mine near Pichon. Happily it had not been set by an expert like our poor booby-trap man, because it had not killed him.

CHAPTER VII

First Act at Gafsa

GAFSA, the Capsa of the Numidians, is a very ancient town on a very slight hill. Warm springs gush from the foot of the hill under a fifteenth-century Arab citadel, which was wrecked by our engineers last February. The citadel was still intact when I first saw the place. There is an oasis around the town, which used to be an important knot in the cord of caravan routes between the Sahara and the Mediterranean. Gafsa had last winter, and by now probably has again, about ten thousand inhabitants, of whom five or six hundred are Europeans, eight hundred are native Jews, and the rest Arabs. The male Europeans, some of whom have their families with them, are government functionaries or employees of the railroad; the Jews, whose ancestors came there not a great while after the Destruction of the Temple, are traders and traditionally middlemen between the Christians and Moslems.

The climate there even at the end of January, when Norgaard and I reached the place, was warm and dry. A battalion of the Twenty-sixth Infantry was stationed in the town, with some batteries of French 75's, a battalion of Senegalese, and some Algerians, Zouaves, or Tirailleurs. The Americans, who were out of the First Division, were the only ground troops we had south of Sbeitla, which was about fifty miles away. They had been there for a month and were quite at home in the place, which, as almost every enlisted man you talked to was sure to say, looked like a set in a *Beau Geste* movie of the Foreign Legion. Old Jews sold surprisingly good native pastries, and Arabs peddled dates in the square in front of the American barracks. The soldiers had adopted Arab kids as mascots and clothed them in G.I. shirts and shoes. There was a great outdoor Roman swimming pool, filled by running warm water from the spring, which had a good deal of sulphur in it but was still pleasant to bathe in, and the Americans spent a lot of time swimming in it. The French soldiers preferred to dangle fishlines into the stream near its source and catch small blue fish, extremely voracious, which apparently were used to living in hot water. There was also a clean Arab bath, in a narrow *Arabian Nights* alley, where the attendants would stretch you on the floor and twist your arms and legs out of joint and then pound you with a hot brick before allowing you to steam yourself in peace. I remember seeing the English booby-trap man, pink and jolly from the steam, in the Arab bath, wearing a towel around his loins. People leave you with curious last pictures of them, in a war.

The men of the Twenty-sixth had carried out numerous raids against Italian detachments that occasionally appeared in the no man's land to the east, between Gafsa and Maknassy. Neither adversary had any fixed garrison in this flat, desolate stretch of about seventy miles. Once the fellows from Gafsa had bagged eighty-four prisoners—that was reckoned a big haul for southern Tunisia in January. But during the entire night that followed the arrival of Norgaard and myself the sound of armored vehicles moving into and through the town never ceased; morning found most of the First Armored Division in readiness for the big thrust to the sea we had heard about.

Here, in the words of the old Yorkshire song, is where we get our own again. Earlier in the book I have described the fight that Norgaard and I saw between Gafsa and Sened, and I can continue here from the end of it. After we returned from the battlefield and heard that the offensive had been countermanded and our 200-odd casualties would apparently have to be written off to training, we went over to the mess of a French battery to have dinner. The battery was commanded by a captain named O'Neill, whose family had emigrated to France from Ireland in the seventeenth century. He looked like a conventional O'Neill, blue-eyed and florid and saddle-nosed, but he spoke English to Norgaard with a heavy French accent. Captain O'Neill had a battery of three guns, one of the original four having been found useless, and he had as prime mover for the three guns one old motor truck that burned alcohol, so the battery moved in installments, one gun at a time. Their shooting, he said, was very good, but they never arrived at any place in time to shoot. We showed up at the mess before O'Neill and his officers, who were accustomed to dining late, whereas American Army chow is usually dished up early. A young native Jew who wore a blue beret and a European business suit invited us into his house for an *apéritif* while we waited. He had delicate Arab features and eyes as blue as O'Neill's, and he spoke excellent French.

The Jew's one-story house was large and square, with thick mud walls to insulate it from the summer sun. It was built around a small circular court that let in air and daylight. The house looked ageless, like most of the others in town; the Numidians had probably built in exactly the same fashion—but the rooms leading off the court were wired for electric light and filled with heavy gaudy contemporary furniture from some factory in Europe. The Jew's ancient bearded father, who spoke no French, and his small, comely brunette wife and gray-eyed daughter kissed our hands. He poured sweet wine for us and gave us olives and sliced turnips pickled in lemon. His name was Chemouni. When a servant who had been left on watch outside came in and told us that O'Neill had arrived, we left the Chemounis, feeling faintly embarrassed by their fervor. I remembered them a few weeks later, when I heard that we had abandoned Gafsa to the advancing Germans and Italians.

At Gafsa, Norgaard and I slept without blankets on the concrete floor of a former French barracks. A captain in a regiment of armored infantry had spread his bedding roll in a corner of the same building. His regiment was not in the fighting; he had been sent up by his colonel as some sort of observer. The captain was a Virginian; he and Norgaard got to talking about a book by Douglas Freeman, called *Lee's Lieutenants,* that they had both read. The captain, like us, had been out on the battlefield, observing. He seemed pretty tired. He said that he knew old Freeman well; the author was a friend of the captain's family, and as a boy the captain had accompanied the already adult writer on long rambles over the Virginia battlefields. The captain told us he had a house at Yellow Tavern, where Jeb Stuart had been killed. There were Yankee musketballs imbedded in the stair rails, he said. "People down in my part of the country talk about battles as if they were some kind of fine antique, like old lace," he said. "I always used to daydream about them as a kid. But, my God, if I'd known a battle was like this——"

It reminded me of Stendhal writing in his diary: "All my life I have longed to be loved by a woman who was melancholy, thin, and an actress. Now I have been, and I am not happy."

Next morning every soldier in town knew that the offensive had been called off. A part of the armor had already pulled out during the night, roaring north on the road to Feriana and Sbeitla. But the troops who had taken Sened Station held it firmly. We heard that there were captured enemy guns and tanks there, and since captured matériel, like prisoners in quantity, was still a novelty at that stage of the campaign, Norgaard wanted to drive out to have a look. As soon as we had got out on the naked road between Gafsa and Sened both of us, I think, were again sorry we had quit the shade of the palm trees and anti-aircraft guns. The hot metallic sky that it hurt your eyes to look into hung over the road and weighed down on your brain with its implicit Messerschmitts; every group of tanks or guns you met parked off the road seemed an invitation to air attack, and you hurried to get away from it. Then, until you reached the next collection of armor, you felt lonely. Signs along the road warned drivers to keep a 300-yard interval and look out for strafers. Sometimes as we passed an outfit we would see a man off by himself squatting on his hunkers and looking up into the sun, his right hand shielding his eyes, afraid to concentrate entirely on his most personal functions.

There was no temptation to drive across fields as we got close to Sened, for the fields had almost certainly been mined by the retreating enemy. Sened Station was sinister—a wooden *gare* full of wasps' nests, a *buffet,* in a separate building, which two of our booby-trap captain's noncoms were busily rigging with their trip wires, as happy as parents decorating a Christmas tree, three or four buildings, a water tower, and a church, all shattered by shell-fire. The booby-trap men at work meant that we in our turn were going to abandon the place almost immediately. You don't booby-trap where you are going to stay. We talked to the trappers, both Royal Engineers, one of whom was carrying so many one-pound cakes of dynamite under one arm that they seemed always on the point of wriggling loose. It looked like coarse white laundry soap. "Lord love you, sir, it wouldn't explode if it did fall, not without a deetonyter, it wouldn't," he said. They wore a fixed, slightly fatuous smile which seemed a mark of their curious vocation. "We 'ad some nasty ones to tike up before we put ours in," the man with the dynamite said. "We've rearrynged them so Jerry will 'ave a time with them, when 'e comes back. 'E won't be surprised, not 'alf."

There were three American medium tanks in a triangle where

282

the main road went by the station, looking as if they had been punched clean through and then ripped with a giant can opener. Armor-piercing shot from German 88's had gone into them, bounced around inside like a buckshot in a rattle, and then gone out the other side, leaving something to be grilled by the flames as the fuel burned. The broken bits had been extracted that morning and buried; a soldier's web belt, stiff with blood, remained outside the hole through which they had drawn the crew of one tank. A couple other soldiers were looking at this tank and the belt. One of them seemed to feel the same blood excitement as the fellow we had seen go wild at the fallen German plane by the airfield. He was saying, over and over again, "I'll never take no more prisoners, the bastards, I'll never take no more prisoners!" A couple of 88's had laid doggo and caught the tanks with crossfire as they entered the town.

The artillery was still firing in the hill ridge about five miles away.

We asked a bearded, wild-looking soldier who was sitting in a parked jeep what the guns were pounding at. "We got a lot of Germans trapped up there on the mountain," he said. "How many?" Norgaard wanted to know. "About a division, I guess," the soldier said. "I don't see how you could hide a whole division on that hill," Norgaard said calmly, and the soldier answered, "They got the mountain all hollowed out, and that's where they're hiding." A couple of days later, when we had got back to Second Corps headquarters, we asked the G-2 what had happened to the Germans trapped on the hill, and he said, "Oh, you mean those last nine Heinies? They surrendered." We got back to town fast. There was an uncomfortable feeling about Sened, a tacit menace that made me feel worse than actually being bombed or shot at. Norgaard said he had exactly the same reaction.

The reason why none of our early operations in this area could amount to anything was that we had no infantry available to occupy the tactically important hills and stay on them. A war conducted almost exclusively with planes and armor is in its essence a medieval conception. The armored knights ride out, the armored knights ride back again, but they would become helpless if they dismounted, so war is resolved into a series of raids. And the strategic air-force scheme of destroying the enemy's factories is strangely like the medieval one of burning his crops.

I did not get back to Gafsa for six weeks after the affair at Sened Station. In the meanwhile we had executed in rather ragged fashion a previously determined withdrawal from Gafsa, Feriana, Sbeitla, and the old airfield on which Norgaard and I had lived during the private war. We had lost almost all of two battalions of armor and two battalions of infantry, and for the moment at least all our prestige with the French and Arabs. The Germans, pushing on our heels, had tried to get through to Tebessa, but they had failed. I had missed all this unpleasantness by going off on a frivolous trip in another direction, which has nothing to do with the story of the war, and I was rather glad I had missed it. I had had my bellyful of retreat in France.

When we prepared to go back to Gafsa it was in a substantial, intelligent manner, with plenty of infantry. It was more than just infantry, it was the First Division. I didn't have to file a daily dispatch, like the newspaper correspondents, so I decided to travel into action with the division and live with it. Major General Terry Allen, the division commander, whom I had met at Oran and again in Algiers, said it was all right with him as long as I kept out of his way, so I brought my bedroll down to division headquarters at Bou-Chebka, on the Algerian-Tunisian frontier, on the night of March 16. The division was moving to Gafsa that night, fifty miles across territory occupied neither by us nor the enemy, where we might bump into anything or nothing. It turned out to be nothing.

CHAPTER VIII

Gafsa Revisited

THE TENTS OF DIVISION HEADQUARTERS at Bou-Chebka stood on a hill covered with cedar trees. They were still standing when I arrived, but by the time I had had supper at the headquarters mess almost all the tents had been struck and loaded on trucks for the advance, and it was raining. The G-2, chief of the intelligence section of the divisional staff, a 34-year-old West Pointer with a high forehead and an almost prim manner, was worried during supper because he said a reconnaissance party had reported seven Italian tanks moving around on the very site which he had chosen in advance for the divisional command post, and whither the headquarters vehicles would be heading. The colonel commanding the tank-destroyer battalion had wanted to go down and get the Italian tanks while there was still light, the G-2 said, but the appearance of the tank destroyers down there might have given the show away. So General Allen had decided that the tanks should be left alone. "They'll probably go away anyway," he had said. The divisional chief of staff, who takes life seriously, let off a bit of steam by "eating out" the headquarters mess officer for serving C-rations at the last meal before the jump-off. "You know we have a limited quantity of C-rations, and it's the only form of ration the men can carry with them when they're fighting," he said. He did not say that we would have preferred a tastier meal ourselves because we did not know when we would get another. Brigadier General Teddy Roosevelt, the assistant division commander, was as restless and wriggly as a little boy whose family is taking him to a circus and who wants to get started early. Allen was in good enough humor but preoccupied. He had the responsibility.

I was to travel with a lieutenant named Ted Liese, who had once been in the display-advertising business in New York. He was now in charge of the liaison officers attached to division. A division is divided into three combat teams, each made up of a regiment of infantry and a battalion of artillery. Each team has a liaison officer, generally a young lieutenant, at headquarters. He travels back and forth between the CT command post and division, maintaining direct connection between the two. The division reconnaissance, or "recon" troop, the tank-destroyer battalion, the French, the British, and division artillery also maintain liaison men at division. Liese was a kind of housekeeper for the entire group. I permitted myself to be separated from my bedroll and typewriter, which were loaded on a truck that would follow us into Gafsa after the division had captured it, and retained only my musette bag with my mess kit in it and my rifle belt and canteen. I had no rifle, but I preferred a rifleman's belt to the usual pistol belt officers wear, because the cartridge pockets are ideal receptacles for ration chocolate and chewing gum.

The first echelons of the division started moving at dark, but we were not to get off until one o'clock in the morning. We waited in the rain. The jeeps assigned to us were being used on various errands in the early evening, but they got back in plenty of time. We climbéd in and, after waiting around awhile, moved into the procession of vehicles of all kinds that now filled the Gafsa road. I had been over the main road a dozen times; it would have been of no interest to me even if I could have seen. The sensation of being in a great caravan of vehicles moving forward through the night is soporific; I had the comfortable certainty for once that if shooting started it would be well up ahead of me in the early echelons, and not from a plane diving out of the sky directly over my head. I slept. I woke up when we turned off the road somewhere south of Feriana. The tracks through the semidesert had been marked out with white tape, and there were M.P.'s everywhere to guide us. The parking spaces for the various units were marked with signs illuminated by blackout lights; I had the feeling I was being driven into the parking area around the Yankee Stadium on the night of a prize fight. We reached divisional-headquarters area at a little after four o'clock. I got out of Liese's jeep and then could not find it again in the dark, so I threw my mackinaw coat on the ground and flopped on it and went to sleep. The rain had stopped.

When I awoke it was daylight and the divisional artillery was making a loud, comforting noise. I find nothing objectionable in the sound of artillery fire when I know it is going out. I got up and looked around for my jeep, but somebody said Liese had already been sent on a mission to one of the combat teams. Our jeeps and trucks were widely dispersed on the plain, and as soon as the men awoke they picked themselves off the ground and started digging themselves foxholes. I would like to say someplace that foxhole is a widely misused term, being applied freely to deep, carefully constructed slit trenches as well as hasty burrows. The kind men make when they are out in the open in fear of imminent attack really are foxholes. But the German planes which had dived-bombed or strafed even single vehicles in the small-scale Sened'thing six weeks earlier never put in an appearance to bother this divisional attack. It was a tipoff that the enemy had not awaited us in Gafsa but had already pulled out. We could not see the town from our first CP of the day, but at about eight o'clock we heard an explosion heavier than any of the artillery and saw a mighty column of gray-black smoke on the horizon toward Gafsa. The last elements of the enemy had blown a great munition dump.

I strolled over by Allen's tent and heard him successively telephoning his combat-team commanders, asking, "How you doing, kid?" The infantry were closing in on Gafsa through the hills. "It's all going like a maneuver," Allen would say at the conclusion of each call, "too good to be true."

Sergeant Jimmy Mimms, the general's driver, and an M.P. named Cawthorne who acts as bodyguard, were frying Deerfoot sausage and making coffee by the gasoline-burner process, and every time Mimms got an especially fine color on a sausage he would send it over to the general, to tempt him to eat. "He's just got to eat, Cawthorne," he would say. Allen paid no attention to the first six or seven burnt offerings. Finally he accepted one and sent Cawthorne back for more. "The battle must be going all right," Mimms said. "I guess we're in now."

We were. That afternoon the First Division moved into Gafsa, which had been deserted by the Arabs during the bombardment. The Arabs came back very slowly, as if they had bad consciences. Rain had begun again at noon. A waddy between division headquarters and the town appeared so swollen that headquarters decided to stay where it was for the night.

General Allen's aide, Major Kenneth Downs, had been a war correspondent for International News Service when I first knew him, and he now invited me to share his jeep and tag around with him for the rest of the offensive. Downs and his jeep driver and I charred some Spam and heated some soluble coffee in the shelter of a tarpaulin held against the side of a hill, and after the meal Downs and I pitched a pup tent. The driver decided to sleep under the tarp in what he thought was a sheltered nook in the hillside. We crawled under cover at seven o'clock. I never slept sooner or harder in my life. It must have been about two in the morning when Downs banged me on the head to awaken me, which he did. I said, "What's the matter?" and he said, "The tent has blown away." By that time my blankets were soaked through, but I was not concerned about that, because I had borrowed them anyway. I sat up in the jeep for the rest of the night. The driver, who had been rained out of his burrow, was in the jeep already. Downs, I think, managed to scrouge into the general's tent. Next morning we moved into Gafsa.

The French inhabitants of Gafsa had been evacuated in American Army trucks before the arrival of the Germans, so there were more good billets available in town than when I had been there before. Division headquarters moved into the Gendarmerie Nationale, a fine modern place. Gafsa was the capital of an administrative area with a population of about 150,000 natives, so the government buildings were out of proportion to the size of the town alone. It was the first town I had ever been in that our side had recaptured from the enemy, and was in its small way a symbol that this particular breed of bug could be dislodged like any other. But the science of booby-trapping has taken a good deal of fun out of following hot on an enemy's heels. Our engineers had been through the lower floors of the gendarmerie already, looking for booby traps, but they hadn't had time to do the living quarters in which Downs and I were billeted. It caused me acute distress to turn a doorknob or draw a shutter. In the end the division engineers decided that the Italians who had last been in Gafsa had lacked the time or possibly the skill to put any booby traps in the buildings. They had mined the roads and shoulders of the roads leading into and out of town, however, and protected most of their heavy mines with things the engineers called "bouncing babies." The babies were metal containers that were blown into the air by a charge of black powder when a soldier stepped on a hidden trip wire. They were packed with high explosives and steel ball bearings, and were timed to explode when about chest high in the air. The steel balls did the killing. Knowledge that there are bouncing babies about is disconcerting when you are in a jeep during a road strafing. You hesitate to dive for a roadside ditch.

Soon after we pulled into Gafsa I went for a walk about town to see how it had been affected by the occupation. The old Moorish citadel had been partially wrecked by an explosion. The engineers had used it as a storehouse for explosives and had blown it to save the stuff from the enemy. The destructions had not been well carried out; it had been planned, for example, to run a number of locomotives north over the railroad and then blow a railroad bridge north of town so that the use of the road would be barred to the enemy, but somebody had blown the bridge first, so that the loco-

288

motives were trapped in Gafsa. Then, since no preparations had been made to destroy them, they were abandoned and fell into German hands.

I met an Arab in the market place in front of the old citadel who said he had been some sort of a government employee, a police-court interpreter, I think, and had remained through the occupation. He was frightened, because the French notion of justice for Arabs is summary. The houses of all the Frenchmen had been thoroughly pillaged. So he was eager to talk and to convince me that his heart at least had been with the Allies. Most of the Moslems of Gafsa had fled to join their kin in the hills during the occupation, he said, because they wanted to escape the exactions of the Italians and because a great force of American bombers had come over shortly after the evacuation and flattened a lot of Arab houses. The bombers had killed about four hundred Arabs who were in a bread-line on the market place, he said. "The people were much impressed, and those who had gone about talking of the victory of the Germans as certain were discredited," he said, indicating that there are several kinds of propaganda. "They realized that the Americans must have mistaken them for Italian troops.

"When the Germans and Italians first came here they encouraged the people to rob the houses of the French and Jews," he said, "and some of the more ignorant elements of the population complied with their wishes. The Germans did not stay here long, but went on, leaving an Italian garrison. The Italians were revoltingly poor. They pulled up even the young onions out of the gardens in the oasis and ate them as if famished. They broke into Arab houses and stole carpets off the floors and sold them to other Arabs living in the surrounding country, to get a few *sous*. They are a people without shame." The German words, *Araber Laden,* or *Araber Geschäft* had been scrawled in chalk on the doors of a great number of shops, and the Arab said this had been done immediately after the evacuation, according to instructions from the Axis Arabic-language radio in Tunis, to protect Arab-owned businesses from pillage by invading troops. "I never listened to that radio, of course," he said, "but so I have heard it related." I had never imagined that so many Arabs knew even a couple of German words, but he said that a number in Gafsa had been prisoners of war in Germany in 1914–18 and had learned the language there. It was easy to guess that the place had been full of Arab Axis agents during our previous stay there; some of them were probably still wearing the G.I. shirts compassionate doughboys had given them.

I walked out to the house of the Chemounis, near the roadblock where the Feriana road entered town. It was still standing, but when I looked inside it seemed that nobody had lived there for years. There was nothing in the place but a few pages of Hebrew printing on the hard earth floor and a chandelier that swung crazily from the roof of the room where Norgaard and I had drunk wine. I wondered whether the family had escaped from Gafsa or been destroyed. I asked a lad I met on the road near by what had happened to them, and he said that they were in town, living in the old Jewish quarter, a couple of fetid alleys where only the poorest and least Europeanized Jews had lived in January. The boy was Jewish himself. He guided me to the house where the Chemounis lived. A scarecrow of a man, wearing a beret and a long blue robe, precipitated himself upon me, blubbering and trying to kiss me. "They have stolen even my trousers," Chemouni sobbed, pressing his face against the front of my field jacket. Other Jews, those who had recently been outwardly European now like my friend indistinguishable from the most Oriental, flocked about with their stories of the occupation. The Germans had come to the houses of the leading Jews on the first night, but had taken worth-while things like money, jewelry, and stocks of raw wool, leaving furniture and minor personal possessions alone. Then they had gone on, but not before inviting the Arabs to help themselves to the leavings. There had been a wild competition between Arabs and Italians to gut the Jewish houses. The Italian commandant of the place had ordered all the Jews into a few houses in the old quarter and had put them on a ration even smaller than that accorded to the Arabs, which had been minuscular. No Jews had been killed, although two young men had almost gone before a firing squad because an Arab accused them of having betrayed an Axis parachutist to the Americans in December. The two young men had escaped to the desert. The caïd of Gafsa, the chief Moslem official, had remained on the job through the occupation, and so had the spahis, the French-trained native police. The caïd had fled with the Italians, fearing the returning French would shoot him, but the spahis were still on the job, again under the orders of their original French superiors. They were recovering stolen Jewish and French property from Arab houses, but what they found was ruined or of slight original value.

Israel had been spoiled again, but naked as they had been the members of the community had apparently hoarded a few hens and roosters against the day of their deliverance. The *shochet,* the ritual slaughterer with his matted beard, was killing these chickens for the family feasts of celebration, holding the blade in his lips between strokes while he smoothed back the neck feathers of the chicken he was going to slit next. A couple of big Jewish soldiers from the Bronx, with tremendous hands that could palm a basketball and great feet that could kick a football sixty yards, had their arms comfortingly on the shoulders of ancient, tiny matriarchs with whom they had no means of communication except signs, because the Tunisian Jews speak no Yiddish. The Bronx Jews and the Tunisian Jews looked as different as a Percheron and an Eohippus.

"The Arabs are very bad," Chemouni said to me. "They have always been bad." "How long has your family lived in Gafsa?" I asked him. "I think for two thousand years," he said. His little girl, who spoke French as easily as any child in the Parc Monceau, looked at me with large frightened gray eyes. I asked him if she would go to live in France after we had won the war. He said no, of course not, she would marry and live in Gafsa. "Not a single bomb touched a Jewish house," he said. "God protects his people."

The *controleur civile,* the chief French administrative official for the district, had returned, and I went to talk to him. The Axis radio, he agreed, had had an important effect on the *indigenes.* Also the attitude of the Bey of Tunis had had an important effect. The Bey, Moncef Pasha, of the old Beylical Hoceinite family, had allowed the Germans to put him at the head of an "autonomous" Tunisian government in Tunis. It would be necessary to install another bey as soon as the Allies got to Tunis. Since the beylicate was not hereditary from father to son as long as it remained within the Hoceinite clan, that would be easy. Moncef Pasha had dozens of cousins. The *controleur* was much concerned with the problem of bringing the wives of himself and the half-dozen other leading French officials back to Gafsa. "There are so many soldiers in the streets," he said, "I am afraid it will be very embarrassing for them." We moved out a couple of days later, to spare their blushes.

CHAPTER IX

Under the Acacias

GENERAL ALLEN HAD BEEN PLEASED with the smoothness of the Gafsa operation, but he was uneasy, too, because he could not believe that the enemy would relinquish the region without a fight. The First Division had been ordered to capture and hold Gafsa as a railhead for the supplies of the British Eighth Army when the Eighth made its junction with the forces in our part of Tunisia, but you cannot hold a town unless you hold its approaches. There are two or three ranges of hills around the oasis of El Guettar, which is twelve miles southeast of Gafsa, and Allen thought of them as a dentist thinks about the possibly infected roots of a tooth. So the division slipped out of Gafsa with the same noiseless ease it had achieved in the other night move and attacked two of the ridges south of El Guettar.

Downs and his jeep moved with the division headquarters, and naturally so did I. This night ride was a short one. The headquarters vehicles turned off the main road at a point where hundreds of palm trees were silhouetted against the night sky, the oasis proper. I had recovered my bedroll after the first advance and had it in the jeep with me. After the driver had stowed the jeep under a tree, Downs and I dragged out our rolls and spread them near the side of the road, on the highest ground we could find. The oasis was on low ground, and we knew there must be a lot of mosquitoes in the grass. The Numidian frogs, which make a noise like parrots, sang from the shallow irrigation ditches that intersected the fertile land. When I awoke, to the accustomed thunder of the guns, I found myself in a Josef Urban stage set, appropriate to the last act of a musical comedy but not a war play. There were hundreds of acacia and almond trees in blossom under the palms. The white acacia blossoms and the pink ones of almond dripped down on us all through the battle.

A Ranger battalion attached to the division had attacked at four in the morning at one spot, and at six the infantry attacked at another. They found the enemy forces in strong positions, but these troops were sleepy, half-starved Italians who surrendered in droves and wept for joy when presented with C-rations, to our men the most despised form of army nourishment. First Lieutenant, now Captain, Ralph Ingersoll, the former editor of *PM*, was with the Ranger battalion which executed the first attack, and made of it the central episode of his book, *The Battle Is the Pay-off*. Our men made more than a thousand prisoners, but there was not one German in the lot.

Allen, who at first meeting appears to be a slapdash, reckless sort of fellow, perhaps because of his old-line cavalry personality and mannerisms, is in fact a worrier. He felt that things had been going too well to be on the level. He ordered an advance on Djebel Berda, the only ridge left unexplored, for the next morning.

Brigadier General Teddy Roosevelt, the assistant division commander, likes to circulate among the units in action during a battle. He invited me to make the circuit with him in his jeep on the day when the Djebel Berda attack was scheduled. Just as we were leaving the oasis a couple of the division engineer officers came up with Ingersoll in tow. One of them said, "General Roosevelt, I would like to have you meet Lieutenant Ingersoll." Roosevelt, who hadn't been thinking of the *PM* Ingersoll, said, "How do you do, Lieutenant?" and we walked away. I said, "That was Ralph Ingersoll, the *PM* editor." The general likes to descant on the thesis that all the prominent interventionists stayed safe at home while he, a hard-shell America Firster, went to war. He stopped sharply. "Hell," he said, "I always thought that man was a sonofabitch."

I had got to know Roosevelt pretty well at Sainte Barbe, near Oran, where the First Division headquarters had been when I first arrived in Africa. As assistant division commander he spends much of his time between battles visiting battalions and reporting back to division on their needs. His staccato, gamecock walk serves to identify him as long as he is within field-glass range. He always carries a short cane, head down, in the pocket of his field jacket, and he always makes a point of speaking to the mess sergeant of each outfit he visits. He asks the sergeant, for instance, if the company has enough baking powder. The sergeant invariably says no, and Roosevelt leaves him with the impression that if he, Roosevelt, were Secretary of War, there would be enough baking powder.

Simple as this device is, it makes men feel that the divisional command is on their side. Roosevelt has a special way of saluting across his face, a little like Dave Chasen's celebrated gesture, and when he is on one of his tours of the division he goes out of his way to get saluted by as many soldiers as possible. He says that saluting is a criterion of division morale. He was in the First Division in the last war, in which he earned several wound stripes and decorations. After holding a reserve commission in the tranquil years between wars, he came back to the Army and his division in April 1941. He speaks of himself as an old First Division soldier, and when he visits regimental headquarters in back areas, bands play "Old Soldiers Never Die, They Simply Fade Away" for him. He has a memory for the first names of the veteran First Division noncoms he encounters. He is at his best, however, in battle; his gamecock strut and his slightly corny humor take on a new and attractive quality when they are being exhibited under fire. The men consider Roosevelt an intellectual because he carries a considerable stock of books in his blanket roll. His library includes anthologies of verse, which he memorizes in vast chunks; works on anthropology, a subject which he discusses on any provocation; and a large number of detective stories, with which he reads himself to sleep.

Roosevelt's aide, Lieutenant Mike Stevenson, drove the jeep for us on the Djebel Berda morning. The German ground troops had not appeared on the previous day, but their planes had put in some energetic dive-bombings of American gun positions in the late afternoon. The Stukas had destroyed two field pieces and killed their crews, by far the heaviest loss of the day. The skies were full of German planes on the Djebel Berda morning, too, and the general, the lieutenant, and I spent considerable time clambering out of and into our jeep. I wedged myself so hard into the interstice between a parked truck and a bank of earth on one occasion, I remember, that when the planes disappeared I could hardly get out. I seemed to have contracted with fear, and when I expanded to normal size again I was stuck. I went in so hard that both pockets of my field jacket were completely filled with pebbles, as if I had been a human steam shovel. The general didn't seem to mind. The command post of the Eighteenth Infantry Combat Team was at the foot of a high hill which had an observation post on top of it. When we had got that far Roosevelt, who changes his mind as quickly as another man, decided that he wanted to stay at the observation post and watch the attack, which the Eighteenth was going to make. This was all right with me, and we all climbed up to the O.P.

This action took place on two ridges of hills which form an amphitheater that is open at both ends. The Americans, who already held the ridge which forms the northern side of the amphitheater, moved infantry by truck to both ends of the arc opposite them. The infantry detachments at the two ends then worked inward toward each other, for the enemy was supposed to be, if he was in the neighborhood at all, on the southern ridge at the center of the arc, at the point where the amphitheater was widest. If the battlefield had been a football stadium, the enemy would have had a seat on the fifty-yard line. The O.P. was in a correspondingly advantageous position on the American ridge. American artillery fired over our heads, blasting a spot on the hills across the way, where the enemy was supposed to be. G-2, the intelligence section of the divisional staff, had reported that two thousand Italian troops with three batteries of artillery were on Djebel Berda, but some skeptics still insisted that they must have pulled out. A force that size could not hope to hold out against a division, they argued, so it had probably vanished toward the coast.

Our infantry detachments, using ground cover and visible from the observation post only occasionally, and then just for a moment or two at a time, carried out their slow advance for four hours without a sign of enemy activity, as our guns continued to pound his ridge. The situation was beginning to get slightly embarrassing for General Allen, and adherents of the no-enemy theory, who had ordered the attack, were starting to speak up when puffs of white smoke broke out on the opposite ridge at points in front of the advancing infantry. The enemy was firing on our men with mortars, and our infantry was temporarily pinned down. Our artillery searched for the mortar positions and evidently found them, for the mortar fire ceased and our infantry moved on again. Allen, in the O.P. with us, looked pleased with himself, like a dentist whose probe has at last hit the sensitive spot. He had found trouble.

By nightfall our infantry reported that the enemy apparently was caught in our pincers, where he could be finished off by a night or dawn attack. The Americans were now on both ridges, and our artillery was comfortably tucked in behind our infantry—like a fighter's chin behind his left shoulder.

We drove back to the oasis well pleased with the day's results, but I still sensed a lack, and I think in their hearts the others did too. American troops had not yet beaten German troops in battle in this war. The forces in Tunisia had won a few skirmishes against Germans and had a few hard knocks, but hadn't won an action on a large scale. The First Division had been broken into its component units and fed into the fighting a battalion at a time during the winter, and the individual battalions had fought well. As a division it had a success against the French at Oran, and now it had a victory over Italians. It is safe to say that all its officers felt it could hold its own against a German division, but it had never had a chance to try. Until American troops had beaten German troops in a fair fight, there would always remain a doubt in the back of the minds of the people at home. It was all right to demonstrate mathematically that we had enough men and enough factory capacity to make victory sure, but the Germans had done such a job of self-advertising that even Americans wondered whether they weren't a bit superhuman. The First Division was scheduled to furnish the answer, and other American divisions as they gained experience would amplify it.

At five o'clock next morning, as I slept in the oasis, a peremptory voice broke into my dream, which I have now forgotten. Half awake, I realized that it was no dream voice; then as I became fully conscious I knew that it came from inside a half-track equipped with radio which was parked about ten yards from me. This half-track belonged to the liaison officer of a tank-destroyer battalion. The battalion communicated with division headquarters through the radio set in the half-track. And now I could hear the voice on the radio saying, "Baker reports German tanks threatening to overrun ——— Field Artillery." Lieutenant Colonel Herschel Baker was the commander of the tank destroyers. A moment later I heard, "Baker recommends infantry on lower slope ground fall back toward soft ground and resist tanks with rocket guns." I rubbed my eyes, spat, and walked over to G-2 to find out what was happening. It was the test match.

When I could find a G-2 man who had time to talk to me I learned that some tanks of the Tenth German Panzer Division had appeared on the plain between the two ridges that morning. They had entered the stadium through gullies in a part of the ridge still held by the Italian infantry, and they had begun the day by trying to climb a slope and overrun the batteries of American artillery which had been posted below our ridge. Our infantry and gunners stood firm, and our artillery had shot through several of the tanks. The T.D. outfit, coming to the rescue of the artillery, engaged the tanks, which moved off and started to make their way down the center of the field toward the western exit, which meant, incidentally, toward us at headquarters. The only combat troops in the oasis were the men of the headquarters defense platoon, which had four 37-millimeter cannon. The universal belief in the division was that these cannon would puncture nothing more heavily armored than a Kiddiekar.

Apparently the German intention was to come around the rear of the American position in the north stands and cut the main road back to Gafsa, then retake that town and thus leave the First Division stranded. If the maneuver succeeded, the entire disposition of Allied forces designated to contain the German Army in Tunisia while the Eighth Army smashed its way through the Mareth Line would be upset. We would have to retreat from them while they retreated before the Eighth Army. The German commander also probably hoped to cause panic among the cut-off American troops and get a lot of equipment and prisoners. "They think they can push us over and laugh at us because Americans can't stand up to German armor," my G-2 man said in a hard tone. Since the tanks were coming in our direction I decided that the oasis was as good an observation post as any.

The oasis was cut up into the small holdings of individual Arabs by crumbling mud walls and irrigation ditches. The Arabs had used the earth from the ditches to make the walls. There were red earthen water jugs nested in the tops of some of the palm trees—I suppose the owners, who climb like gibbons, carry water from the ditches up to the tops of the trees in dry spells and sprinkle the choice dates. In some of the others there were whitened bovine skulls, to frighten the birds from the ripe fruit. Under the palms were the acacias and almonds with their blossoms, and at ground level there were the thin green blades of spring onions and the flowers of black-eyed peas. The sun filtered through the blossoms;

the drone of bees was so strong that it was hard to distinguish at once an approaching airplane motor.

A young liaison officer named Troup Howard Matthews, who was on call to carry messages to the First Armored Division, but who had nothing to do for hours at a stretch, suggested that we move to the outer edge of the oasis and observe. We strolled over there and sat on a mud wall. Matthews was twenty-five years old and one of the few mildly intellectual young officers I had met, a low-voiced New Orleans boy. He had worked for the National Broadcasting Company in New York before entering the Army, and as we sat on the wall waiting we tried to enumerate the bars in Rockefeller Center. We had had about one drink apiece in the previous month. Italian troops had occupied the oasis before us, and I tried to piece together a couple of torn Italian letters to see what their folks at home had been writing to them about. There was a low plain between the oasis and the ridges we had watched on the previous day, and I hoped our engineers had put out some mines beyond the oasis' edge. There was a small salt lake in the middle of the plain, but the tanks would not have to cross it to get to us.

Matthews looked through his binoculars and saw a couple of small dots creeping hesitantly toward us like lice across a panhandler's shirt front. He said they were tanks. They came nearer, very indirectly and with frequent halts, until they got as big as bedbugs on a wall, and then geysers of black smoke and dirt began to appear near them. There were about a dozen dots now. Matthews said he could see twenty. They would stop sometimes when the geysers spouted up, and then I would think they had been hit, but soon they would come crawling on again. The geysers were shellbursts; our howitzers, firing from their position back of the ridge we held, were shooting at them. The foremost tanks got within two miles of us, which is close for motorized battle, but I do not think they knew that the palm trees concealed the C.P., or they would have made a more determined effort to overrun it. Then the howitzers got to them. Four tanks were shot through. Their clumsy black bodies, belching dark smoke, remained on the field right below the command post now. You could see them with the naked eye, and they had outgrown the bedbug stage. They were about as big as caramels. The American 105 and 155 mortars are not ideal anti-tank weapons, because of their high arching trajectory. But they had served. Matthews and I went to breakfast.

All day long, that day of the stadium battle, the German tanks toddled about the field and in the first rows of our hill grandstand while the artillery potted at them and the tank destroyers, waddling into action like bull pups, drew their fire and returned it. Finally, all eighteen tank destroyers were knocked out, but only after they had wrecked thirty-one tanks. By the time this tank-destroyer battalion was finished, another had arrived from the rear, so our position was not weakened. Old Baker, the tank-destroyer commander, came rolling into the oasis late in the afternoon to say good-by to General Allen. He said he had had surprisingly few casualties and was loading his men into trucks and taking them back to Feriana to get some new guns. Baker, with white hair, apple-red cheeks, and bright blue eyes, looks like Father Christmas minus the whiskers and is always full of bounce. He had been riding around among the tanks in a jeep and had somehow captured a German who had a lot of pornographic postcards in his wallet. Baker was as happy as a lark.

During all the fighting our infantry held firmly to the hills. Without it, the artillery, which was in this battle the striking arm, would have been overrun. G-2 had somehow picked up the information that the Germans would make their big attack at 4:45 in the afternoon. I went out to the edge of the oasis with some other idlers to wait for it, repeating to myself idly,

"The Spartans on the sea-wet rock, sat down and combed their hair,"

and understanding for the first time that they had sat down not because they were heroes but because there was nothing else to do. Promptly at 4:45 twenty Stukas flew over the oasis, paying us no heed, and dived on our gun positions. The only American plane in sight all day had been a Piper Cub used by the artillery spotters. The echo of the Stukas' bombs and of the whistling devices between their front wheels had hardly died down before the enemy began his attack, but it was out of our sight. We could hear the guns and see the German shellbursts on our ridge. This time, as I learned a little later, the Germans sent forward some armored infantry, known as Panzer Grenadiers, whose mission apparently was to

299

climb through our infantry lines and reach our guns. German tanks followed the grenadiers. The guns killed all but nine of the two hundred grenadiers of the leading platoons, and the rest of the attacking party stopped and went away. The American guns fired time shells, and the divisional artillery commander, a calm, professorial kind of brigadier general, told me afterward that he was highly pleased with their effect. As it turned out, that particular battle ended at that particular instant, because the Tenth Panzer Division never resumed the attack. It had lost forty or fifty tanks, most of which remained in our hands and were blown up by our engineers so that they would be beyond repair. What was more important, it was licked.

If one American division could beat one German division, I thought then, a hundred American divisions could beat a hundred German divisions. Only the time was already past when Germany had a hundred divisions to spare from the Russian front, plus God knows how many more to fight the British, plus garrison troops for all the occupied countries. I knew deep down inside me after that that the road back to Paris was clear.